THE GLIDER WAR

THE GLIDER WAR

JAMES E. MRAZEK

Robert Hale & Company
London

St. Martin's Press, Inc.
New York

St. Martin's Press, Inc.
175 Fifth Avenue
New York, N.Y. 10010

Library of Congress Catalog Card Number 74-33917

Robert Hale & Company
Clerkenwell House
Clerkenwell Green
London EC1

ISBN 0 7091 4495 4

Filmset and printed in Great Britain by
BAS Printers Limited, Wallop, Hampshire

CONTENTS

ILLUSTRATIONS

MAPS

To Randy Clarke
My Canadian Grandson

ACKNOWLEDGEMENTS

I am indebted to many people for their contributions and for their assistance in preparing this exhaustive (and exhausting) work. Ever since I served as a gliderman during World War II, where I collected some of the first data about transport gliders, I have gradually compiled material from many sources and had the help of many people. I trust that I have not omitted attributing contributions from any person or source whatsoever, but if I have inadvertently done so, it has not been intentional.

Regrettably some German material I had used in the manuscript was lost when I mailed it to the U.S. from England, where I had been working with the publisher. The data from the material had already been used, but the names of individuals and archives in Germany who had so generously provided the information were recorded in the correspondence lost with the material. Thus I may not have given credit to those sources.

UNITED STATES

General John R. Alison, wartime Deputy Commander 1st air Commando Group

The late Captain Homer Ambrose, U.S.N. Ret., editor

Captain R. S. Barnaby, U.S.N. Ret., test pilot and wartime chief engineer Naval Aircraft Factory, Philadelphia

Robert Bovey, wartime glider pilot

Richard M. Bueschel, author and Japanese and Chinese aviation historian

Eleanor M. Burdette, reference librarian, National Aeronautics and Space Administration (NASA) headquarters library, Washington, D.C.

Jack Coogan, actor and wartime transport glider pilot

Colonel Carl F. Damberg, U.S.A.F., wartime chief, Aircraft Laboratory, Wright Field, Ohio

Major Fred Demousse, U.S.A., linguist who assisted in translating of Russian material

The late Major General Frederick R. Dent, U.S.A.F., wartime chief, Glider Branch, Wright Field, Ohio

Dr. Cortez F. Enloe, Jr., military surgeon on the staff of General Orde Charles Wingate

Marcia Frances, U.S. resident of Vienna, Austria, who translated German material

René Francillon, PhD., author of *Japanese Aircraft*

Royal Frey, Curator, U.S.A.F. Museum, Wright-Patterson Air Force Base, Ohio

Virginia G. Fincik, archives technician, 1361st Photo Squadron, Aerospace Audio Visual Service, U.S.A.F.

Colonel John R. Galvin, U.S.A., author *Air Assault*

Elsie L. T. Goins, office of Naval Aviation History

Jane S. Hess, head, General Reference and Cataloguing, NASA Langley Research Center Library, Hampton, Virginia

Colonel Joe A. Hinton, U.S.A., wartime chief, Airborne Section, general staff, G-3, Supreme Headquarters, Allied Expeditionary Force (SHAEF)

Chief Warrant Off. Michael Lansing, U.S.A., German linguist, assisted in translating German materials

Lieutenant Colonel Robert C. Mikesh, U.S.A.F. Ret., assistant curator, aeronautics, also Louis S. Casey, curator of aircraft, National Air and Space Museum, Smithsonian Institution, Washington, D.C.

Rose F. Mrazek, author's mother, translator of Czech material

Colonel Mike C. Murphy, U.S.A.F.R., wartime glider pilot and glider staff officer, AAF, the Pentagon

Lieutenant Colonel Dan Harris, U.S.A. Ret., Japanese linguist

Thomas E. Holman, archivist, Military Archives Branch, National Archives, Washington, D.C.

Colonel O. W. Howland, U.S.A.F. Ret., wartime commander, 435th Transport Carrier Group

Key K. Kobayashi, assistant head, Japanese Section, Orientalia Division, Library of Congress, Washington, D.C.

Colonel Edward H. Lahti, U.S.A. Ret., wartime commander, 511th Parachute Infantry Regiment, 11th Airborne Division

Charles B. MacDonald, author, *Company Commander*; deputy chief history, Office Army's Chief of Military History, Washington, D.C.

General Anthony G. McAuliffe, Commander of the 101st Airborne Division at Bastogne

Leeds Mitchell, author, wartime transport glider pilot

Dr. Hector Nadal, wartime surgeon, glider-borne medical unit

Herbert Naylor, multilingual linguist

Colonel Virgil Ney, U.S.A. Ret., author, military historian

Rudolf Opitz, wartime *Luftwaffe* assault/transport glider pilot residing in Stamford, Conn.

J. C. Parker, president, Northwestern Aeronautical Corporation, Minneapolis, Minn. during World War II; partner, Auchincloss, Parker and Redpath

Lady Alice Pennington, linguist, widow of Sir John Pennington, concert orchestra conductor

John A. Powers, wartime transport glider pilot

Colonel Robert Rentz, U.S.A.F. Ret., wartime transport aircraft pilot

Michael Rosen, historian

Max Rosenberg, Deputy Chief of History; Carl Burger, Chief, Histories Division; David Schoen, Chief, Support Division; Mary Ann Cresswell, archivist; Office of U.S.A.F. History, Washington, D.C.

William T. Sampson, wartime transport glider pilot

Lloyd Santmyer, wartime test pilot

Paul Schweizer, president, National Soaring Museum, Elmira, N.Y., and president of Schweizer Aircraft Corporation

Albert F. Simpson, Historical Research Center, Maxwell AF Base, Alabama

Ted Solinski, editor *Nashville Tennessean*, wartime transport pilot

Michael Stroukoff, Jr., son of the designer of XCG-14, -14A and the XCG-20

Colonel Floyd J. Sweet, U.S.A.F. Ret., NASA Headquarters, Washington, D.C., wartime commanding officer for a period, AAF Training Detachment, Twenty-nine Palms, Cal. and later glider project officer and test pilot then Chief, Glider Branch, Wright Field, Dayton, Ohio

Dorothy Taylor, manuscript typist

Major General Louis A. Walsh, U.S.A. Ret., contributor, information on Japanese transport gliders

Paul L. White, archives technician, National Archives

Arthur A. Whiting, wartime aeronautical engineer for Curtis Wright Aircraft Corporation

Robert Wolfe, Chief, Captured Records Branch, Military Archives Division, National Archives; also George Wagner, reference specialist, same office.

and   )

Thelma, my wife and editor who assisted me immeasurably during the writing

GERMANY

Edmund Auer, *Luftwaffe* test pilot, engineer

D. C. Consbruch, *Zentralstelle für Luftfahrtdokumentation unde Information ZLDI*

Hans Karl Becker, wartime assault, transport glider pilot

Werner Davignon, historian, *Luftwaffe* chief navigator, air transport group

Wilhclm Fulda, *Luftwaffe* assault, transport glider pilot, captor, the bridge at Corinth, Greece

Generalmajor Walter Gericke, *Bundeswehr*

Colonel Walter Hornung, *Luftwaffe* air transport group commander

Heiner Lange, *Luftwaffe* assault, transport glider pilot

Alexander Lippisch, aeronautical engineer, pioneer German aircraft designer

H. J. Meier; W. A. Thurow, *Vereinigte Flugtechnische Werke GMBH*

Generalmajor Friedrich Morzik, *Luftwaffe*, wartime commander of Germany's air transport on eastern front

Eugen Moser, *Luftwaffe* assault, transport glider pilot

Dr. Sack, *Zentralbibliotek der Bundeswher Der Leiter*

Hanna Reitsch, wartime *Luftwaffe* test pilot

Dr. Friedrich Stahl, *Bundesarchiv-Abt. Militararchiv, Freiburg*

Generaloberst Kurt Student, *Luftwaffe*, pioneer in the use of the glider as a military weapon

Dipl. Ing. Heinz Trautwein

Woldmer Voigt, Head of the Departments of Advanced Design and Hardware Design, *Messerschmitt*, Augsburg.

Oberstleutnant i.G. Volker, *Militargeschichtliches Forschungsamt*, Freiburg

Helmut Wenzel, wartime paratrooper, key figure in capture of Fort Eben Emael

Colonel Rudolf Witzig, *Bundesheer*, captor of Fort Eben Emael

also

Messerschmitt-Bolkow-Blohm, and *Hamburger Flugzeugbau GMBH ein internehmensberger der Messerschmitt; Heinkel Flugzeugbau, Vereinigte Flugzeug Werke VFW*, Speyer

BRITAIN

Jean Alexander, author, forthcoming work on Russian military aircraft

Jack Beaumont, aviation authority, proprietor Beaumont Aviation Literature

J. M. Bruce, Deputy Keeper, aircraft collection, R.A.F. Museum

Brigadier George Chatterton, author *Wings of Pegasus*, wartime commander Glider Pilot Regiment

Edmund Creek, collector German aircraft data, collaborator on several works on aircraft

Colour-Sergeant T. Fitch, Airborne Forces Museum, Aldershot

J. S. Lucas, Senior Museum Assistant, Photographic Library, Imperial War Museum

E. A. Mundey, historian, R.A.F. Archives

Major G. G. Norton, Honorary Curator, Airborne Forces Museum, Aldershot

Lieutenant-Colonel Terence B. H. Otway, D.S.O., wartime commander of 9th Battalion the Parachute Regiment

C. W. Prower, coordinating engineer, Hawker-Siddelcy Aviation Ltd., formerly on the staff of General Aircraft

Gladys Puddock, my typist in the U.K. whose spirits never flagged and who had an uncanny ability to interpret my illegible scrawl

Anne Tilbury, archivist, photo collection, *Flight* International

Hessel Tiltman, head of team that designed the Horsa glider

W. J. P. Wigmore, general secretary, Glider Pilot Regiment Association

K. G. Wilkinson, Managing Director, Mainline, BEA

Lawrence Wright, author *The Wooden Sword*, wartime transport glider pilot

also

Public Archives

AUSTRALIA

Warrant Officer A. H. McAulay, Australian Army, historian and sailplane pilot

W. A. Smither, Department of Air, Canberra

BELGIUM

Henri Lecluse, Liége, Belgium

Jean-Louis Lhoest, Editor, *Le Peuple*

CANADA

S. F. Wise, Director, Directorate of History, Department of National Defence, Ottawa

FRANCE

M. Henri Michel, *Directeur de recherche au Centre national de la recherche scientifique*
Raymond Danel, aeronautical engineer, historian

INDIA

Squadron Leader B. S. Hatangade, Assistant Air Attache, Indian Embassy, Washington, D.C.

ITALY

Ing. Angelo Ambrosini, designer and builder of transport glider AL-12P
Colonel S. SM Vittoria Castiglioni, Army Office of Military History

JAPAN

Lientenant Colonel Hideo Aoki
Ikuhiko Hata, Chief Historian, Ministry of Finance, Tokyo
Commander Sadao Seno
Yoshisuke Yamaguchi

SWEDEN

Rudolf Abelin, aircraft designer and test pilot, president and general manager of Saab-Scania, Malmo
Kjell Lagerstrom, SAAB, New York

INTRODUCTION

This is the story of the fighting glider, and of the stirring and valorous deeds of the gallant soldiers and glider pilots from many nations who flew into combat in this stealthy weapon. They made their hazardous flights in these fabric-covered, motorless, and unprotected craft, while buffeted by gusting winds and their tow-plane's propeller blast; flew so slowly that they became sitting ducks for enemy ack-ack; and finished their one-way ride skidding or crashing into enemy strongholds. Americans appropriately called them the 'towed-target' infantry.

Their story has few antecedents and fewer residues. It is contained in a five-year span of history. The glider had no wartime predecessor, in contrast to many weapons used during World War II. The crawling British tanks that surprised the Germans at Cambrai in World War I were the forerunners of the fast-moving, powerful Sherman, Churchill, Tiger, and Stalin tanks of World War II. Modifications made to the famous French 75-mm artillery piece used in the first war enabled armies to use it during the second war. The dog-fighting Spads, Fokkers, and de Havilands of the first conflict evolved into the sophisticated fighters and bombers of the second one.

But the story of the glider is different. No one had ever flown a glider into combat before World War II. The first glider used in combat was a novel by-product of the fragile, translucent, sports sailplane; and only two nations, Germany and Russia, had dreamed of the possibilities of transforming the sailplane into a weapon of war. Suddenly, early on 10th May 1940, the world was rudely awakened to the startling news that a Nazi force using some unheard-of weapon had landed stealthily on the top of the key Belgian fort of Eben Emael. That weapon was the glider.[1]

No less to American officers than to the beleaguered Allies striving desperately to stem the onrush of the Wehrmacht, the glider was an ominous, strange weapon. American and British generals had some experience with paratroopers, and some jelled ideas about them; but gliders, none—absolutely none.

Eben Emael proved that the glider could be used with devastating

[1] For a complete account of the fall of Eben Emael, see *The Fall of Eben Emael* by James E. Mrazek (Robert Hale, London 1972; Luce-McKay, Washington D.C.—New York).

tactical surprise. Its potential, once studies were undertaken by U.S. military leaders, appeared awesome. Gliders might now change the character of war. Rivers were no longer formidable barriers to armies, nor would they run red with the blood of troops hit while they ran unprotected across foot bridges, or tried crossings in defenceless assault boats. Gliders could form air bridges over the rivers. Gliders could simplify the supply of ground operations because, loaded with supplies, they could be towed to units in critical need of supplies and there released. Visionaries said that gliders could be built to transport tanks into combat; a job that no aeroplane then in existence could do.

Little did our generals realize that they were laggards in their estimate of the value of the glider. Long before the Germans were defeated, in fact by 1942, their glider effort had reached a pinnacle of technical achievement that the United States, with its tremendous resources, could not attain in a five-year intensive glider-production effort. The United States did out-produce the Germans by ten to one; a not unexpected accomplishment, in view of America's greater industrial resources. Nevertheless, America neither produced a glider that was nearly as large as the German *Gigant*, nor attained the excellence in design and technical innovations that was reached by the Germans.[1]

In no comparable effort did America bumble so horribly from the beginning to the end of a programme. The Americans were 'johnnies come lately'. They were conservative; they were not daring in the development and procurement of the glider; and in its strategic and tactical application in combat the Americans fell far short of what might have been expected. A huge U.S. glider arsenal lay largely untested and unused during the war. Tied to American operations, the British could do little better.

On 7th December 1941, neither Britain nor the U.S.A. had combat gliders; there were no qualified combat glider pilots, no glider infantry regiments, and no trucks, tanks or artillery pieces suitable for transport in gliders. Moreover, neither had doctrine for the operational employment of gliders, and few people had any idea of how, when, and where gliders could be used.

---

[1] For a complete description of the *Gigant* and some fifty other transport and assault gliders see *Fighting Gliders* (Robert Hale—forthcoming).

CHAPTER I

Capture of Eben Emael

At 0505 on 10th May 1940, a mile east of Fort Eben Emael in Belgium, sturdy *Luftwaffe* gliders, heavy with Hitler's glidermen, guns, and secret explosives, one by one cut away from the tow-ropes of the straining Ju 52 tow-planes. Majestically, like an enormous hawk, each glider soared upward momentarily then banked, while its pilot quickly searched for and found the fortress walls below. From every direction they swooped in shrieking dives, and quickly levelled off as the ground raced up. One by one they skidded silently on to the very roof of the 'impregnable' fort, virtually into the mouths of its huge casemates.

Led by Lieutenant Rudolf Witzig, seventy-eight Germans in ten gliders dared to attack a concrete and steel monster manned by 780 Belgians. Hardly in the history of warfare had such a small force faced such incredible odds. To crack Eben Emael's defences the gliders carried machine guns, grenades, assorted ammunition and explosives, and, most important, twenty-eight of the new hollow charges, totalling five tons of explosives. The highly secret hollow charge, a fiendish invention never before used in war, was a 100-pound hemisphere of dynamite with a small part scooped from the flat undersurface. When exploded, great pressures focused in this hollow. Unknown to the world until recently, the hollow charge was the forerunner of the atom bomb, and made the atom bomb possible.

In their eagerness to attack the huge Belgian casemates, the glider-men catapulted out of the doors and burst through the fabric sides of their gliders. Two squads found that the craft that had carried them now rested in a mat of barbed wire that had snagged the gliders to a sudden halt. Belgian machine gunners, quickly recovering from their stupor, started firing at the Germans as they struggled towards their assigned casemates with the heavy hollow charges in tow. The Germans frantically clipped the wire and picked their way through, as bullets twanged and ricocheted.

Getting to the tops of the casemates, they centred their hollow charges on the thick steel observation and gun turrets, triggered the fuses, and fled to safety. Across the enormous surface of the fort the charges

DFS 230, the German glider used to attack Fort Eben Emael

Gliders on the ground after the assault on the fort. The cupola in the foreground has been damaged by a hollow charge

began exploding in miniature atomic blasts, marked by tell-tale mushroom-like clouds.

So violent was the shock, so unsuspecting were the Germans themselves of how strong the force would be, that it blew many to the ground while they were still racing away. It burst the eardrums of Heine Lange, one of the glider pilots who had placed a charge on a steel gun turret, the largest in the fort, making him virtually deaf for life.

The steel atomized under the fiery heat. Extreme pressure jetted it into the bowels of the casemates, incinerating men, blowing guns from their stanchions, and creating indescribable havoc and confusion in the depths of the fort. In a matter of twenty minutes the Germans had almost sealed the Belgians in the fort's maze of tunnels.

Meanwhile, thirty more gliders were descending out of the grey morning mists along the Meuse River on to the surprised defenders of three bridges that Hitler had also ordered to be seized. Captain S. A. Koch, leading a glider element carrying four officers and 129 men, landed close by the bridge at Vroenhoven. A platoon led by Lieutenant Schacht moved off to take the bridge, while Koch and his staff set up a headquarters and made radio contact with glider forces at the fort and at the two other bridges marked for capture. The Germans hit the defenders of the Vroenhoven bridge with such ferocity and speed that they overwhelmed the Belgians, and disarmed the explosives set to destroy the bridge before the Belgians could set them off. Less than thirty minutes later the bridge was open to German tanks, and within three hours all significant Belgian resistance in the area was liquidated. Despite strong Belgian efforts to dislodge the glidermen, the Germans held firm. However, Schacht's platoon paid a heavy price, losing seven killed and eighteen wounded.

At the Canne bridge the story was different. Belgian Sergeant Pirenne, in charge of destroying the bridge, set off the fuses to the charges inserted into the bridge just as the gliders were landing. Before the Germans could get out of their gliders and to the bridge the charges exploded, and the bridge folded into the Canne Canal.

In a short time, Captain Koch's radio operator had the reassuring signal from the Germans at Fort Eben Emael that all was going well, and thenceforth Koch intermittently got word that Witzig's force was maintaining control. However, Koch had no word from Lieutenant Schächter at the Canne bridge. About noon he sent a patrol to find out what was up. Two hours passed. The patrol returned. Its commander reported that the bridge was demolished, and Schächter's team had taken a beating. The patrol had found four glidermen dead and six severely wounded. Disappointed at not having captured the bridge, Schächter's glidermen nevertheless captured forty-nine officers and 250 men, and left 150 Belgians dead, before they were relieved on the 11th.

Aerial photograph of Fort Eben Emael taken by a German reconnaissance plane before the attack

At the third bridge, Veldwezelt, the German success was comparable with that at Vroenhoven. Several Belgian officers, hearing the alert signalled by the fort's guns, pleaded for permission to blow the bridge immediately. A wavering senior officer advised that it was necessary to get formal orders first. Several minutes later gliders appeared and virtually hypnotized the gawking Belgian soldiers into inaction. None could venture a guess as to what the mysterious silent machines could be, for none had ever seen aeroplanes without engines. The order to blow the bridge never came; and the German glider force, commanded by Lieutenant Altman, descended into the midst of the Belgian defenders and skidded to a stop right on target. Using a hollow charge against the casemate protecting the bridge, while aggressively attacking the Belgians entrenched close by, Altman's platoon seized the bridge ten minutes later and disarmed the charges set to blow it up. In the brief but violent struggle, and during the combat that ensued for the remainder of the day, the Germans lost eight dead and twenty-one wounded.

Back at Eben Emael, Major Jean Fritz Lucien Jottrand, its commandant, ordered several counter-attacking sallies from the fort. Backed by dive-bombing Stukas, the glidermen repulsed the Belgians each time.

By the next morning, with his men choking from the acrid smoke filling the tunnels, no help forthcoming, and the situation utterly hopeless, Jottrand raised the white flag. Assault 'Granite'—the German code name for the operation—became history only hours after it began.

At Eben Emael, ten gliders and seventy-eight men started a new phase of Nazi conquest, at the cost of six killed and twenty wounded. The lives of an estimated 6,000 crack German ground troops were saved; the force the German High Command calculated it would have had to sacrifice to take Fort Eben Emael by conventional attack. The Germans had also estimated that it would take six months of hard fighting.

The idea for this utterly sensational attack on Eben Emael was Hitler's, and his alone. It was not just a hare-brained gimmick dreamed up to boost German morale. It was a brilliant stratagem, the most crucial strike by any element of the German military machine during that opening day of the attack against France, Belgium and Holland.

If Eben Emael had held off the glider attack force successfully, the *Wehrmacht* would have had to grind the fort into submission by a methodical, time-consuming, costly air-bombing and ground attack. Worse for Hitler's time-table of world conquest, had he been unable to seize Eben Emael (and the bridges that the fort protected) with glider forces, his panzers would have had to make their way through the tangled Ardennes. This would have been a gruelling contest. The

German generals had pledged that they could win it; but there was great danger that the attack might have come perilously close to bogging down into World War I-style trench warfare, a method of fighting they had no taste for.

Hitler had to have speed, and he sought to achieve it by a total surprise. He had to have speed to overwhelm France and the Low Countries before the British armies could come to the aid of a beleaguered France, as had happened during World War I when the Kaiser's forces were about to destroy the French armies.

The glider was Hitler's surprise weapon. Never before used in waging war, gliders were potent weapons. They could disgorge tens of men and tons of violence on the heads of an unwary foe. They could be released from tow-planes many miles from an unsuspecting enemy and, in utter silence, stealthily land on and about his fortifications, as Eben Emael proved. Because they were quiet and could get low quickly and skim the treetops, they could easily sneak through or avoid anti-aircraft fire.

After the Germans moved into Denmark and Norway, but subsequent to the capture of Eben Emael, they began to fly gliders to Oslo, with the plan of using them in the airborne operation to seize Narvik. When parachutists took off from Oslo for Trondheim, a staging point for Narvik, gliders accompanied them. Narvik at that time had no airfields usable for making air landings with Ju 52s to bring in artillery and other heavy equipment to support the parachutists.

Glider pilots, and those who were to fly to Narvik, grew beards, and the gliders carried boxes containing a change of civilian clothes for each man. Orders were to change into civilian clothes after the operation, cross over into neutral Sweden, and return to Germany.

Because Britain controlled the sea and access by land was difficult, Narvik had to be captured by airborne assault. However when the parachutists took off, several of the air staff decided the weather conditions were unsuitable for gliders. Thus, gliders were never used, although their use had been planned. According to Lieutenants Walter Fulda and Heiner Lange (glider pilots who were to participate), the judgement that the weather was unsuitable was bad. Gliders, they are convinced, could have made the trip to Narvik without any problems.

The speed at which the Germans liquidated Eben Emael jarred and baffled World War I-orientated generals and politicians alike. For sheer breath-taking swiftness and shock-power nothing like it had ever occurred in any war.

Hitler had kept the forthcoming attack on Eben Emael a closely guarded secret, limiting those who knew of it to the handful directly involved in planning and carrying out the operation. Pleased with his gliders, he clamped even tighter security over them after the fort was taken. German newsreels featured the capture and had shots of the action, but showed no gliders or hollow charges, leaving the impression in Germany that it was a conventional military operation carried out by dauntless German soldiers. The German and other Axis-country presses carried accounts of the capture, but nothing about gliders. Abroad, legends grew; the world guessed wildly. The Germans had used nerve gas—some said sabotage. *Life* magazine published an 'endive-tunnel-treachery' fairy tale, beggaring the imagination, yet published as fact; German workers, married to Belgian women during the construction of Eben Emael in the years before 1940 had, under the guise of endive farmers, planted explosives as well as endives in the tunnels scraped under the fort.

The fall of Eben Emael had a great deal to do with building an image of German military strength, if not invincibility, in the minds of many Allied leaders. Until the end of the war most of Germany's highest ranking officers really never knew the true facts, so closely was the secret kept. In fact, it would be years after the war before the true role of the 'secret weapon', Hitler's gliders, would be generally known.

Eben Emael was the culmination of German far-sightedness, for in 1922 Hermann Goering—years later to become Marshal Goering, Chief of Hitler's *Luftwaffe*—outlined Germany's glider programme to E. V. Rickenbacker:

> Our whole future is in the air. And it is by air power that we are going to recapture the German empire. To accomplish this we will do three things. First, we will teach gliding *as a sport* to all our young men. Then we will build up commercial aviation. Finally, we will create the skeleton of a military air force. When the time comes, we will put all three together—and the German empire will be reborn.

Towards this end the German government subsidized glider research in the postwar period and, although there was a certain interest in gliding in other countries, it was in Germany that the sport had its most extensive and advanced development. There was little opportunity for the Germans to channel their enthusiasm for flying except in this sport, owing to a condition imposed by the Treaty of Versailles. (When Hitler later re-armed Germany, it was done at first secretly and then in open defiance of the treaty regulations.) So the energies of a nation that would normally have been devoted to powered and unpowered flight were expended on gliding, with interesting consequences.

The government, strongly influenced by Goering's viewpoint, encouraged all young Germans to fly. The Hitler *Jugend* dominated by the *National Socialistische Flieger Corps* (N.S.F.C.), supplied facilities for those who, for financial reasons, would not otherwise have been able to take up glider flying. It kept the records of all pupils, gave tests, and issued proficiency certificates. From the beginning it kept a detailed log, countersigned by his instructor, of each student's progress. This was the authority for the issue of various glider certificates.

N.S.F.C. also encouraged independent organizations, especially those with means such as gymnasiums and universities, to establish glider clubs at their own expense. These clubs came under the supervision of the Reich's *Luft Ministerium* (Air Ministry) which issued the necessary records and certificates.

At ten years of age a boy became eligible for the Hitler *Jugend*. The leaders encouraged him to build model aircraft, and gave him frequent opportunities to exhibit his workmanship and fly his models. The principles of elementary aerodynamics were gradually instilled. When he reached the age of fourteen a boy became qualified to join the *Flieger Hitler Jugend*. Thereafter he started primary flying instruction on straight flight and lateral control, using the *Zegling* glider, a single-seater of the open type. The youth then advanced to a closed cockpit single-seater, such as the *Baby Grunau* and learned to make turns. Coupled with flying instruction, the instructors showed films depicting the flight of birds. He was also taught something about wireless, aircraft recognition, and navigation.

Work with either the *Flieger Hitler Jugend*, the N.S.F.C., or the university gliding clubs, qualified youths for elementary gliding certificate A, awarding a badge with one white seagull in flight, B with two seagulls, or C with three. The youngsters had to have soared once for the duration of at least thirty seconds, sixty seconds, or 120 seconds, in that order, to obtain these awards.

Advanced civilian flying qualified the budding glider-pilot for one of three certificates. Certificate I called for two hours flying time calculated from the pilot's log book in flights of at least sixty seconds duration, made over an unrestricted period of time. In addition he had to be released, fly on his own at least once, and fly turns and circles.

Certificate II called for twenty hours of flying, including a minimum of twenty flights of not less than one minute each, in a two-seater glider; while Certificate III required twenty towed starts, in a glider with three or more seats.

The prerequisite glider-training for aspirants to the German *Luftwaffe* was to hold a Class II certificate. (During the war, civilian clubs lacked three-seater gliders, hence the Class III certificate had fallen into abeyance.) Many young Germans were trained up to this standard in the various gliding clubs, thus the *Luftwaffe* had a wide choice of ready-trained personnel and itself provided no facilities for elementary glider training.

Much of the early soaring and gliding centred in the high rolling hills around Wasserkuppe. Its enthusiasts at the time were not interested in getting ready for another war; they wanted to fly, and it is there that soaring and sail-planing matured. And it was volunteers from their ranks—Brautigam, Ziller, Raschke, Brendenbeck, Stapper, Lange, Scheidhauer, Distelmeier, Schulz, Kraft and Pilz—who were to be in the attack on Eben Emael.

In the late 1920s Oeltschner, Klemperer, Hirth, and a host of other Germans captured virtually every national and international glider prize. By 1929 Robert Kronfeld, an Austrian Jew (later to escape to Britain), using a variometer in his *Rhon Geist* sailplane, was the first to exceed a flight of 100 miles. Soon from the heights of the Wasserkuppe he was making equally long flights in his *Wein* (Vienna), and through these flights he gained mastery over ridge and storm-front flying. However it was left to another German, Wolf Hirth, while on an exhibition trip in the United States, to make the first use of thermals in order to soar.

The seed that was to grow into the military glider germinated during the period 1930 to 1933, when technical knowledge of civilian soaring aircraft used for sport, was applied to the development of a 'flying observatory' glider—'Obs' as it was called—by Dr. Alexander Lippisch of the *Rhoen-Rositten-Gesellschaft*.

Dr. Lippisch brought together the best knowledge available from the sports glider and aircraft industries in Germany. By 1933 he had produced a totally new aircraft, much larger, but similar in appearance to some sports gliders. Although retaining their grace and taper, its gull wings were proportionally much thicker and somewhat wider than those of the soaring glider, to enable it to carry the meteorological equipment and several scientists. In keeping the features of the sail-plane, it was to differ radically from the true combat glider of which it was the progenitor. The new craft had to be towed by a powered aircraft from takeoff to within gliding range of its landing area, and then released for a gradual glide to earth. As a general rule, it could not sustain its altitude by riding the air currents as could a sports glider. Its loaded weight and its design committed it to a descending glide, with little or no option for soaring. However, when the glider was lightly loaded, many pilots found it handled so much like a sports glider that they could, on occasion, take advantage of prevailing air currents to enjoy a few minutes of soaring.

For meteorological readings at high altitudes the glider was ideal. When in free flight it was noiseless, vibrationless, and free from the electrical emanations usually found in aeroplanes, that are likely to disturb sensitive instruments. The flying observatory was first towed in tests by the diminutive woman test pilot Hanna Reitsch.

General Ernst Udet, when inspecting the flying meteorological laboratory on one occasion, saw in its design and performance possible military applications. He felt it might be used to supply encircled

A Focke-Wulf FW 56 with a DFS glider

The Go 242A in flight

units, or, perhaps, serve as a kind of modern Trojan Horse, by landing soldiers unnoticed behind an enemy's front lines.

German imaginations also visualized that the total cargo lift capacity of an aeroplane could be almost doubled through the use of a transport glider in tow. A large number of skilled sailplane pilots existed, who could be drawn upon to fly the new gliders. The glider also offered the advantages of low-cost production, ease of manufacture, and expendability.

Along with General Udet, some of the more visionary members of the Air Force, General Jeschonnek in particular, began to press for a combat model. They got one. The design and development of the project was given a 'secret' classification right at the start. It was turned over to the *Deutsche Forschungsanstalt Fuer Segelflug* (DFS), an affiliate of the *Rhoen-Rositten-Gesellschaft*. An aircraft engineer, Hans Jacobs, assisted by glider pilots on the staff of the company, masterminded the project. The glider that grew out of this effort was designated the DFS 230.

The project got under way despite serious controversies between the technical staff and the airborne proponents. The controversy was caused, in part, by the varying viewpoints on the tactical doctrine for glider operations.

The German military forces had experimented extensively with parachuting, and had developed combat tactics for parachute airborne operations. On the other hand, no one had yet seen a combat glider, much less experimented with it. One thing the Germans realized was that landing men by glider had certain advantages over dropping them by parachute. The glider could carry a unit of men—perhaps a squad of seven to nine—and land them together ready to fight. In contrast, parachuting scattered the men into patterns 150 to 200 yards long and for this reason they had difficulty in getting assembled and lost much time in the process. If they were under fire while reassembling, there might be heavy losses. The gliders landed quickly, in small areas, and the men were ready to fight upon landing, without having to cope with the problem of getting out of a parachute harness.

Another feature that helped to sell the advantages of the glider was its silence. It could be released miles from its target and probably land without detection. Rarely could a parachute operation have the surprise of a glider landing. But because there was no agreement on just what the objectives of the programme should be, controversy raged for some months before Jacobs' team received a clear directive to go ahead.

Jacobs was to design a glider that could carry nine fully-armed soldiers, glide and dive noiselessly, and land on short, uncultivated fields. The Germans aimed at keeping the cost at 7,500 Deutsche Marks. This was based on the expense of landing 10 men by parachute.

In other words, the price was equivalent to the cost of manufacturing 10 parachutes.

In early 1939 the strange new craft was finished. It looked very much like a large light aeroplane without a motor. The fuselage was made of a steel tube framework covered with canvas. The wings were set high, and braced. The wheels, once the glider was aloft, could be jettisoned, and the glider landed on a central plywood ski-like skid. It weighed 1,800 pounds and carried 2,800 pounds of cargo. A bench for passengers ran down the centre. Hanna Reitsch, a Captain in the Luftwaffe and a test pilot, was soon test-flying it near Munich.

A number of high-ranking generals including Ernst Udet, the World War I fighter ace, Von Greim, Albert Kesselring, Walter Model and Erhard Milch observed an experimental flight of the DFS 230 and were enthusiastic about its possibilities. Contracts were soon negotiated with the Gothaer Waggonfabrik, a manufacturer of railroad cars in the city of Gotha.

Despite the enthusiasm of a few high-level people, however, the glider's failure to win broad acceptance in German military circles worried some of the more enterprising members of the High Command. What was needed was someone to inject leadership and imagination into the project.

General Hans Jeschonnek, at the time Chief of Operations for the *Luftwaffe* (later to become Chief of the General Staff), called General Student, then still a Colonel, to his office. The two were long-time friends and military associates. After some preliminaries in which he described what was being done in the glider development programme, Jeschonnek, uncertain of Student's sympathy with the idea of building a transport glider, almost apologetically said, 'Nobody gives a damn for the new glider. The best that could happen is that you should take it under your personal wing. Otherwise the whole damn thing will lie dormant.'

This surprising disclosure was the first intimation to Student that anything like a glider transport programme was in progress. He was excited by the challenge and willingly agreed. He took over the project and personally test-flew the glider many times. In his opinion, the glider was of excellent construction, with a good ratio between empty and loaded weight; moreover, it had outstanding flying characteristics. From the start he planned to use this glider not only as a medium of transport but, owing to its noiselessness, as a weapon of attack. It went into production soon thereafter with his strong endorsement, and he personally named it the DFS 230 'attack glider'.

However, the usefulness of the glider from a military point of view continued to be seriously debated. The chief objection came from the parachute enthusiasts who saw in it a source of unwelcome competition. As a consequence, wide differences developed in military circles.

A second demonstration was held, this time before the Army General Staff. Ten *Junkers* (Ju) 52s transporting paratroopers, and ten gliders, carrying glidermen and towed behind ten more Ju 52s, flew to the airfield at Stendal. There the gliders were cast off, and the paratroopers dropped. The gliders dived steeply and came to rest in close formation, discharging glidermen in units ready to fight. The parachutists, on the other hand, who had the ill luck to encounter a stiff breeze—from which the gliders had actually benefited—landed widely dispersed. In some cases they were a considerable distance from their ammunition, which had been dropped by parachute. Though this experiment did not, of course, obscure the importance of paratroopers in a future war, it at least proved conclusively that the troop-carrying glider could become a weapon of great value.

Initial models of the DFS 230 showed the need for some alterations. Loading doors had to be modified to accommodate a greater variety of loads—including bicycles and anti-tank guns—without the need to disassemble them beforehand. It was also desirable to change flight characteristics to enable the DFS 230 to be towed at higher speeds, thus enabling its use with several models of tow-plane. A drogue parachute was added. If the pilot needed additional braking when landing, he released it to billow out behind and slow down the glider.

Soon large-scale production was launched under the supervision of the Gotha works. Many different companies participated in the manufacture of the DFS 230; one of them, was the Hartwig Toy Factory in Sonnenberg, Thuringia. By the time the war broke out a large number of DFSs were ready for combat. By 1942, manufacturers had delivered 1,477 to the *Luftwaffe*.

In 1937 when General Jeschonnek saw that the DFS was going to be produced in quantity, he ordered the *Luftwaffe* to establish transport-glider schools. The government equipped each glider school with DFS 230 gliders. The schools used many different tow planes, the Ju 52, 68, 87, as well as the Me 110 and 111. Even some Gloucester Gladiators that had come into German hands via Finland (to whom these planes had been supplied by the British Government) found their way into the programme.

During 1940, while Churchill valiantly worked to bolster British morale, badly battered by the debacle at Dunkirk and the defeat on the Continent, the Germans began the first phase of 'Seelöwe' (Sea Lion), the invasion of England; a hope that had long tantalized Hitler. According to General Major Fritz Morzik, head of the German Air Transport Command, some consideration had already been given to this operation as early as January. The German staff drew up no formal plan, however, since the lower echelons of the staff were busily engaged in working out details for other urgent military operations. The invasion plan got a further setback on 10th January 1940, when the Belgians captured Major Hallmuth Reinberger, a German officer carrying highly secret strategic plans for the invasion of the west. It is held that this incident delayed further planning for the invasion of England until the summer of 1940.

When France capitulated, Hitler determined to invade England via the southern counties, with gliders playing a major role in operation operation given the code name 'Seelöwe'.

According to the initial plans, gliders were to land in the Folkestone-Hastings area, and isolate and secure it for the main invading (sea-borne) force, by blocking the movement of the British defence forces towards the beaches until the seaborne forces had obtained a secure foothold in England. Glidermen, followed by parachutists, were to secure a landing area. Infantry in gliders and in transport aeroplanes were to follow as soon as the landing area had been reasonably secured. To fly the momentum going, gliders and planes were then to start shuttling back for more troops and supplies until German forces had secured the 'airhead'. Diversionary airborne forces were to land near Oxford to draw British reserves away from the southern beaches, where the German seaborne forces would land.

One of the foremost needs was to support the airborne invasion with heavy artillery and tanks, without which it was doomed to failure. Although five hundred[1] DFS 230s were to carry troops and the lighter equipment, they did not have the cargo capacity necessary to carry tanks or heavy artillery. To fly the heavy equipment over, the Germans conceived an enormous glider, the Messerschmitt (Me) 321, which was to become known as the *Gigant* ('Giant' in German). The *Gigant* would carry tewnty-four tons or 200 fully-equipped men. This is four times as much as the largest British glider ever developed, five times as much as the largest U.S. glider and an equal cargo-capacity to the Boeing 707-320B jet. The *Gigant*'s wing was twice the length of the British Hamilcar's, thirty-five feet longer than the 707 jet's, and has been exceeded since only by the 450-passenger Boeing 747.

The German Air Ministry did not wait for production models to be built. It began to shift forces in the direction of the Channel, and set September as the month for the invasion.

The plan called for tow-planes to haul gliders to a position above the western coast of France, where at 11,000 feet altitude glider pilots would release. This height would give glider pilots enough range, it was calculated, to glide from above the coast of France to landing areas in England. Moreover, the scheme had the advantage that tow-

---

[1] Although this is the number most often given by interrogation reports and other military sources, Colonel Walter Hornung, a former member of the *Luftwaffe*'s Air Transport Command considers the figure 'optimistic' and estimates that only 150 gliders were then available, and somewhat fewer qualified glider pilots.

planes would not be fired at by British anti-aircraft guns and would be less likely to be attacked by British fighter aircraft.

German planners were convinced that the comparative silence of gliders, along with the fact that British radar would have difficulty in detecting them because of their low metal content, gave a strong possibility that the glider assault would take the British by surprise.

Over 15,000 parachute and infantry units assembled at Grosslar and nearby camps in Germany, in mid September 1940. Tension heightened when they got final orders and advance parties departed for St. Quentinand, close to the take-off air bases. All was in readiness.

Meanwhile, sensing peril, the British hastily began to construct anti-airborne defences. German reconnaissance aeroplanes, daily photographing British progress, showed it to be rapid.

Suddenly Hitler cancelled 'Sea Lion'. The German invasion threat to England vanished for the duration of the World War II.

German General Kurt Student contended that the German failure to carry out an invasion of England resulted directly from the lack of a concrete plan prior to the fall of France. He considered it one of the greatest mistakes of the war to allow England to prepare her defences during the summer of 1940, while the German staffs were completing their invasion plans. He believed that an airborne invasion of England should have been launched at the very moment when the British troops were being evacuated from Dunkirk. He felt that he could have captured London in a short time.

The cancellation of plans for the invasion of Great Britain did not stop the Germans from producing new and better models of gliders. After the phenomenal results with the DFS 230 at Eben Emael, a new kind of twin-boom, rear-loading glider, the *Gotha* (Go) 242, went into production at the *Gothaer Waggonfabrik*. An outgrowth of military demand, it could fly light trucks, guns and critical cargo for long distances.

The Air Ministry went on with the development of the Me 321 despite loud outcries from many industrialists and from the military forces involved with other war production. Messerschmitt quickly produced the first developmental model. Because the pressure to get the glider into production was so great, much testing had to be improvised, often with tragic consequences. Except for the Ju 290 (incidentally powered by American engines), the *Luftwaffe* had no aeroplane that could tow the *Gigant* into flight alone. As a result, test engineers resorted to an ingenious arrangement whereby three Me 110s were hitched (like three horses to a chariot) by tow ropes to the nose of a Me 321. This arrangement became known to the Germans as the *Troikatow*, after the Russian word for a team of three horses abreast.

The Me 110, a fighter-bomber, was not designed for towing. It took great dexterity and on the part of the pilots to attempt the delicate task of towing into the air the *Gigant*, which needed 4,000 feet of runway. For some reason the most frequent problem was with towing aircraft on the left, particularly at take-off, which was made at the unduly low speed of 120 miles per hour maximum. The Me on the left frequently had to release prematurely, leaving a task too much for the remaining two and frequently forcing these pilots also to cut off; the Me 321 was then at too low an altitude to land safely. Power differences between the tow-craft set up tow-cable tension variations, adding to flight problems. This matter was never successfully resolved. Finally, multi-towing proved most sensitive to winds and turbulence. It was pure luck when any of the early experimental flights overcame all these problems. Most of them ended with the abortion of the mission and the loss of one or all the test craft involved.

Because take-off speeds were proving too slow to get the *Troika* combinations airborne, and it was thus proving extremely dangerous, designers and test engineers began to use a rocket attached to each wing of the Me 321 to give the thrust needed to get the glider up to acceptable speeds. This worked, and thereafter rocket thrust was habitually used to get the craft off the ground. Incidentally, the Me 321 became one of the first aircraft to use JATO as standard propulsion.

Even though procedures were evolved to make the *Troikatow* safer, still as a way to haul the Me 321, it was costly in tow-craft. Every Me 110 in the *Troika* was one less available for aerial combat. Moreover, *Troikatow* was inefficient at best, and was very tiring to pilots, who had constantly to fight to maintain wingtip distance and flight speed in suitable balance, and to communicate under precarious circumstances.

Searching for a better solution, designers hit upon an idea even more novel if even not more daring than the *Troikatow*. This was to join two He 111s together. Within three months of getting the contract, Heinkel designed and built a five-engined glider tug by fusing two He 111s at wingtip and placing a fifth engine at the wing junction. They built twelve of these grotesque aeroplanes. The pilot sat in the port fuselage. Because it was such an unusual-looking plane, for a long time its mission remained a mystery to Allied intelligence. Unfortunately, the He 111Z—also called the *Zwilling* (twin)—though powerful was a cumbersome craft, and Allied fighters found it easy prey.

Although Messerschmitt manufactured two hundred Me 321s, early tests and later operational experience led *Luftwaffe* generals to the conclusion that these enormous craft were proving too difficult to operate. In addition, they were too difficult to maintain, especially against the ravages of weather in climates found in several of the theatres of war. For these reasons, production was terminated, as were plans for a 60- to 70-ton adaptation of the Me 321. The Germans converted all existing Me 321s into the six-engined Me 323.

To tow the giant Me 321, two He 111 aircraft were joined at the wing-tips and an engine added. This became the He 111Z

Go 242As towed in formation.

Another giant glider produced by the Germans was the *Junkers* (Ju) 322, called the *Mamut* (Mammoth), sometimes incorrectly referred to as the *Merseburg*. The *Mamut* was an enormous wooden all-wing glider, with a 207-foot span and a cargo compartment in the centre of the wing. It never flew well, and with the production of an adequate supply of Me 321s, the Air Ministry decided to put an end to its production.

CHAPTER II

Blood, Sweat and Tears

Pre-war Britain, like its future ally the United States, had not considered using transport gliders as military weapons, although the Soviet use of gliders for this purpose had long been reported. As early as July 1934, the London magazine *Flight* carried a photograph and an account of the GN-4, a five passenger glider built by the Moscow Glider Works.

On the other hand, in pre-war years the British had developed a rich background of experience with sports gliders. During the early 1920s soaring had taken hold in England, and by 1929 a gliding association had been formed. Three years later there were enough enthusiasts flying gliders for the association to sponsor a national championship. By 1937 British gliding techniques and glider construction had progressed enough to earn respect in international circles and to draw a group of young German glider enthusiasts to England, ostensibly to obtain instruction from British experts. Actually, it is likely these Hitler *Jugend* had a better reason for being in England: to collect information on the terrain and on military objectives, especially in southern England; for soon most of them reported for flying training with the Luftwaffe, where this knowledge could prove invaluable in any future conflict.

Whether the British learned anything about German military gliders, or whether at any time during the 1930s information leaked out of Nazi Germany about the closely kept secret of that country's military glider programme is not known. That such activities could have escaped the observation of the highly efficient British intelligence service is extremely doubtful. Nevertheless, whatever the straws in the wind, the British military leadership was apparently unmoved by the potential of the glider as a military weapon. The more serious thought, of a possible cross-Channel glider invasion by an enemy based on the Continent, apparently never crossed military minds.

There was understandable complacency, the result of British history and the belief that the Royal Navy would keep any invasion from British shores. To the British, an invasion of England by sea would be utter madness for an enemy to contemplate. A mood prevailed leading to the conclusion that if fight they must, there would be a drenching bombing from the air in the haphazard style of World War I. Certainly the nation would again show the guts to withstand such an annoyance until victory came again. Nor could they imagine for their islands an invasion such as Hitler later unleashed on Crete. Finally, innovation in the form of a massive glider counter-attack, in retaliation against an enemy preparing to attack from France, was not in the style of the British naval-orientated, sea-immersed mind.

However, much to his credit the Prime Minister Winston Churchill sent a brief instruction to his Chief of Staff in June, 1940. It called for the creation of a 5,000-man parachute force with a proportionate glider element, by the spring of 1941. It was a bold demand, considering that remnants of the British Expeditionary Force in France were still being evacuated from Dunkirk. His wish might have been contested by his staff, who were involved in more urgent matters, had he not adamantly signed it 'P.M.W.', Prime Minister's wish (in other words *no arguing*!). What made the task even more formidable was that the British had to start from scratch in developing their airborne arm, accomplishing in little more than a year what the Germans had taken six years to do.

With traditional British vigour the airborne programme was got under way. To their credit, once at the task they seemed to do better at it than either the Germans or, a bit later, the Americans. This was true of the way the British converted their industrial effort to the task, the manner in which they organized and trained glider pilots, and generally the way they went into combat operations.

Within two days of Churchill's 'wish' having been expressed, the War Office summoned Major J. F. Rock, Royal Engineers, and ordered him to organize the British airborne forces. How he was to do so, of what those forces were to consist, what arms they were to carry, what method was to be used to train them and to transport them to war— these points were not explained. 'It was impossible,' records Rock in his diary, 'to get any information as to policy or task.' Rock was a regular soldier; his acquaintance with aircraft was not more intimate than that of a frequent passenger. He knew nothing of parachutes or gliders beyond what he had read, or was soon to read, concerning their use by the enemy in the attacks delivered against Holland and Belgium six weeks before.

In short order Rock, now a Lieutenant Colonel, formed the Central Landing Establishment, at a private airfield that was soon to be taken over by the R.A.F. At first, the Central Landing Establishment was conspicuous mainly for an almost total lack of the equipment necessary to train parachute soldiers, glider pilots, and air-landing troops. Information was equally scanty. A damaged parachute and jumping helmet captured from the Germans were the only models available, and for aircraft he had four Whitley Mark IIs, which were seldom simultaneously serviceable.

The first glider exercise was a modest one. On an autumn day, 26th October 1940, two single-seater sailplanes moved slowly by, behind two Avro 504 tugs. That was the glider exercise; for that was the *only* serviceable equipment that Rock had to put into the air. Those who witnessed it must have required no little imagination to picture the huge fleets of large gliders which only four years later were seen, by the battered and triumphant inhabitants of Britain, on the wing for the Netherlands and the Rhine.

On 26th April 1941, six months later, Colonel Rock's units staged an exercise for Prime Minister Churchill, although it was again no more than a demonstration. A formation of six Whitleys dropped their full complement of parachute soldiers, five sailplanes landed in formation, and one Hotspur was towed past the Prime Minister. By then it had been realized that to train 5,000 airborne soldiers was a task requiring a great deal of time. Soon after this demonstration Rock organized a Glider Exercise Unit, and experimenting with it Rock and Wing Commander P. B. N. Davis gradually developed usable tactics and techniques for gliders. Expansion continued, and the number of glider-training units considerably increased, until they occupied several stations of the R.A.F.

Although Churchill had been quite definite about the number of paratroopers he wanted in the force, he was vague about what the War Office was to do with glider forces. It is possible that the development and production of gliders, and the recruiting and organization of glider pilots and airborne forces, would have been relatively neglected had not circumstances dictated otherwise. Gliders came into their own somewhat by default. Although Churchill had directed the equipping of a 5,000-man parachute force, it was discovered that due to lack of planes only 800 men could be lifted for a parachute mission. Looking around for a solution, planners turned their attention to the glider as a means of increasing the number of troops that could be airlifted, while minimizing the drain on the already heavily committed powered aircraft available to the nation. They saw that gliders could fill the void. Gliders would supplement the meagre number of powered aircraft available to the airborne establishment, and help to get the 5,000 men 'off the ground' as per the P.M.'s wishes. This led to the production of the eight-passenger Hotspur, the 30-passenger Horsa and the Hamilcar, a first rate competitor to the German *Gigant*. They also developed a 15-seater Hengist, as insurance against the Horsa not proving satisfactory.

The size of the first glider to come off the production line was to a great extent dictated by a number of the exigencies of the time. The

A Stirling taking off with a Horsa glider

Troops emplaning into a Hotspur glider; November 1942

British had no aeroplane in military or commercial use in large numbers, as a transport, that could be converted to tow gliders, such as the Germans had had in the Ju 52. Glider-towing aeroplanes, for the time being, were going to have to be bombers, then in short supply, or old biplane fighters, of which the Hart was one. The largest glider it could tow, according to calculations, was 'About an eight-seater with a wing span of somewhere between 50 to 60 feet.'

The Air Ministry dispensed with the usual design and development procedures and other red tape, and in June 1940 it ordered the eight-place Hotspur glider into production, even though the glider had not yet left the drawing board at General Aircraft; so keen was the need. General Aircraft miraculously delivered Britain's first glider four months later.

The Hotspur proved ideal for the circumstances. Being made of wood, Hotspurs could be built in furniture factories, and their manufacture would thus not create an added burden on the aircraft industry, which was heavily committed to war production. Its most important asset was that it could be quickly mass produced and was immediately ready to fly into combat.

The Hotspur I, first to come off the line, looked much like an over-sized sailplane. It had a stream-lined fuselage and a tapered 62-foot wing. Pilots sat in tandem, and troops squeezed in behind.

General Aircraft constructed several other models of the Hotspur. The Hotspur II had a shorter wingspan and a larger fuselage than the I. The Hotspur III served widely as a trainer. General Aircraft also built a twin Hotspur, in an attempt to speed up the availability of a glider that could carry at least 15 troops. For the 'Twin', engineers joined two Hotspurs by means of a special centre wing section, the pilot and co-pilot flying the craft from the port fuselage. But because of its unpopularity with pilots the R.A.F. did not order quantity production.

Ideal for training, Hotspurs I and II were not large enough to transport the heavy equipment that airborne forces would need to enable them to hit hard once landed; and in time the idea of using the Hotspur for operations was discarded as the Horsa began to make its appearance. No Hotspurs were ever used in combat.

The former Airspeed Aviation Company designed and built the Horsa at its Portsmouth works. Typical of the whole aircraft industry, Airspeed was involved in other R.A.F. projects and was pressed by the unending demands of the R.A.F. for bombers and fighters. Production of the sorely needed Horsas dragged, and it was not until well into 1942 that the first glider came off the production line.

This aircraft was the ugly duckling of the war, its excellent behaviour in flight disguised by an ungainly appearance. Of all-wood construction, it had a high unibraced eighty-eight-foot wing, jettisonable wheels, and a central landing skid. Its length was sixty-eight feet and it stood

The interior of a Hotspur, with glidermen in position for the flight

almost twenty feet high at the top of the large fin. Loaded, it weighed more than seven tons, carrying almost its own weight in troops or cargo. Its interior has been described as not unlike a section of the London Underground in miniature. Unhandsome though it was, it admittedly impressed with its stern, determined dignity.

It was not until 27th March 1942 that the British were able to test-fly the tank-carrying Hamilcar. Seeing this glider for the first time, Colonel Frederick Dent, the American officer in charge of glider production in the United States, remarked, 'It was the biggest hunk of airplane I have ever seen put together.' Tip-to-tip its wing measured 110 feet. By the time several Hamilcars had been produced, the British had also turned out a light fast tank called the Tetrarch, designed to fit snugly into the Hamilcar. A sophisticated aircraft, it was far ahead of its day.

Now that the British had their Tetrarch and Hamilcar, the need for a powerful towing aeroplane arose; reminiscent of the German experience with the *Gigant*. Fully loaded, the Hamilcar weighed more than sixteen tons, even more than a fully-loaded Whitley bomber, then the best available tow-plane.

The Halifax Mark III, a yeoman craft with new four-bladed pro-pellers and the most powerful engines in service, first towed the Hamilcar. Later the still more powerful Halifax Mark V took over the towing task, but even then it was a great strain for the machine to tug the British giant, for in wing-span and wing-area the Hamilcar overwhelmed the Halifax.

By November 1941 the initial period of experimentation, and the training of Britain's first airborne forces had been completed, and a fine base laid for its forthcoming expansion. In that month Major-General F. A. M. Browning, C.B.E., D.S.O., M.C., was appointed General Officer Commanding Airborne Forces and provided with a skeleton staff. From that time on, despite a multitude of difficulties and disappointments, there was no looking back. Airborne forces were now an integral part of the British Army. Presently they wore on their heads the maroon-coloured beret, soon to become famous, and on their shoulders Bellerophon astride winged Pegasus.

In January 1942 the War Office formed the 1st Airborne Division and appointed General Browning its commander. The division con-sisted of an airlanding brigade that would be transported and landed in combat by gliders or aeroplanes, a parachute brigade, and a number of divisional support units. According to this type of organization, and the requirement for military operations visualized by the War Office, it became obvious that more than half of Browning's division would go into combat in gliders.

Concurrently with the formation of the division, the War Office also ordered the formation of a glider pilot regiment in the Army. By this step, and doctrinal policies developed through their training and combat operations, the British took off on a path widely at variance with that of the Germans or the Americans.

The division and the Glider Pilot Regiment were billeted on Salisbury Plain near the Netheravon Aerodrome; the Glider Pilot Regiment was stationed at Shrewton. The 38th R.A.F. Wing, which was to support the Airborne Division and tow its units in gliders, was also stationed at Netheravon. This concentration of units, all to be involved in airborne operations, enabled them to collaborate effectively.

Not only the Airborne Division but also the Glider Pilot Regiment introduced a new concept of war for which many agencies engaged in the war effort were not prepared, especially when it came to providing new and lighter equipment, different clothing and helmets of a new design.

When Colonel Rock went to a flight training school with forty Army officers and other ranks, in order to learn the business of flying gliders, Major George Chatterton, D.S.O., got the task of raising the regiment, a task he found to be no easy matter. That there were a large number of enthusiastic volunteers available was most fortunate; but what they were to be trained to do beyond flying a glider had not been fully determined.

Chatterton made it his goal that glider pilots should reach the high standard, as soldiers, that he required of them as pilots. Not only must they be able to fly with the utmost skill and resolution, they must also be equally at home manning a Bren gun after landing, driving a jeep, or firing a rifle, an anti-tank gun, or a mortar. Out of the many thousand volunteers interviewed for the purpose of choosing glider pilots, very few were accepted. From these, many were unable to pass the stiff flight tests on their way through pilot training, and dropped from the chosen ranks. It was thus only a select band who were judged worthy to follow this arduous and gallant calling.

In the end Britain had in her glider pilot regiment quality pilots and a workable organization such as American airborne commanders wanted but never got. The wisdom of the British as against the short-sightedness and disorganization of the Americans was to come into stark relief in the test of combat.

Colonel Rock was killed in a flying accident late in 1942 and the then Lieutenant-Colonel Chatterton took command of the Glider Pilot Regiment. Chatterton now began to build an organization, constantly insisting upon loyalty and discipline.

Soon the 1st Airborne Division was ordered to North Africa to prepare for the invasion of Sicily. Several hundred glider pilots from the regiment accompanied the Division, thus splitting the regiment. Pilots went to Africa with training incomplete and no night flying experience, although it was the opinion of many that when they made

The Horsa was adopted by U.S. airborne troops in Britain, hence the American markings on this British glider

Men of the 101st Airborne Division unloading a jeep from the mid-section of a Horsa

the flight from Africa to Sicily to begin the Allied invasion it would be a night operation. Few had experienced formation flying over long distances, especially over water.

Situations had evolved over which Colonel Chatterton had no control. He felt that glider pilots had been superbly trained by the Royal Air Force but that, except for brief periods, they were out of touch once the R.A.F. had finished training them. Colonel Chatterton objected to the fact that many of his glider pilots had not been around an airfield for months, arguing that a pilot is a pilot! 'After all, a horseman must live with and in the atmosphere of horses. Is it not the same for pilots? Whatever their employment or the type of aircraft they fly, they must live with and around aircraft,' he said.

While he wanted closer association with the Royal Air Force, at the same time he shied away from the camaraderie and relaxed outlook of the Air Force, feeling this was special to their needs and good for them, but not especially good for the Glider Pilot Regiment, which was a unit of the British Army. Since glider pilots would have to fight as infantry once gliders were landed, he felt they had to have the high and unique standard of infantry discipline for which there was no substitute on the battlefield, where '. . . once committed there is no going back'. He thus sought a compromise.

Colonel Chatterton had major obstacles to overcome to sell his point, however, since during the months after the regiment was first organized it had been handled rather haphazardly, and there were many in the higher echelons who had their own ideas as to how they wanted the regiment to work. Certain of the brigadiers commanding airborne forces would have liked to have the glider pilots serving under their direct control in all matters. Chatterton felt the regiment and its men must be completely independent of any command except his, and he determined he would not bend on this point. He got his way after taking on the single-handed struggle to convince the R.A.F. and the War Office of the logic of his viewpoint. Soon orders made Chatterton commander of the Glider Pilot Regiment. It then started to take on more of an R.A.F. character.

Battalions became squadrons; companies became flights. A 'flight' had four officers and forty other ranks, all glider pilots; and among them they carried four pistols, two tommy guns, two light machine guns and thirty-two rifles. An expansible organization, his squadron could have as many as five flights; and when concentrated after landing its 200 men, backed by their arsenal of weapons, could add up to an infantry battalion in combat power. The regiment became unique not only in the British Army but in history, as a fighting force. While the new units of the regiment might work with, and support, the operations of the R.A.F. groups with which they were to fly, they would at all times remain independent.

At the same time that the War Ministry was organizing glider forces, the R.A.F. had to decide which aircraft could do the job of towing, from among the Hector, Master, Albemarle, Halifax, Stirling or Dakota. For a long time Hectors and Masters towed the lighter Hotspur, but they were quite unable to deal with the larger Horsa. In June 1942 the R.A.F. decided to use the Albemarle, a fairly fast medium bomber, as a troop carrier or a glider tug. They carried out much good experimental work using this aircraft for towing, at a time when nothing else was suitable or available. Later in the Sicilian operations they did use Albemarles, but these were succeeded in other operations by Dakotas, Halifaxes and Stirlings.

During early training the Albemarle and glider pilots had to learn to fly in combination, in an unremitting effort to learn the demanding flight skills needed for combat operations. Through weary months of training they learned that the tug and the glider must be not only a physical but a mental and moral combination. In other words, only the closest feeling of comradeship between the aircraft crew and the glider pilots could achieve the high standard of efficiency required.

That this lesson took some time to learn was due not so much to the pilots themselves, as to the fact that for many months they were located at fields some distance apart. By the autumn of 1942 hundreds of glider pilots had been trained, and awaited action in army camps on Salisbury Plain. An adequate supply of gliders and tugs was not available, however, to keep them in training, and the pilots' skills grew stale. Moreover, they were having no contact with the crews of the tugs. Colonel Chatterton remedied the situation by gradually obtaining quarters for the glider pilots at the main airfield, but this took time to achieve.

Meanwhile glider pilots gradually built up their flying hours. Soon Hamilcars carried tankmen and their tanks on familiarisation flights. One led to an extraordinary crash. The Hamilcar touched down at between ninety and a hundred miles an hour at one of the fields. It careened wildly across the airfield, demolished two Nissen huts, and stopped in the wreckage. Colonel Chatterton rushed to the site. He found that the tank had shot forward right through the glider and the buildings, and had come to rest unscathed fifty yards further on; rushing towards it, Chatterton met the tank driver crawling out, with some remarks that were coolly casual considering that he had just been zipping along at eighty miles an hour, a speed unsurpassed by any tank in history.

On 19th November 1942 the British initiated their glider operations with 'Freshman', a mission to destroy the Norsk Hydro Plant at Vermork, eighty miles inland and sixty miles from Oslo. This was a heavy water plant reportedly connected with German research on the atomic bomb. Two Halifaxes, each towing a Horsa, took off from Skiffen in Scotland. Each glider carried fifteen sappers (army engineers), all volunteers, with Lieutenant G. M. Methuen in command. Two of the pilots, Staff Sergeant M. F. C. Strathdee and Sergeant P. Doig, came from the Glider Pilot Regiment. The other glider pilots were Australian; Pilot Officer Davies and Sergeant Fraser, R.A.A.F. Squadron Leader Wilkinson, R.A.F., piloted the first tow plane, and was accompanied by Group Captain Cooper, and a Canadian, Flight Lieutenant Parkinson, piloted the second aircraft.

The small force faced many difficulties. The worst of them was the fact that the Halifax crews had little experience in towing gliders. The Halifaxes were modified for the mission, but their performance was marginal for the job they had to accomplish. The cooling system was inadequate to keep the engines from overheating, as they worked harder than normal while towing gliders. No one was certain that the straining engines could pull the load the 400 miles across the North Sea. The flight over water almost all the way called for pin-point navigation, so that the two combinations could cross the Norwegian shore almost on target. Plans dictated that once Methuen's men had destroyed the 'heavy water' and the plant, he then had to lead his men through snow-covered mountains to Sweden. The Norwegian underground stood ready with guides for the long and arduous trek.

At 2341 monitors at Skiffen got a faint voice by radio, believed to be Parkinson's, asking for a course to bring him back to Skiffen. The monitors worked frantically trying to plot his location. By intersection of radio beams they located Parkinson over the North Sea. Fourteen minutes later, monitors heard a voice grimly stating, 'Glider released in sea'. But could it be? For a quick calculation on a signal received from Wilkinson showed him to be above the mountains in Southern Norway. The mission was in trouble—that much was certain.

The full story did not become known until some years after the war. Trouble plagued the mission from the start. Weather was thick, although meteorologists promised a clear sky and a moon over the target. Before take-off one tug's wing-tip light, and both tow-rope telephones, failed; as the use of radio was frowned upon, a simple code of light signals had to be improvised. By the time they had accommodated to these faults, darkness had fallen; and what was worse, night take-off with full load had not been practised before. Given the option to postpone the operation until the next day, the pilots chose to take-off at night and get on with the job. By 1750 Wilkinson's combination had taken wing into a darkening sky, and twenty minutes later the second followed. Wilkinson chose to fly high, picking his way through broken cloud and reaching Norway at 10,000 feet altitude. Then just as he needed his Rebecca radio beam system, to tie into the Norwegian agents' Eureka to direct the airplane to the target, he found the Rebecca did not work. Cooper, doing the navigation, could now only rely on maps, but a heavy layer of snow disguised all landmarks.

Wilkinson passed over what might have been the release point, but lacking clear identification made another circle to find the target. The Norwegian agents in the landing zone had heard the aircraft flying almost directly over them on its first attempt but, since the Rebecca radio beam had failed, they could make no contact. By now he had been flying for five and a half hours and still had 400 miles to go to get back to Skiffen. He flew into thick cloud about forty miles northwest of Rjukan, and could not climb out of it. By this time there was barely sufficient petrol to get the tug and glider home. Ice began forming on the craft, and worse still, on the tow-rope. Both tug and glider lost height rapidly. They sank into unbroken cloud and somewhere in the void above Stavanger the two rope parted. Staff Sergeant Strathee now started a descent in zero visibility. Dense cloud turned into swirling snow. It was at this point that the wireless operator had sent out his signal. The plane, unable to do any more, just succeeded in returning before its petrol ran out. The glider crash-landed at Fylesdalen, on top of the snow-covered mountains overlooking Lysefjord, killing Lieutenant Methuen, Strathee, Doig and five others, and injuring four more severely.

Meanwhile Parkinson flew low above the sea, trying to keep beneath the clouds until just short of the Norwegian coast, there hopefully to encounter the promised clear weather. Parkinson crossed the coast near Egersund and was heading towards Rjukan when his plane hit a mountain beyond Helleland. As the plane crashed, somehow the tow rope snapped but the glider, with little chance for manoeuvre left, made a heavy landing close by, killing three. German troops soon captured all survivors. The Gestapo then took over. They poisoned the four injured in the first glider crash while they were in a hospital recovering. On Hitler's standing orders the Gestapo then shot the nineteen uninjured men as saboteurs.

Was this grim tragedy to prove an omen for British glider combat experiences of the future? This was soon to be tested on the barren soil of Sicily.

CHAPTER III

America Hops the Bandwagon[1]

We're going to build 350 gliders a month.
                                    General B. E. Meyers
This programme started in confusion and will undoubtedly end that way.
                                    John C. Warren

While the Germans were acquiring a notable proficiency in the construction and use of the glider as a military instrument, American gliding enthusiasts found little encouragement in official circles. Neither in the War Department in general nor in the Air Corps was there any appreciable sympathy for the ardour of the 'glider people'; nor, for that matter, was there any real appreciation of the military value of gliders among the civilian devotees of soaring.

As early as 1922, Glenn Curtiss designed a glider which he thought might be useful as a target. Curtiss believed the glider might be towed by a motor boat, then released and fired upon. During the next two years thirteen target gliders were actually built at McCook Field, and distributed throughout the service for use instead of the conventional tow targets. Beyond this, however, the Air Corps did not go. While acknowledging the 'considerable enthusiasm' for gliding in the United States and abroad, McCook Field reported that it was adhering to Air Corps policy not to undertake any 'large scale' investigations.

By 1930 gliding was still primarily a sport, and when a glider enthusiast invited the Air Corps to participate in a national glider meet at Elmira, N.Y., the Assistant Secretary of War replied that 'there exists no appropriation whereby an officer on the active list could be dispatched to a duty such as you mention.' The following year the Secretary of War said: 'It is considered that the military value of glider flying is negligible, and that the expenditure of time and funds required to teach the art is not warranted.'

As late as 1938 the War Department was not convinced that the glider had any real value as a military weapon. Harry Malcolm, of

---

[1] John C. Warren's *Airborne Operations in World War II European Theatre* (U.S.A.F. Historical Study 97) has been consulted for this chapter.

Lombard, Illinois, suggested in August 1938 that gliders might be utilized to carry bombs or troops, or they might be built as aerial torpedoes. Military officials dismissed the idea by pointing out that an equivalent load could be carried more efficiently by the towing plane. Malcolm was informed that 'the plan of your suggested method of towing gliders as practical weapons is not of sufficient military value to warrant further consideration and development.'

In 1940 U.S. Military Intelligence of the War Department General Staff quoted reliable evidence indicating that the Germans had used gliders in the capture of Fort Eben Emael in Belgium, that glider practice was being carried out on many German aerodromes, and that the Germans had already built gliders 'in some numbers' and were 'prepared to use them for troop and possibly tank transport.'

The United States Military Attaché at Bern reported that glider trials were carried out at Brunswick and Naunheim in March and April 1941, and related that 'General Kitzinger (probably a cover name) told Swiss Staff Officers that the German General Staff attached much importance to the trials of transportation of troops by glider.' Twelve days after the submission of the report from Bern, thousands of glider-borne German troops began the spectacular invasion of Crete. Here was the final proof that gliding was more than a Sunday pastime.

Even after the initial German successes with gliders in the war had aroused a new interest in gliding in the United States, the Air Corps was not in a position to accede to the more vehement proposals of soaring zealots because of the urgent military demands for powered aircraft and aeroplane pilots.

As the evidence on German use of military gliders accumulated, the U.S. Army Air Force (A.A.F.) began to develop a positive glider policy. On 25th February 1941 General Henry H. Arnold, Chief of the A.A.F., decided that 'In view of certain information received from abroad a study should be initiated on developing a glider that could be towed by aircraft.' He directed that the study be completed by 1st April. To gear up for production, his staff soon issued two classified technical instructions to its procurement offices, one for glider design studies, the other for the procurement of '2, 8, and 15-place gliders and associated equipment.'

Almost before the ink was dry on the technical instructions, on 8th March 1941, Air Force technical officials sent preliminary engineering requirements for 15-place gliders to eleven companies, and by May they ordered experimental models of 2-place training gliders, and static- and flight-test models of 8 and 15-place transport gliders. The stage was now set for a programme that was soon to blossom into a monumental effort. It remained unheralded, plagued with vicissitudes, shunned and neglected. Yet it was a production miracle.

53

In October 1941 General Arnold appointed Lewin B. Barringer, well-known in civilian soaring, as co-ordinator of the glider programme. Barringer served until January 1943, when a plane in which he was flying disappeared over the Caribbean. Although his was largely an advisory job until his death, Barringer played a vital part in the glider programme, swinging a big stick merely by virtue of being Arnold's man.

In reviewing the role of the glider programme after Barringer's death, General Arnold decided to give it the staff prestige it needed by establishing an office of 'Special Assistant for the Glider Programme'. It carried the same power as the several assistant chiefs of air staff in matters relating purely to the glider programme. A day later Arnold appointed Richard C. DuPont to this position. Richard DuPont was a soaring enthusiast, an important reason for the appointment. Equally important, however, was his family background as scion of the DuPont family. Arnold hoped through the association to bring the enormous DuPont enterprises into active support of the glider programme, as a way to draw industrial backing. Within five months Richard was killed in a glider crash. Arnold immediately appointed Major Felix DuPont, Richard's brother, to the office.

Arnold's attitude toward the glider programme, and his relationship with Barringer, are indicated in the following comments made by General Frederick P. Dent, Jr., then a colonel in charge of the glider development at the Aircraft Laboratory at Wright Field, Dayton, Ohio. General Dent made these comments in an interview with the author held at his residence near Eglin Air Force Base, Florida, in January 1969.

I would like to talk a little bit about a part of the programme that is a little touchy. I think General Arnold was one of the finest leaders we ever had. He was dynamic, and he certainly did one hell of a good job during the war, not only to produce airplanes and gliders but also to fulfil the military requirements of two different theatres. There was certainly an awful lot of pressure on him to go one way or the other.

General Arnold did, however, have one very serious weakness. He did not understand engineering, and he did not understand Wright Field, although he had commanded it at one time. As a result, anything concerned with development and production was a burden to him; and he was not interested in it. As a matter of fact from about 1938 to 1943, a period of five years, I think the records show that General Arnold visited Wright Field only once. The only time he saw a glider was when it was a completed product.

General Arnold had another weakness, which was that any civilian knew more than anyone in uniform. This attitude was reflected not only in the progress of the glider programme but also in different parts of the Pentagon itself. As an example, at about this time we realized that we had to set up an office in Washington as a central place for co-ordinating the glider programme. In addition to production and development of gliders, there was also a very active glider training programme in progress. My office had stepped out of the training business at the conclusion of the training of the first class of pilots. General Arnold picked a chap by the name of Lou Barringer, a real fine individual and one of the nicest people I ever met, to head the Washington office. Lou Barringer had spent quite a bit of time as a soaring pilot, but he knew absolutely nothing about the military. He did not speak the language; he had no idea what the military requirements were; and in heading the office he really did not give us much help. As a matter of fact, he got interested in several other developments, and these other interests hampered our programme. Lou Barringer was ordered overseas to take a look again at what the British were doing when he was killed. General Arnold then had to look around for someone to take his place, and he found Richard DuPont, again a very fine man who had had several successes in international flying meets. Again, he knew nothing about military requirements and did not speak our language!

The effort of experimenting with and developing tactical gliders taxed the ingenuity of the engineers of the Air Force's Experimental Engineering Section at Wright Field, and those in civilian industry. In the absence of previous American experience with transport gliders, originality and design skill became essential in the glider programme.

Of the eleven companies to whom preliminary engineering requirements went out in March, only the Frankfort Sailplane Company, the Waco Aircraft Company, Bowlus Sailplanes, Inc., and the St Louis Aircraft Corporation sent favourable replies. The other firms said that they had previous manufacturing commitments, which they did not prefer to alter, or that the proposed glider was too large for their facilities.

Thus, early in its development work, the Materiel Command at Wright Field, which was saddled with the job of procuring the gliders, ran into one of the major obstacles of the entire programme. This was the inexperience and limited capacity of the concerns that might be willing and able to manufacture gliders. Most of the established aircraft companies in the United States were expanding to produce urgently needed fighters and bombers for the European war. The Air Corps regarded the need for powered aircraft as paramount, and instructed the Materiel Command to place glider orders with companies not already engaged in the manufacture of powered combat aeroplanes. This policy severely hampered the glider effort.

Anxious to begin work at once with available facilities, Wright Field officials negotiated at once with the four companies interested in the preliminary proposals.

It finally placed an order with the Frankfort Sailplane Company, on 7th May 1941, for the XCG-1 and XCG-2 (X for experimental; C for cargo; G for glider) experimental transport gliders. Unfortunately Frankfort's first glider did not meet specifications or pass structural tests. At that time Frankfort were achieving recognition for the construction of the Frankfurt utility gliders for the A.A.F.'s glider-pilot training programme, and gave evidence of being better suited for

Waco CG-4A landing in Lubbock, Texas

Henry Ford Senior (right) celebrates with Col. Dent and Lt.-Col. Price
the first glider to come off the Ford production line in October 1942

producing training gliders than for developing and manufacturing transport gliders. Since this was the situation, the Air Force felt it better to cancel the transport contract, and did so towards the end of the year.

Another contract signed with the Waco Aircraft Company of Troy, Ohio, called for one static-test and one flight-test model of an 8-place XCG-3 glider, and one static-test and two flight-test models of a 15-place XCG-4 glider. Although Waco was a small company, it had been a pioneer in manufacturing commercial aircraft and was better prepared to handle a development contract than were most of the corporations to whom the Wright Field turned in the early days of the glider programme.

Waco completed one XCG-3 wind-tunnel model within a few weeks. It delivered a structural static-test model to Wright Field laboratories on 26th December 1941, and a flight-test model on 31st January 1942. Early in February, after flight tests, the A.A.F. found the XCG-3 satisfactory, and in April accepted it and ordered quantity production. However, numbers were later substantially reduced in favour of the XCG-4 which, from the standpoint of cargo capacity, came nearer to meeting forecast needs.

Waco delivered the static-test model of the XCG-4 on 28th April 1942, and the first flight-test model arrived at Wright Field on 14th May. In a significant test conducted shortly afterwards the XCG-4, carrying fifteen passengers, flew successfully in tow from Wright Field to Chanute Field, Illinois, and back—a distance of 220 air miles!

Designed by the engineers at Waco and the Materiel Section at Wright Field along the same general lines as the XCG-3, the XCG-4 differed primarily in size. It was bigger, had a gross weight of 6,800 pounds, and carried a 3,750-pound load; substantially more than its own unloaded weight.

In this glider the Air Forces found the solution to the urgent need for a reliable, easily manufactured, durable combat craft. The glider enthusiasts had now established the basis for a production effort of remarkable proportions, achieved despite many problems and disappointments along the way.

Before Waco was able to deliver the static-test XCG-4, the Air Force was forced to conclude that other contractors for experimental tactical gliders could probably not supply an acceptable 15-place glider. As a consequence, and in view of the urgent need for gliders, and the satisfaction with Waco's progress on the XCG-3 and XCG-4, Wright Field gave production contracts for the Waco gliders before other companies had completed their experimental models. In fact, before the first flyable XCG-4 was delivered on 11th May the need for CG-4As had become so pressing that Wright Field went ahead and contracted with eleven companies for a total of 640 CG-4As.

These contractors, and those to be involved in the design and development of other models, brought in many subcontractors to provide wings, steel cable, steel tubing and fittings, finally swelling the total to more than 115 companies. These companies included the H. J. Heinz Pickle Company, which manufactured wings, the Steinway Piano Company, which also produced wings, Anheuser-Busch, Inc., the Brunswicke-Balke-Collender Company, and a canoe manufacturer.

The Air Force continued to investigate many other glider models of comparable size to the CG-4A, to determined if they had more desirable characteristics. For various reasons, primarily the need to settle on one model and get it into mass production, only one prototype was built of most other gliders, for it soon became clear the XCG-4A (the Waco) was the favoured 15-place glider.

During the next few months, contractors were plagued with conflicting directives about the production future of the combat glider. Although Air Force officials had reason to complain about contractor performance, contractors could legitimately complain about the plague of conflicting directives issued by the Air Force.

In March and April 1943 the Wright Field officials resolutely pressed Washington to get a firm decision on the models and quantities of gliders required. There was a note of desperation in the testimony of one Wright Field executive who, lamenting the absence of a clearly defined policy with regard to future glider procurement, summarized his view of the glider effort by observing, 'This programme started in confusion and will undoubtedly end that way'.

General Arnold unsettled all those involved in the endeavour by saying that the glider they were producing '. . . was not built to meet the purpose for which it was intended.' In his opinion the CG-4A involved too much engineering, cost too much, and took too much time to build. 'It should be cheapened,' and be good for only one flight. Further, he believed it should be made entirely of wood.

General Meyers did even more to upset designers when he expressed the belief that glider fuselage should be telescopic, its parts nesting together so that shipping space could be saved.

General Lee felt that the problem of shipping-space could be solved by resorting to British producers. He announced that British production in 1943 was 1,340 Horsa gliders, and in 1944 approximately 1,400. Revised schedules showed that British production could be considerably in excess of requirements. They were therefore planning to curtail the production of gliders at two plants and transfer these to aeroplane construction. General Lee stated that as a result of several conferences with British authorities, an agreement had been arrived at. If the American government would immediately consider placing orders for gliders within the British Isles (with these two plants), then the British production of gliders would be held steadfast, and both men and equipment maintained until a decision could be arrived at about American requirements.

A full discussion took place at this time about the number of gliders that might be required for American operations in the British Isles. The conference agreed that 600 should be ordered to be constructed in Britain during 1943, and an additional 900 in 1944; the entire 1,500 to be delivered on or before 1st July 1944. This discussion proceeded to the point where it was decided that orders definitely would be placed; but they never were.

From the 14th through the 17th of April a series of meetings took place in Washington to unscramble the mess. On 15th April Brigadier General O. A. Anderson reported that the War Department General Staff had not completed its requirements for gliders, but expected to have them ready soon. General Anderson *expressed doubt that gliders could be used in a major operation*, stating facetiously that 'haste should be made slowly in the whole matter'.

In April 1943 General Meyers had submitted data on the glider manufacturers to Lieutenant General William S. Knudsen, Director of War Production, and requested Knudsen to come to a decision about marginal or high-cost contractors. General Knudsen recommended that the contract of Robertson and three other companies be cancelled. However, on 1st May the Under Secretary of War, Robert P. Patterson, notified General Meyers that he believed it would be cheaper to continue all CG-4A contracts than to cancel those of the poor producers. The A.A.F. allowed Robertson to continue the production of CG-4As, and by August the company had delivered sixty-three gliders.

A major tragedy finally drew public attention to the glider programme and broke the spell of apathy surrounding it. On 1st August 1943 the 65th CG-4A manufactured by the Robertson Corporation of St Louis, Missouri, carried on a demonstration flight the corporation president, Mayor Charles L. Cunningham, other executives of St Louis, and military officials. High over the field a wing suddenly disintegrated, and the glider plummeted to earth, killing all its passengers.

The A.A.F. rushed investigators to the scene of the crash. The complex system of subcontracting, involving several stages of sub-assembly at various factories, and a complicated flow of materials from contractors to subcontractors and back, made the problem of establishing responsibility for the tragedy exceedingly difficult. The investigation finally revealed that an over-machined, weakened inner-wing fitting (manufactured, ironically, by the Gardner Metal Products Company in St Louis, former manufacturers of caskets) had snapped.

The investigating board reported that inspection personnel at Robertsons were inexperienced, and had inadequate inspection equipment. Furthermore, the Air Force Inspector General, Colonel L. M. Johnson, reported that his investigation of the Robertson crash left him 'firmly convinced that the conditions which were in existence at St Louis prior to this accident are prevalent throughout the country. There is little that the Materiel Command can do to correct conditions.'

Poor workmanship, improper methods of manufacture, and general inefficiency of contractors at the plants, were all unfortunate aspects of the glider programme.

On 16th March 1942 five representatives of the Ford Motor Company conferred with representatives of the Air Forces Aircraft Laboratory to discuss the possibility of Ford's participation. Subsequent negotiations resulted in the award of a contract, approved on 30th June 1942, for 1,000 CG-4As. In view of the resources, facilities, and experience of the Ford Motor Company, it is interesting to note that Ford delivered only six gliders by February 1943. While this accomplishment was not by any means unsatisfactory for a company that had not been brought into the programme until some three months after the majority of companies had been given contracts, nonetheless it indicates that the problems of getting into full production were not resolved in a matter of a few weeks.

In fact, serious delays in beginning production were common to all the glider manufacturers with the exception of Cessna, and Cessna received extensive government aid not given to other contractors. The experience of the Ford Company, viewed in relation to the performance of other contractors, suggests that the agencies responsible for glider procurement should have allowed for at least a six months period between the award of a contract and the start of quantity production. Without a well-organized programme for preparing tools and equipment, and ready access to materials, this preparatory organizational period should have been much longer.

If Ford's performance demonstrated the need for an unavoidable six months to prepare for production, it also soon proved the advantage of placing orders with experienced, financially sound concerns that were familiar with quantity production. The Ford glider plant at Iron Mountain, Michigan, produced more than twice as many gliders as any other company in the years 1942, 1943, and 1944. It is true, of course, that Ford was not handicapped by concomitant work on experimental glider projects. Initial delays in no way detracted from this contractor's contribution to the glider programme, which was sizeable from the standpoint of numbers manufactured.

In March 1944 Wright Field procured an additional 1,200 CG-4As from Ford, and in September the contract was further increased by 725 gliders. As part of the October 1944 procurement for an extended CG-4A programme, Ford was awarded a letter contract for an additional 2,000, making a total procurement of 4,925 Wacos from this contractor. By 31st October 1944 Ford had delivered 2,418 CG-4As and twenty-six CG-13As, or twenty-three per cent of the tactical gliders supplied for the entire glider programme. Ford's unit cost of approximately 15,400 dollars on these gliders proved the economy of efficient, experienced mass production. Most other companies did not produce a glider for less than 25,000 dollars.

While the CG-4A programme was being carried out, the Materiel Command went ahead with the development of larger gliders. In June 1943 Major DuPont's office foresaw a requirement for 30-place gliders. This was soon approved.

In April 1942 the Air Force contracted with the Laister Kauffmann Aircraft Corporation for three XCG-10 30-place troop-cargo gliders of wooden construction.

By the fall of 1942 the CG-4A was in production and Waco, the designer of the glider, in a position to undertake a new development project. The Air Force desired to apply Waco's experience with 15-place gliders to the problem of developing gliders of larger capacity. A contract was awarded to that company to develop a 30-place troop-carrier glider, the XCG-13, having a towing speed of 174 miles per hour, a gross weight of 15,000 pounds, and a useful load of 8,000 pounds.

XCG-10 production lagged, and the first flight-test, and static-test models were not delivered until October 1943. In the meantime the Waco Aircraft Company had completed its XCG-13 30-place glider. When the XCG-13 was approved for production in the fall of 1943, work on the XCG-10 was stopped and the Laister-Kauffmann contract was changed to call for the XCG-10A, a 42-place glider of wooden construction. Laister-Kauffmann delivered the glider to the Clinton County Army Air Field on 30th April 1944, and in August the Air Forces declared the glider suitable for production.

The first flight model of the XCG-13 was delivered to Wright Field on 10th March 1943. The XCG-13 was the first of the large gliders to meet military requirements, and the Air Force quickly ordered service-test and production models.

Numerous suggestions came from the front, as America gained combat experience with gliders. These ideas led to landings on packed snow and on water. Therefore it was suggested that gliders could be used for the routine supply of fixed and mobile ground and air-force units of all types, with weapons, ammunition, food, and personnel. It was pointed out that this kind of supply operation would be especially useful for armoured units. Another suggestion was that an airborne repair depot might be dropped wherever mechanized ground-force equipment and ordnance material needed repair. Gliders might move airborne field hospitals from one location to another, and they might evacuate wounded from combat areas. They might also be used as carriers for raiding parties, and in rescuing ground-force elements that had become isolated.

Many of these suggestions, which at first might have been thought far beyond the scope of gliders, were made feasible by the improvement of a pick-up device that enabled a flying tow-plane to whisk away a loaded glider from a field. It became known as the 'snatch' technique. The A.A.F. used this method extensively to recover thousands of gliders that had landed in combat. Medical units used the system to evacuate litter-patients in gliders.

During 1944 the A.A.F. conducted studies to determine whether the Hamilcar, or any other glider, could be carried in a pick-a-back fashion as the Germans had done with some of their gliders. The effort was concentrated on using the P-38 attached to the top of the Hamilcar, although consideration was given to the P-38 and XCG-10 combination as well. This arrangement of aircraft had some decided advantages but no tests were ever made.

Beginning in December 1941 the Materiel Command procured several experimental tow-target and bomber-loaded gliders. The Bristol Aeronautical Corporation of New Haven, Connecticut, built twenty-one C-1 tow-target gliders. In May 1942 the Fletcher Aviation Corporation of Pasadena, California, delivered ten XBG-1 radio-controlled bomber-gliders. Another project undertaken in 1943 was the development of the XFG-1 fuel-glider, an unconventional tail-less glider with swept-forward wings that would fuel a powered aircraft in flight.

On 1st April 1942 General Arnold directed the Materiel Command to make a study and perform tests to determine the suitability of combat and transport aircraft to tow gliders. Wright Field conducted extensive tests of tow-planes, beginning in the summer of 1942, and by October 1944 the Air Force listed the A-25, B-25, C-46, C-47, C-54, C-60, P-38, and any four-engine bombers or transport planes, as suitable for towing the 15-place CG-4A and CG-15A gliders. The 30-place CG-13A could be towed by either a C-46, C-54, B-17, or B-24. By the end of November 1944, however, tactical considerations as well as the performance and availability made the C-47 the outstanding tow-plane.

For the development of suitable tactical gliders the Materiel Command awarded twenty-two contracts to sixteen companies between April 1941 and 31st October 1944. In addition, the Aircraft Laboratory modified a C-47 transport, and evaluated foreign gliders. Four production-model tactical gliders were developed: the CG-3A, CG-4A, CG-13A and CG-15A. The XPG[1]-2 was also approved for production, but no procurement of it was authorized. The converted C-47 (XCG-17) was tested and considered to have tactical utility.

The production programme was plagued by discord, a mixture of misdirection and lack of direction, absence of firm goals, and bad

[1] PG: Powered glider.

management at several levels. That this condition was permitted to exist in the production of such a sensitive piece of Air Force material was criminal negligence on the part of many involved in the programme from the War Department down, and their dereliction was not long in showing.

The development of tactical gliders was one of the most difficult tasks undertaken by the Air Force. Working with few precedents to guide them, and handicapped by provisions that excluded the larger aircraft companies from participating, Air Force engineers were none-theless asked to develop acceptable gliders in the shortest possible time.

Key leaders vacillated to such an extent in advancing the programme that they plainly lacked a good understanding of the potential of the glider. Or, having this understanding, either they were still uncertain of the glider's potential, or lacked the courage and strength to push the programme. It probably survived mostly through the conviction and dedication of a few subordinates in the Air Force, saddled with the working-level responsibility, whose foresight gave them a basis for continuing despite the obstacles.

Meanwhile, defective gliders were coming off the line, to be flown by glider-pilots and ridden in by troops, all blissfully unaware of the danger inherent in the defective product they were using, in training and combat missions already supercharged with peril.

CHAPTER IV

Crete—Gliders Lose Hitler's Favour

In two different attacks, Greece was to feel the glider's sting. On 23rd April 1941, General Alexander Papagos, commander in chief of the Greek Army, surrendered. Forces consisting of Australians, New Zealanders, men from the United Kingdom, and miscellaneous Greek units, were now in deep trouble. An evacuation from Greece was the alternative to annihilation.

The Germans had sensed another Dunkirk in the making and were doing everything in their power to trap the British. In hard-driving pursuit they rapidly converged on the ports of Porto Rafti and Rafina east of Athens, through which any evacuation must take place. Lieutenant-General Henry Wilson leading a mixed corps of New Zealanders, Australians and British, began withdrawing towards the ports, meanwhile fending off the probing German elements, and determined to set a trap for them.

Wilson realized that the Germans might soon capture the ports. When they fell, he must then evacuate from the small ports of Nauplia, Kalamata and Monemvasia, a hundred miles to the south, nestled within the fingers of the Peloponnese and connected to the mainland by the sandy narrow Isthmus of Corinth.

The Corinth bridge spanned the gorge-like Corinth Canal which sliced that isthmus. It carried the main artery towards the ports, vital to the operational effectiveness, if not the survival of Allied forces in Greece. Some anti-aircraft guns, several artillery pieces manned by Greek troops—all wearied by days of combat and harassment by dive-bombing Stukas—defended the bridge. Several companies of equally harried troops had been dropped off from units crossing the bridge on the night of the 23rd, to bolster the strength of the defenders. They had barely dug in. A handful of engineers had managed to mine the abutments and girders and stood ready to explode and topple the bridge eighty feet into the bed of the canal.

General Student, who was in Plovdiv, Bulgaria, along with selected elements of his 7th Flieger Division, watched and waited, his attention focused on the Corinth Canal, and the sensitive bridge whose capture would cut Allied forces in two and prevent their withdrawal, and over which German forces could speed into the Peloponesus to destroy Allied resistance there. He ordered Colonel Alfred Sturm, commanding the division's second regiment, to take the bridge in a parachute attack.

Months before, the Germans had studied ways to take the bridge. Most of the top military commanders, and staffs involved in the planning for such an operation, felt that the bridge could be seized only by parachutists. Apparently they held the view that regardless of the stunning victory at Eben Emael, military gliders were no longer a secret, and their surprise value as a weapon had been lost; thus, they could not, by any stretch of the imagination, be thought of as having any value for an operation similar to Eben Emael again in history.

Most of the experienced glider pilots held an opposing view. If the 'establishment' view was valid, then, contended Wilhelm Fulda, it followed that one could not expect infantry to make a surprise attack either, since surprise by infantry attack had been forever lost after the first infantry attack in history, whenever it was. Fulda had piloted one of the gliders in the attack against the bridges near Eben Emael.

The majority of glider pilots felt the establishment viewpoint as very narrow, short-sighted and stupid. They worked hard to change it, but with no success in the quarters that counted. They refused to let the matter rest, and felt their best opportunity to prove their point would be in pressing for a chance to make another successful Eben Emael-like raid.

Few higher-ranking sympathizers dared to voice their support of the glider pilots' views, with one surprising exception.

One day in March 1941, Fulda, then a lieutenant glider instructor at Fassburg near Hannover, got a telephone call to report to Colonel Stein in Hildesheim. Stein was in charge of ground operations there and had been a student of Fulda's before the war, when Fulda was an instructor in Germany's glider training programme. Stein held Fulda in high esteem, respected his ideas, and agreed with his view that the glider could be used again for surprise raids.

Stein astonished Fulda. He said there was a possibility that gliders would be used in a raid now under study, and said, 'Maybe there is a chance for a raid. I don't know. We must do what we are told now and wait and see.' He told Fulda to select twelve glider pilots—'The best!' Also Fulda was to take charge of the operation, including the shipping of twelve to fifteen gliders to Plovdiv in Bulgaria. Stein warned that the mission was top secret.

By 13 March Fulda had his small force assembled at Graf Ignatiev airfield outside of Plovdiv. There he waited for orders. Days turned into weeks without a word from anyone.

Finally things began to bustle at the field. German parachute units set up camp nearby; but the action seemed to bypass Fulda. Finally, one day Colonel Stein flew in. He seemed depressed and paid little heed to Fulda. Fulda finally insisted on a meeting. It was very unsatisfactory, and Fulda got the impression that the possibilities of a raid had evaporated, which apparently they had. Fulda had never been so frustrated in his life. He sensed some great event was about to break and wanted to participate.

He got a motorcycle, and a sidecar and driver, and instructed the driver to take him from unit to unit of troops. At 2200, tired and cold, he drove into a parachute artillery camp where he met an equally frustrated Lieutenant von Sooden. Von Sooden's outfit could not become a part of General Seussman's task force, that was preparing to go in an operation, because there was no way to air-land them by Ju 52s in the area where the jump was to take place.

Fulda said: 'I can do it for you. I have gliders!'

The lieutenant had to be told what Fulda meant. Von Sooden didn't know that a military glider existed. Words stumbled pell-mell from Fulda as he hurriedly explained he had done just such an operation at Eben Emael. Von Sooden was soon convinced.

They raced to Plovdiv to see Major Graf (Count) Uxkull, the operations officer for the raid. He at first ridiculed the idea. Fulda and von Sooden pleaded. He relented; he would think it over. They left.

Uxkull called the next morning. 'I have thought over your idea. It is good. We will use your gliders. Tell Stein.'

Fulda objected to going to Stein because he did not want Stein to know he had gone over his head. Soon Stein called Fulda to his tent. 'The raid is on!' They went off to a staff meeting, where again they had to convince those present; but once given the details all were enthusiastic about using gliders *to seize the bridge at Corinth*.

Fulda was given command, and was to have six gliders and some thirty-six parachutists, among them engineers, to take the bridge. He was to land first, and ten minutes later Ju 52s would drop parachutists on high ground nearby to assist him.

That afternoon Fulda, Lieutenant Franz Phenn, Walter Lassen, Raschke, Mende and Brendenbeck took off for Larissa piloting DFS 230s towed by Ju 52s led by Lieutenant Schweizer; this officer had led the Ju 52s that towed gliders to Eben Emael. They got to Larissa late in the afternoon of the 25th April 1941. There were no German support troops there to help them—no food, little water, no advice. They were on their own. Worst of all there were no troops for them to fly to Corinth. Had the mission been scrubbed? No one could hazard a guess.

It was a miserable night, bone cold and bleak. Everyone was hungry.

The bridge at Corinth just after it had been blown by the British.
Against it, the wreckage of a German glider

Commonwealth prisoners detailed to move a glider used in the Corinth
attack

At midnight a unit of German troops appeared, led by an engineer lieutenant. He had a mistaken idea he was to parachute onto the bridge. When he and his men found they were to land in gliders they became more and more terrified as Fulda explained what was involved. This took another selling job by Fulda. Soon he had the parachutists calmed down and confident of the operation. Under the wing of a glider they made their plans, organized men into glider groups, stowed the guns, explosives and ammunition in the gliders, and got set for an early morning take off.

At 0430 they were on their way. Forty airplanes filled with paratroopers were taking off from other fields.

At 0658 German planes began bombing and strafing the Allied forces defending the bridge. Their attack was barely completed when Fulda's glider released at 6,500 feet altitude, and began the descent on the bridge. As Fulda had so often reassuringly told doubters, the defenders, thinking the approaching gliders to be another flight of bombers, ducked into their emplacements until the bombing was finished. It never came.

At 0740 the gliders swooped down on the bridge, Fulda, Brendenbeck and Mende bringing theirs down on the north side. Fulda's force caught the Australian and New Zealand defenders completely by surprise. In a few minutes the force took eighty prisoners. Lieutenant Phenn's glider, carrying the engineer officer in charge of operations on the south side of the bridge and his party, rammed the abutment of the bridge. One man was seriously injured but, miraculously, the others were unhurt.

In a few minutes, the Germans on the south had taken the six Bofors guns and disconnected the wires leading to the charges on the bridge.

Now Fulda wanted to get the charges removed from the bridge structure. The engineer lieutenant adamantly refused. He had orders to disconnect the wires, but was not to touch the charges. Apparently the plan was to blow the bridge if the enemy became too aggressive. Fulda argued with the lieutenant. The charges stayed put. Almost a half hour later wave after wave of Ju 52s appeared and parachutists started dropping.

Then what Fulda had feared happened. From a position about 250 yards away, a position from which no enemy fire had yet come, Fulda heard shells that must have been pumped from a Bofors start to hit the bridge. The shells were tracers, and they were getting closer to the charges on the bridge with each round. He ordered those who could be freed from guarding the prisoners to start shooting with machine guns at the Bofors. Too late!

A well-placed round hit the charge. Lieutenant Phenn was on the bridge, along with a German cameraman. The bridge rose into the air, hung there uncannily, then in a crackling, splintering roar toppled into the canal. Phenn was killed in the explosion. The Germans had seized the isthmus at 0625. They had lost the bridge by 0655.[1]

Despite the loss of the bridge the Germans were elated by the results of the operation; gliders had again won the day. General Seussman landed at the bridge that afternoon in a Storch and congratulated Fulda. Several weeks later Fulda was given the *Ritterkreuz* (Knight's Cross), primarily in recognition of his foresight and determination in seeing a glider raid on Corinth through to a successful conclusion. With the award, he became one of three glider pilots to receive this decoration.

Unknown to Fulda, Lieutenant von Sooden's parachute artillery had started out not far behind his own flight. Four of the gliders were too heavily loaded, did not reach sufficient altitude, and had to release before crashing into the mountains of Southern Bulgaria. Two were high enough, and got to Larissa. The other four were flown out from the place where they had made emergency landings in Bulgaria, took more time to gain altitude, then headed for Larissa. From there the six took off again and by 1500 had landed at Corinth.

On the 27th Lieutenant Heiner Lange landed at Corinth in a Ju 52 charged with the job of getting the gliders back to take-off fields, there to be used for the assault on Crete. He got twenty 'Tommies', as he called his detail of Australian and New Zealand prisoners, and marched them to the bridge, and there the prisoners helped to dismantle the gliders too damaged to fly, and moved the others to take-off positions.

Everyone was hungry. Heiner and several 'Tommies' dropped grenades into the canal with satisfying results, and soon all were feasting heartily on fish fillets. The prisoners did their part by brewing tea in a petrol can from which the top was removed to make a pot. Later that day Heiner accompanied the detail while they dug a grave and buried one of the Australians who had died early that day. Heiner heard one of the prisoners remark, 'That's very nice of him' when he stood at the graveside and saluted the fallen soldier. With the spade with which the grave had been dug, Heiner removed a daisy plant nearby, dug a hole and placed the plant in it.

Earlier that day Heiner had found a copy of 'Gone With The Wind' in the debris of a British camp. After the detail had completed the work on the gliders, Heiner went alone to the grave of his good friend Phenn, now marked by the tip of his glider's wing, upright over the grave. He turned up a few handfuls of earth, laid the book in the depression, and covered it over. So had gone one of his best friends.

With the mainland of Greece under German domination Crete

---

[1] Before giving the above account to the author in Hamburg on 13 February 1973, Fulda, who finished the war as a captain flying the ME 163 rocket fighter, had never given a public statement of what transpired prior to and during the raid.

became not only the last foothold for the king and government of Greece, but also a collecting point for many disorganized Greek, British, and Commonwealth units driven from the mainland. Although the Germans had air superiority in the Balkans and over the Aegean Sea, and the enemy forces on Crete posed no threat to the Germans in the foreseeable future, the nation that held that island could control the eastern end of the Mediterranean by having air bases from which fighters and bombers could interdict shipping routes. The idea of taking Crete gained greater favour with both Hitler and the German High Command as General Erwin Rommel sped along the African coast to Alexandria. Crete could become a stepping stone for other German forces on the move south over the Mediterranean towards the strategic Suez Canal. Moreover German air-power on Crete would help to protect the German shipping that moved men and supplies to Rommel's divisions.

On 25th April 1941, Hitler ordered 'Merkur', code name for the operation against Crete, named after Mercury, the winged god of Greek mythology. It became the first full-scale airborne invasion in history.

Hitler placed Student in command of the operation and gave him two divisions for the task, one being Student's own 7th Flieger Division, elements of which had taken Fort Eben Emael and the bridges of the Meuse by glider forays, and the other the newly organized *Lastensieglergruppe* 1 (LLG 1). Although he immediately ordered the concentration of the divisions for the Crete operation, Student soon found himself in a tight time-squeeze.

Five days after Hitler ordered the invasion of Crete he directed the *Wehrmacht* to invade Russia and gave 22nd June as the date to open the attack. Crete had to be securely in German hands by that time, for after the 22nd June Student's divisions had to be available for Russia.

By the end of April, Colonel Walter Hornung, Commander of LLG 1 had concentrated 74 DFS 230s at Hildesheim and prepared them for rail shipment. By 2nd May all had been loaded on three trains of flat cars and by nightfall the first train left for Salonika in Greece.

In two days, Hornung's Ju 52s of LLG 1 took off from Hildesheim and nearby airfields for Salonika. Meanwhile many trainloads of parachutists and air-landing troops were also heading towards assembly areas in Bulgaria.

More than usual security precautions were taken, for the trip was long and Student had no desire to awaken suspicion of what might be afoot as his forces moved through many countries towards marshalling areas in Greece. Men wore no unit insignia, and none could carry private papers. Identification cards bore men's names but not their unit's. The trains wended their way through German and Bohemian

70

towns and villages and a silent, hostile Prague, crossed Hungary (one glider pilot noting that the Danube was in flood), and then, amid increasingly friendly and enthusiastic people, entered Bulgaria, where the troops detrained and went into bivouac for about a week. It had seemed as though the farther away they went from the countries that bordered Germany, the more friendly were the people they met.

By 12th May the trains with the gliders had arrived at Salonika. There mechanics of LLG 1, who had arrived in the Ju 52s some days earlier, assembled the gliders over the next few days. As they were assembled and checked out, Ju 52s immediately shuttled them to fields at the ancient Greek city of Tanagra, and to Eleusis just outside Athens. By 15th May, the glider build-up at each was complete.

On 15th May the troops started arriving from Bulgaria and moved into tents near the airfields. Two days later, after lunch, glider pilots formed up silently on the airstrip at Tanagra in front of a row of gliders parked along the edge. At 1400 a staff car drove up. General Student stepped out. There was little formality. He walked slowly along the ranks, stopped at each pilot, asked where he was from, and details of his experience. Occasionally he would ask about the pilot's family. Student inspected the troops in a leisurely relaxed way, closing each chat with a handshake. It was at this ceremony that Student made it known that the objective was—Crete! Pilots then got clear-cut orders— the squadron that would tow them, the flight, and their position in the flight.

On 18th May, glider and plane pilots got together with the leaders of the troops they were to carry. Details were worked out on the dis- tribution of the troop units, down to each glider; pilots got their courses and glider pilots their precise targets in Crete. As one pilot remarked, 'Now with a little luck the operation will be a hundred per cent successful'.

That afternoon glider troops loaded gliders with mortars, ammuni- tion, explosives and equipment for the attack. On returning to the camp, supply sergeants passed out to each soldier a full allocation of combat ammunitiion for his personal weapon. No detail was over- looked. Company commanders saw to it that each man carried his standard issue of contraceptives, as well as a short glossary of German- English phrases spelled phonetically, including 'If yu lei yu uill bi schott'.

On the 19th the same pilot told in his diary of 'extreme and feverish preparations', and in the afternoon 'there was discussion about the attack once more'. That evening the troops marched to the gliders and loaded their weapons, packs and gear. 'I am quite calm,' the glider pilot reassured himself and finished his entry for the day, '0715 Tuesday is to be the time of landing on the island of Crete.'

At 0300 the shrill warble of top sergeants' whistles aroused them all. The first glider at Eleusis took off at 0503. Confusion delayed take-offs at one field until 0525. The glider pilot reported that on his 'first attempt a lorry ran into my tow-rope; on the second the towing aircraft fell out of formation, but I managed to get away.' Four hundred aeroplanes carrying paratroopers followed the forty-eight-glider echelon from Tanagra headed for Maleme, some to drop parachutists following the glider landings, others to chance hazardous landings on Maleme and other airdromes in Crete, bringing in airlanding troops, artillery ammunition and supplies. Other aeroplanes, twenty-six DFSs in tow, took off from Eleusis and Megara.

The flight was a gruelling ordeal for the glider pilots. Several gliders became separated from their tow-planes and had to land in the sea. Another crashed on the island of Aegina killing Lieutenant-General Wilhelm Seussman, commander of the Seventh Airlanding Division. His death was unfortunate and can be judged as an unnecessary, avoidable tragedy. The glider tow over water to Crete, under the best of conditions for the most qualified glider pilot, was a delicate, hazardous task. When asked by Colonel Wilke, the overall commander of the air transport part of the operation, 'Who will fly General Seussman?', Heiner Lange, who had to recommend glider pilots to participate, said it should be Lassen. Lassen, a certified engineer in civil life, was not even a sergeant, but was a superb glider pilot and in Lange's estimation the best person for the task. When informed of Lassen's rank, Wilke disapproved and asked for another name. This time Lange suggested Eugen Moser, a sergeant. Again Wilke refused. Was there an officer glider pilot? Lange made the point that in no one pilot did he have what Wilke wanted—rank and glider-piloting ability. Lange then suggested Lieutenant Döge, an able pilot. Döge, however, was at Tanagra. But Döge it was!

Within a few hours, the five glider pilots to fly General Seussman and his headquarters were called to report to meet Seussman. Döge was not there. A hurried call to Tanagra got him on the way. Lieutenant Gruppe would represent Döge at the meeting and inform Döge of what transpired.

In the walk to Seussman's headquarters, Gruppe walked separately with the senior officer taking the five pilots to meet the general. He was in urgent discussion all the way to the headquarters. Döge had not arrived. The senior officer said, to the surprise of the other four pilots, 'Döge is not here. Gruppe will take his place.'

They went into General Seussman's offices. The senior officer introduced each pilot to the general. He said to General Seussman, as he introduced Gruppe, 'This is your pilot.' The general then told the pilots to go about whatever preparations were necessary with his staff and left. Not at any time did the senior officer tell the general of the change.

As the pilots were leaving the headquarters, Döge, had just driven up, sweat pouring from his forehead. He ran to them. Gruppe told him he was too late and what had happened, but not all the story by far. Döge objected to his superiors. It was too late.

General Seussman and other members of his staff entered the glider next morning. It had a complete load, enough for the long flight. An eye-witness states that a vehicle drove up shortly before take-off. Several typewriters and bulky packages were taken to the door and placed to the rear of it. The eye-witness realized that any additional load in Seussman's glider, placed especially where he had seen it placed, would move the centre of gravity towards the rear, dangerously further back than it should be. Gruppe, as pilot, should have insisted that this gear should not be placed where it had been, and if the glider was fully loaded and the new gear added too much weight he should not have allowed it in the glider at all.

Gruppe's glider led his element of five gliders. Right at the take-off, his glider climbed too fast. It got, and stayed, well above the usual tow position as the flight took formation. Glider pilots to the rear were puzzled as to why Gruppe did not descend to normal tow position. The answer is now thought to be that he could not. The weight was causing the tail to come down and forcing the nose up, and he must have been desperately fighting at the controls to keep the glider in level flight.

Twenty minutes out, an aeroplane appeared from the east. It momentarily took the eye of Sergeant Busse, the glider pilot of the right glider, from his intent gaze at his own job. Then he saw Gruppe's glider porpoising, diving steeply and climbing precipitously.

Gruppe apparently did not have the experience to know how to stop the motion. Sergeant Moser in the left hand glider, across from Busse's, also saw the aeroplane come into view[1]. Almost simultaneously, an explosion and a cloud of debris appeared where Gruppe's glider carrying General Seussman had been. The tug plane and Moser's glider passed perilously close to the rubble, but were not touched by any of it. Gruppe's tow plane, the tow-rope dragging behind, turned back. The others continued.

Sergeant Moser, so as not to alarm his passengers, flew on as if nothing had transpired. He said nothing. There was a good chance that no one in his glider was aware that one of Germany's most pro- mising military leaders, and a key figure to this operation, had just been killed. After some minutes of silence, Major Uxkull who was seated just behind Sergeant Moser, asked in a low tense voice, 'Does this happen often?' Moser did not answer.

What had happened to Gruppe's glider? In technical terms, ex-

[1] Some accounts claim the crash was due to the excessive turbulence caused by the Heinkel bomber.

cessive turbulence developed above wing surfaces; it suddenly lost lift, and pulling down at the nose started to dive. Gruppe pulled it out of the dive, but at the top of the climb the rope again pulled the nose down. The wings finally twisted and exploded from internal pressures.

Meanwhile Gruppe's tug pilot flew towards the mainland. He did not release the tow rope. He landed at Eleusis and asked several officers to come to his plane to see that the tow-rope was still attached. He wanted no one to think he had released Gruppe. Whatever happened, he wanted to be certain everyone understood it was not his fault. Apparently reassured he returned to his plane, took off, caught up with his formation, and again took the lead.

For an hour the *Luftwaffe* bombed the positions around the Maleme airfield, working over the Allied defenders' anti-aircraft guns so savagely that few guns remained in action. Although accustomed to enemy bombings, because of the intensity of the attack the men sensed that something was in the wind. They were right. Suddenly the bombing ceased. Shortly thereafter the Allied defenders saw a new sight that was quickly understood. Gliders, silent as ghosts after the deafening bombing—huge, grey, and menacing—came sweeping in.

At 0704 Heiner Lange saw the tow-ship wings waggling, the signal to release. He hit the release knob. He had been in tow just a minute over two hours. For the next eleven minutes, or some ten miles, he glided towards Maleme, touching ground at 0715.

The German Eleventh Air Corps, formed for the attack on Crete, comprised three attack echelons. Group West had the mission to capture Maleme airport; Group Centre, Canne and Retimo; and Group East, Heraklion. The Retimo and Heraklion landings were to occur on the afternoon of D-day. The elite Assault Regiment, specially trained for glider and parachute operations, had the Group West mission. General Eugen Meindl, its commander, had orders to seize Maleme and keep it free of the enemy, to enable aeroplanes to land, to reconnoitre west to Kastelli, also to the south and east, and to keep in contact with Group Centre. Because the glider troops would get into action after they landed faster than parachutists, Meindl assigned to glider parties special missions near the airport, which was the key target of the invasion. The parachutists would land a mile or two further away, hopefully where the enemy was not too strong. There they would muster and collect themselves and their weapons for a concerted attack.

After shaking off their astonishment at the awesome sight of the gliders, the defenders cleared their wits and opened a torrential fire on these aircraft that had little defence except speed. Drilled with rifle and machine-gun bullets, the gliders began to crumple. Some of them moved relentlessly above the sea, their pilots determined to attack, seemingly oblivious to the sheet of fire. One, in landing, crashed against

(*above*) Gliders coming in to land at Crete. (*below*) One that made it safely

a huge rock. Another, speeding at seventy-five miles an hour, smashed full tilt against the ironwork of the bridge; then, in some way, its tail swung down and its nose became hitched to the ironwork. It was a grotesque sight.

In some of the gliders that had stayed on course through the hail of death and had landed without damage, only silence prevailed; all were dead in their seats. Some, hitting trees with a wing-tip, spun like tops, ripping apart among the trees and rocks. Many of the gliders lay in the midst of a tumble of bodies. Almost every glider landing ended at best in a jarring shock, splintering wood, ammunition boxes, equipment, and men catapulting towards the obstacle that had been hit. Seven dead Germans lay outside the skeleton of one aircraft. In five gliders that crash-landed in a field in rapid succession, every man was killed, either by the impact of landing or by bullets. Ian McD. G. Stewart, in his *Struggle for Crete*, states: 'Often they came to rest under the very muzzles of enemy weapons. Aircraftsman Comeau stood transfixed beside his tent as a glider burst at him out of the bushes, one wing slithering above his head to wedge itself against the hillside. He emptied his rifle into the open doorway, blocking it with dead and wounded, before making his escape up the bank.'

Nine gliders carrying eighty men, part of the skeleton staff of a regiment commanded by Major Braun, had to land on the dried bed of the lower Tavronitis River, capture the Tavronitis bridge, and prevent its destruction. Another group, commanded by Major Koch (who was the organizer and former commander of the now well known—in German military circles—Task Force Koch) had a headquarters staff of the glider battalion and two companies of 108 men each. One of the companies under the command of Lieutenant Plessen was to land at the mouth of the river and destroy anti-aircraft guns there to ease the way for aeroplanes coming in to land at Maleme. This was the most practical course on which to approach the airport from the mainland. Koch and the battalion staff were to land on Hill 107, the highest point in the area, an objective that had to be taken to prevent the British from using it for either artillery observation posts or defensive infantry positions. Either use of the hill would have caused fire to be placed on German aircraft landing on the Maleme airport.

The selection of the dry bed of the Tavronitis proved that the staffs that planned the invasion had done their homework well. Much of the bed could not be fired into by the British soldiers in trenches on the slopes above the river bed. As was soon to be found, this enabled glider passengers to form up quickly, head aggressively toward their objectives, and take positions on the high ground.

Plessen's company landed according to plan, and with great dash it soon overwhelmed the enemy anti-aircraft crews. Successful here, Plessen changed direction, after leaving a handful of men to consolidate the German hold around the anti-aircraft positions. He went after the defenders round the airfield, where he met a withering fire and was soon killed.

Major Koch had less success. His force landed along the south-east and south-west slopes of the key hill. Because of this, the two elements of the force, split by the hill, had trouble in helping each other. British and Anzac forces stubbornly defending, and looking right down on the Germans, soon began to kill and wound many of the invaders. Koch was severely wounded, but the remnants of his force finally made their way to the area of the bridge.

Braun's nine gliders landed on target. The British were ready, peppering the gliders as they swept in, and rifling and machine-gunning the occupants as they struggled from the gliders. Braun soon fell, mortally wounded. But notwithstanding their bloody punishment, after hand-to-hand combat Braun's men seized the bridge and overran machine-gun positions on the east bank of the Tavronitis. General Meindl was quick to seize the advantage of the stronghold Braun's force had captured. He established this area as a base for continued attacks against the airfield. Later that day Meindl was severely wounded.

Parachutists began their descent through the wicked fire almost concurrently with the last of the glider landings. The crescendo of the battle grew throughout that day and the next, until 14,000 Germans had landed on Crete.

By 27th May Major General B. C. Freyberg, commanding the British and Anzac forces, made the decision to evacuate Crete. A force of 14,000 Germans, at an agonizing cost in wounded and dead, and with the loss of aircraft and other critical military equipment that would have served Hitler well in Russia, had cleared the island of 42,500 British, Anzac, and Greek troops.

The German concept of the large-scale use of gliders came to fruition at Crete. Student felt that the greater employment of gliders would have materially reduced the number of Ju 52s lost from crash landings. Gliders were available in Germany, but time and crews were not available to ferry them to bases in Greece. Of the seventy-two gliders used at Crete, six did not reach the island, five landed too far from their objectives, and the remainder landed with accuracy varying from fair to perfect, although many crashed. Overall, the glider phase of the operation achieved eighty per cent accuracy and only forty per cent effective accomplishment of tasks assigned. At Maleme, the glider missions were seventy-five per cent accurate, and influenced the German gains there on the first day. At Akrotiri, the glider sorties were a complete failure because of the poor selection of landing areas, and the absence of air support.

Soured against airborne operations by the huge losses suffered in

Crete, realizing that the Allies had learned their lesson and that gliders in any airborne operation could no longer be used with surprise, Hitler and Goering paid no serious attention to them after Crete. This brought to an end the General Staff's hopes of an airborne operation to take Suez, and along with it hopes of a projected operation to take Cyprus by an airborne attack, and to use that island as another stepping stone towards Suez. In Student's words, 'Crete was the grave of the German parachutists'. Conversely it was the saviour of Suez.

Strong evidence suggests that although Hitler harboured some doubts about ever going through as distasteful a venture as Crete again, where the target was sufficiently lucrative, he and his generals would have given gliders and airborne forces another chance. But for the time being another factor had cropped up that made Nazi leaders shelve any thought of airborne operations on a large scale. Expanding German operations in Russia, and commitments in the west to ward off the anticipated Allied invasion in France, sucked the German military forces into ground operations. Parachutists were being thrown in as ground troops. Transport planes were hauling supplies. The staff had no time to plan for new frills in the art of war, such as Eben Emael and Crete. The glider effort would have to wait, and perhaps take other directions.

In the summer of 1941, after its employment in Crete, the *Luftwaffe* activated the three remaining groups of LLG 1 to bring its total strength to 212 DFS gliders and fifty-two tow-planes. In an experimental programme, Gruppe I (I LLG 1) was equipped with Go 242s, to test their adaptability as assault gliders. Despite its excellent characteristics, the Go 242 did not have the dexterity of the lighter and more easily handled DFS 230, so necessary for highly specialized assault missions. Rather, it was felt, the Go 242 would be more suitable as a cargo glider, and thus the DFS 230s again replaced the Go 242s.

By 1942 it became clear that any extensive use of assault gliders, in the 'assault' terms of the Eben Emael and Crete experiences, was no longer a possibility, in view of Hitler's position on the value of future massive airborne operations, a lack of airborne troops, and general disinterest in such operations on the part of field commanders. The High Command in Berlin, faced with enormous supply problems on the Russian front, and anxious to keep Rommel's forces on the move, gradually began to turn glider units into freight transport organizations. The transition did not come about easily, nor did it seem that there was consensus as to what their ultimate organization and equipment should be. To their credit, the *Luftwaffe* made notable efforts to adapt all glider models to move freight over the many thousands of miles that separated air supply bases from front line panzers, spread thinly over the bleak Russian landscape. For a time the I LLG 1 became a test group, equipped with the Me 321, and flew tanks, men, supplies and equipment into Russia. Instead of the twelve gliders per squadron they had had when equipped with the DFS, each squadron had only six Me 321s. However, the huge gliders did not prove satisfactory, being an excessive drain on the craft resources of the air transport command.

In 1941 the *Luftwaffe* activated the special cargo-glider *Verbindungskommandos* units. In 1943 it redesignated them *Schleppgruppen Fuer Lastensegler* (Freight Glider Towing Groups). Each group had three squadrons, two with twelve Go 242s and Me 111s, the third equipped with twelve DFS 230s and twelve Ju 52s or He 128s.

Concurrently with the activation of the *Verbindungskommandos* the *Luftwaffe* also organized two glider pilot training groups, or *Erguensungsgruppen* to man the units and provide a replacement pool of skilled glider pilots.

Group I specialized in giving transition training for the *Gigant* (Me 321) and occasionally dispatched cadres to I LLG 1 to supplement existing crews and equipment. Group II specialized in transitioning crews to the Go 242 and gave advanced operational training to DFS 230 pilots. The equipment of these two Groups varied in accordance with demands placed upon them by the tactical organizations. I LLG 1 had three squadrons, II LLG 1 had four.

In May 1942 the *Luftwaffe* activated *Luftlandegeschwader 1* at Hagenau, consisting of three squadrons each equipped with six Go 242s.

Groups normally operated under a *Luftflotten* (Air Wing), although this was by no means a hard and fast rule. The assault units, the *Luftlandegeschwader*, on the other hand, were most frequently under General Fritz Morzik's XIth *Fleigerkorps* (Flight Corps). On a few occasions these units operated under the air transport command, supporting a particular army or corps. It was not unusual for Hitler to step in and direct the reassignment of glider units to bolster the ground operations of one of his armies.

In general it can be said that a few generals tried to use gliders imaginatively for the remainder of the war and, on the whole, gliders made a substantial contribution in freight supply, espionage and sabotage missions.

CHAPTER V[1]

Sicily—Tragedy and Turning Point

Ladbroke

Gliders used	144
Taking off	137
Returned	4
Missing	133

British Chiefs of Staff Committee

In January 1943, on the advice of their Combined Chiefs of Staff, Prime Minister Sir Winston Churchill and President Franklin D. Roosevelt decided on the invasion of Sicily. Plans called for General Bernard Law Montgomery's Eighth Army to seize areas below Syracuse and about the south-east end of Sicily, and General George S. Patton, leading his Seventh Army, to get a foothold at Gela, to the west of Montgomery. Montgomery had been assigned the British 1st Airborne Division, and Patton the American 82nd Airborne Division, to seize key positions in Sicily by airborne assault.

The timing of the operation depended upon reconciling airborne requirements for moonlight, and naval demands for darkness. The Combined Chiefs of Staff had set as the target date the favourable period of the July moon. General Eisenhower and his staff interpreted this to mean the period of the second quarter of the moon, when there should be enough moonlight early in the night for airborne troops to drop and assemble, but complete darkness after midnight, when the moon had set, to allow naval convoys to approach. Thus D-day was determined almost automatically as 10th July.

Montgomery decided that the 1st Airborne Division should make a glider assault near Syracuse, to which he gave the code name 'Ladbroke'. The force had to land at about midnight and seize the Ponte Grande (a bridge over which the north/south highway from Syracuse

---

[1] *Airborne Missions in the Mediterranean, 1942–1945*, USAF Historical Studies, No. 74, Dr. John Warren (Air University, USAF Historical Division Research Studies Institute, 1955) has been used as a major source for this chapter.

crossed two canals) and key terrain commanding tactical approaches south of the city. Although the presence of two Allied airborne divisions, and Air Force troop carrier units, presupposed that Montgomery and Patton would use airborne troops to open the invasion, Montgomery's decision to use a glider force shocked experienced airborne subordinates. Glider resources in Africa could best be described as a hodge-podge of available, marginally available or non-existent, disparate airborne resources, unsuitable for launching any reasonably successful airborne operation. To expect it to be made by gliders at such short notice made the outcome of a glider assault in Sicily highly doubtful.

Although Montgomery approved the glider assault, he apparently acted on inadequate information, and may have been unduly influenced by General G. F. Hopkinson, recently promoted, the former Commander of the Airlanding Brigade of the 1st British Airborne Division. The ambitious Hopkinson had conferred with General Montgomery and had carried from the meeting Montgomery's agreement to land glider-borne troops to open the British assault on Sicily. Following his discussion with Montgomery, General Hopkinson called Colonel Chatterton to his headquarters. Chatterton had not seen Hopkinson for weeks. He sensed that Hopkinson had committed the glider force to something; and as Chatterton later said, 'He most certainly had!' In a few short sentences Hopkinson gave Chatterton the plan. Chatterton gasped. He made quick mental calculations. He had three months until invasion night. Glider forces had no airfields, no tow-aeroplanes, and worst of all *no gliders*. He had inexperienced glider pilots spread out in several camps, who for three months had not flown a glider; and none had flown gliders at night. Chatterton now presented the facts.

'Oh,' replied Hopkinson, 'we will soon put that right. The U.S. Air Forces are going to supply tugs and gliders.'

'American gliders?' asked Chatterton, incredulously. (His pilots had no experience with American CG-4As.)

'Yes, what difference will it make?' was the reply.

The conversation continued, ending in a situation in which Chatterton had no option except to support the frightening operation or be relieved on the spot. He grimly gritted his teeth and said no more.

Nor was Chatterton alone in his doubts. In vain did Group Captain T. B. Cooper, R.A.F., an adviser for British Airborne Forces, plead to Montgomery's staff the folly of a glider mission flown at night on a treacherous course. The decision stood.

Chatterton later found that 'Ladbroke' was to be one of four airborne assaults. Parachutists from the 82nd Airborne Division had to jump at Gela in Operation Husky I on the night of 'Ladbroke'. 'Husky II', another parachute operation of the 82nd Airborne Division, was set for the next night, and a British glider-parachute operation, 'Fustian', was scheduled for the third night.

Some knotty problems on the teaming up of units had to be solved before training for the assault started. The U.S. Air Force's 51st Troop Carrier Wing was already in North Africa. The 52nd Troop Carrier Wing arrived early in May. A rush shipment of 500 gliders was en route by convoy from the States. *There were four CG-4As in Africa.* The British agreed to provide thirty-six Horsa gliders, a squadron of thirty Albemarles, and a flight of ten Halifaxes from the 38th R.A.F. Wing, to tow the Horsas.

The Horsas sat at airfields in England. Somehow they had to be got to Africa. No one was for the moment certain how this was to be done. To add to the difficulties, at first it was decided that the 51st Wing was to transport the U.S. 82nd Airborne Division, and the 52nd Wing was to fly the British 1st Airborne. In mid-May the Allied North African Air Forces (N.A.A.F.) reversed the assignments. The new line-up seemed logical, because the 51st Wing had operated with the British in North Africa, and the 52nd Wing had flown the 82nd Division for three months of joint training and manoeuvres before leaving America. It lost its logic at the end of May, however, when Montgomery decided on a glider mission. The 52nd Wing had been trained in glider operations in the United States, but was committed to the paratroop mission of the 82nd Division in Sicily. By then it was too late to change the missions of each wing again. The 51st Wing had modified its C-47s for use by British paratroops, and there were neither time nor materials to modify those of the 52nd. Moreover, since the techniques of dropping American and British paratroops differed, a switch in the middle of the training period would have caused dangerous confusion.

On 30th May the N.A.A.F. announced the line-up of the airborne drops. About midnight before D-day a hundred C-47s from the 51st U.S. Wing and twenty-five Albemarles and eight Halifaxes from the R.A.F.'s 38th Wing, a total of 133 aeroplanes, would tow 125 CG-4As and eight Horsas on Operation Ladbroke. In the companion airborne assault 'Husky I', 227 C-47s of the 52nd Wing had orders to drop parachutists of the 82nd Division in the Gela area. N.A.A.F. decided that the glider column would fly from fields around Sousse in Tunisia to Malta, head for Cape Correnti just east of Patton's zone, turn offshore to follow the Sicily coast almost to Fela, and then finally head inland to the landing zones.

This route which was to be flown at night, hopefully aided by some moonlight, required three very sharp changes in course by the aeroplanes over the Mediterranean. Some aircraft pilots thought the flight a mad risk and fought to get some straightening of the course beyond Malta. Their protestations were to no avail. In a conference on 22nd

June all the commanders concerned agreed, many with resignation, to the routes and schedules.

In mid-May the 51st Wing started three weeks of intensive glider-towing exercises. Until then few of the 500 gliders ordered to Africa had arrived, so little training had taken place although 105 glider pilots had arrived at Relizane early in March. Elements of the British Glider-Pilot Regiment with the 1st Airlanding Brigade had been at Froha for weeks, but its pilots were also very short of training. A British War Office memorandum judged that each pilot needed 100 hours flying time before being fit for an operation. None had anywhere near this amount. Furthermore, all were totally ignorant of how to fly the CG-4As; these had landing characteristics differing greatly from those of the British gliders to which their experience had so far been geared. They also had little experience in night flying, since British doctrine held that glider missions at night were out of the question. The American glider pilots, on the other hand, had little advanced glider training and virtually none in realistic manoeuvres. The lack of gliders caused a serious delay in training.

Earlier, a small shipment of CG-4A gliders had arrived at Accra on the Africa Gold Coast, and troop-carrier pilots were dispatched on 24th March to fly them to Sousse fields in Tunisia. They found the gliders in such bad condition from neglect, and deterioration caused by tropical weather, that not until 22nd April did crews manage to make four of them safe enough to fly back.

On 23rd April the first consignment of the 500 gliders allotted to the Force in Africa arrived at North African ports. Port units unloaded some fifty in several days, and news flashed that the long-awaited and critically-needed gliders had arrived. But authorities were in for a rude shock.

Each glider arrived, unassembled, in crates, five crates to a glider. Stupid logistics routed crates haphazardly to several ports. One port had fuselages galore but not enough wings. Another had an over supply of wings and a shortage of fuselages, and so the story went on. Important instruments necessary to the assembly of the gliders could not be found; for instance, assembly was delayed for several days for lack of tensiometers.

The situation at Blida, Algeria, one of the assembly centres, proved typical. About twenty-five of the first gliders to arrive at Algiers were redirected to Blida, because no provision had been made to assemble them at the depot at Maison Blanche in Algiers. This meant that many missing parts and much equipment that had arrived at Algiers had to be taken by truck thirty miles to Blida; and their assembly at Blida was given sixth priority, and entrusted to one officer and twenty enlisted men, who had never seen a glider and had no technical experience!

Elsewhere, too, the assembly of gliders had a low priority, and,

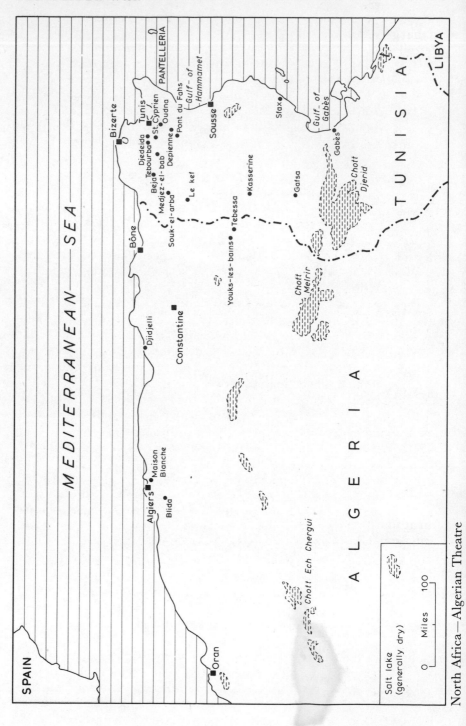

North Africa—Algerian Theatre

despite appeals from the N.A.A.F., Troop Carrier Command stubbornly refused to set a higher priority, claiming that it would upset depot and service-centre procedures. By 5th May only eighteen out of seventy-four gliders delivered to the theatre had been assembled; and by 25th May *only thirty out of 240 gliders delivered were ready to fly*. It was at this time that Hopkinson made the announcement that gliders would spearhead the British assault on Sicily. No wonder General Delmar H. Dunton, commander of the XII Air Force Service Command, referred in late May to an 'extreme emergency' in the assembly of gliders.

Once a crisis was recognized, it was met. The Service Command ordered that work on gliders be given priority even over that of the A.A.F.'s pet P-38s. U.S. troop-carrier units lent experienced glider mechanics. Colonel Chatterton sent fifty glider pilots. His decision to have all his pilots trained as glider mechanics now paid off. By 13th June enterprising men using assembly-line techniques assembled 346 gliders—amply enough, it turned out, for both training and operations. Meanwhile however, irreplaceable training time had been lost.

Gliders were not always usable after they had been assembled. On 7th May, out of twenty gliders assembled only six were delivered to troop-carrier units, because British static cables were lacking. The next day heavy winds tore up all the gliders on the field at La Senia. Extreme temperatures, and indifferent maintenance by inexperienced personnel, caused rapid deterioration. On 16th June the N.A.A.F., alarmed by a flood of mechanical failures, grounded most gliders in Africa for repairs. Ten days before the invasion, so many gliders had weaknesses in the tail wiring that N.A.A.F. had to ground them all for three days. Glider-plane intercom kits did not arrive until the last few days, too late for practice and almost too late for use.

Meanwhile the British found problems in meeting the commitment for Horsas. They had none in Africa. Any that were to be used had to come from England, 1,300 miles away; too great a distance to ferry them in by a glider-tow all the way from England, thought most authorities.

However, enterprising Squadron Leader Wilkinson hitched a Horsa to a Halifax equipped with extra fuel tanks, and 'sauntered' nonstop over England for enough hours to pick up 1,500 air miles, more than enough to make the 1,300 miles tow from England to Africa. From this accomplishment was born Operation Beggar, calling for Halifax bombers to tow thirty-six Horsas to Salé in Morocco.

It was an incredibly courageous enterprise. Each Halifax had to fly many hours, of which the greater number would be spent in towing. They were very heavily loaded, extra petrol being carried in the bomb bays, which meant that a forced landing with wheels up would almost inevitably cause the aircraft to burst into flames. This indeed happened on the only occasion when such a landing had to be made. German fighters sat warmed up at airfields in France, only 100 miles from the leg of the flight that crossed the Bay of Biscay. What is more, for technical reasons the flight had to be made in daylight. British fighters could protect the 'Beggar' flights for only the first three hours out of England, leaving another six hours for the combinations to fly unprotected. Tug and glider had to stay below 500 feet during the entire flight.

The first day, four Horsas attempted the trip. Two reached Salé. Bad weather turned back one combination, and one broke its rope in a cloud. The pilot gingerly manoeuvred the Horsa through the cloud, finally breaking into the clear to find himself 100 feet above a choppy sea. The nose broke away when he ditched, and the sea poured into the fuselage. The pilots worked madly, unlashing a dinghy they had on board, slid it through the water which was rapidly filling the Horsa, and got out of the nose minutes before it sunk below the surface.

Nor were later flights less hair-raising. One was 300 miles from its take-off field at Portreath, in Cornwall, when a Halifax engine failed. As the lumbering craft started losing altitude, the pilot ordered the crew to lighten ship, and they began jettisoning gear. Soon the Halifax stopped losing altitude. Dangerously low, it held on to the glider and made its way, the glider still in tow, to its home field.

The tug pilots had a tougher time on occasion than the glider pilots. One towed a Horsa from Portsmouth to Salé, and landed back at his base in England after a round trip taking thirty-seven hours. Within six days he had completed another tow. On a fourth trip his tug and glider were reported missing, believed shot down. Another pilot delivered four gliders to Morocco in a fortnight. On one of these trips *twelve* Ju 88s attacked. After a hopeless attempt at evasion, with his glider still desperately hanging on, he called upon the glider pilot to release from the Horsa. The Halifax's tail gunner then shot down one of the German attackers and damaged two. Arrived at Salé, members of the Halifax crew counted thirty-six cannon-shell holes in the aircraft. The Horsa ditched, its crew went into a dinghy, and a naval ship picked it up eleven days later.

In all, thirty-one Horsas left Portreath in Cornwall in Operation Beggar. Twenty-seven arrived safely at Salé. The effort had cost two Halifaxes, four Horsas and a number of crews.

The British also had to ferry more than 360 CG-4As from the Froha airfields, where they had been assembled after arrival via Kairouan by ship from the U.S. Many of the gliders had not been test-flown, nor was there time to afford this luxury. Before setting course,

... each tug would make one circuit, giving the glider pilot a few minutes in which to judge the airworthiness of his craft. Of seven that left Froha on the first day, two released and landed back. Next day General Hoppy was watching. When one of ten glider pilots came back and complained of aileron trouble, Hoppy jumped into the glider, made a circuit, reported it fit to fly, and sent the pilot home.[1]

Lawrence Wright goes on to say, 'There were no further complaints at Froha . . .'

The trip was gruesome. None of the glider pilots had had more than one hour of continuous flight before this. Tug and glider had to,

. . . cross mountains up to 7,000 feet high, flying at about 9,000 feet; a towed Horsa took about an hour and a half to reach this height. After early morning, the air was so rough that a thousand feet or more could be lost in one bump; one pilot reported losing 3,000 feet in 10 minutes.[2]

Wright, citing the bone cracking nature of the flight, tells of seeking out the glider that had carried his motor bike.

After it had been lashed into place (in the glider) at Froha, I had asked the Engineer Officer to make a final check. He had added further ropes and wedges that looked sufficient for a battleship in dry dock. But after that switchback ride, it was lying on one side among shreds of rope, and the fabric roof was still dripping the remains of a basket of tomatoes that I had given to the crew. It was on this trip that one Hadrian shed its tail and killed its occupants.[3]

Thus, the 51st Wing was unready during the first two weeks of June for anything but limited training in the fundamentals of loading and towing gliders. By the first week in June members of the Airlanding Brigade, under their Commander Brigadier P. H. W. Hicks, D.S.O., M.C., were having a strenuous time training to be glidermen in a part of the world composed largely of a vast plain of red clay soil, surrounded by mountainous, desolate country. It was hot and the red dust was a nuisance. The only consolation was the local wine, which the pilots discovered to be plentiful, cheap, crude and surprisingly strong.

The first practice manoeuvre mission with gliders and elements of the 1st Airlanding Brigade took place on 14th June, when the wing flew fifty-four CG-4As, with British pilots, over a triangular seventy-mile course, and released the gliders to come down on to the Froha airfield. On 20th June, glider mission 'Eve' was flown, in identical formations and over a similar course with the R.A.F.'s 38th Wing also participating. Although the results were good, the exercises had not been realistic. In both the gliders had been released by day to land on well-marked airfields.

After the second manoeuvre the training period ended, and the move to the take-off fields began. According to the Troop Carrier Command, the British glider pilots logged a mere 4.5 hours in flying

[1] Lawrence Wright, *The Wooden Sword*, London, Elek Books Ltd., 1967, p. 142.
[2], [3] *Ibid.*

Men of the 82nd Airborne Division loading a 75mm Howitzer into a glider during invasion training in Morocco

the CG-4As. *This included slightly more than one hour of night flying.* Pilots had made about sixteen landings apiece. A British observer wrote bluntly, '. . . practically none of our glider pilots has sufficient training, and it is too late to rectify this omission now'. Because the equally inexperienced American pilots were not scheduled to participate in D-day operations, they had received less instruction and practice than the British. Of great importance, there had been no mass release of gliders either over water or at night, and very little practice in landing them under simulated combat conditions. The future of the mission looked ominous.

The training ended on 20th June. Advanced echelons had begun the trek to Tunisia on the 16th, a move which was not completed until 4th July. It is perhaps as well that plans for the employment of the 52nd in a glider mission were never carried out. The towing of gliders loaded with men and equipment during the move to Tunisia was the only glider training the 52nd received in Africa. No full-scale rehearsal had been held. No time had been given to the pathfinder techniques developed at the airborne centre. Above all, the wing was still insufficiently trained in formation flying, navigating, and locating drop zones at night. At least one group commander later felt that the Troop Carrier Command was far too optimistic as to its crews' proficiency.

On the night of 9th July, 109 C-47s of the Troop Carrier Command and twenty-eight Albemarles and seven Halifaxes of 38th Wing were ready to go on 'Ladbroke', the glider mission against Syracuse. One hundred and thirty-six CG-4As and eight Horsas waited to take off. The latter, because they were big, were to be towed by the four-engine Halifaxes. Nineteen American glider pilots who had volunteered for the mission reinforced British ranks. Twelve hundred men of the British Airlanding Brigade, commanded by Major General G. F. Hopkinson, stood by their gliders that were also to carry seven jeeps, six 6-pound guns, and ten 3-inch mortars.

Their goal was the Ponte Grande bridge, located a mile and a half south-west of Syracuse, on the highway by which the British 5th Division was to approach the city. The Horsa gliders were to land between a quarter of a mile and a mile west of the bridge on landing zone (LZ) 3, which was two small strips of land on either side of the Mammaibica Canal. The CG-4As were to land on two zones; LZ 2, between two and three miles south of the bridge, comprised two irregular pieces of land near the shore, having a combined area of about half a square mile; and LZ 1, about a mile west of the bridge and almost a mile inland, was rectangular, about 1,200 yards long and 900 yards wide, with a small adjacent strip and to the south-west. Officers later stated that all zones had been too small.

The bridge was less than a half mile west of the outer harbour of

Syracuse. Nevertheless, the concentration of anti-aircraft guns around that city had made necessary an approach from the south, and had largely determined the location of glider landing zones.

At 1842 the ground crew hitched the first Halifax to its glider and the combination roared off. The tugs and gliders continued to take off in clouds of dust from six fields, at intervals of less than a minute, until 2020. The ground crews controlled the take-offs with flags and walkie-talkies.

The 60th Group of the 51st Wing lined up its aircraft on the runway four abreast, each with its glider behind it. The tugs and their gliders took off alternately in pairs. Once in the air, the American planes lined up in formations of four in echelon to the right, with one-minute intervals between elements. The British flew individually, as was their custom at night.

Each transport group swept in a wide circle, assembling its aircraft; and then it headed north at 500 feet to rendezvous over the Kuriate Islands with other groups.

Trouble began before the formations had crossed the Tunisian coast. A jeep in one glider, its lashings broken by the turbulence, began to pound the glider interior to bits. The pilot hit the release lever and landed. Five other glider pilots, finding their relatively untested gliders unsound, also released. Now three combinations could be seen returning, their gliders in trouble. The gliders cut off near their home fields, landed, and ground crews rolled other gliders out from among reserves standing by for just such an emergency. Quick work got two glider combinations into the air and on their way to try to catch the remaining 135 combinations, then well over the island of Linosa.

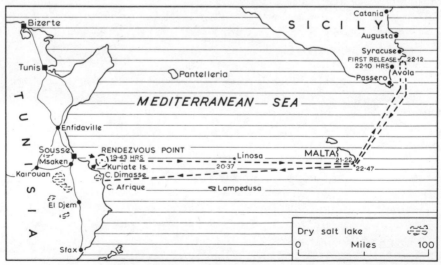

Operation Ladbroke (Sicily): (i)

From the Kuriate Islands the 137 gliders in the main force set out toward Malta, 200 miles to the east. The C-47s flew below 250 feet at 120 miles an hour, the Albemarles at 350 feet at 125 miles an hour, and the Halifaxes at 500 feet at 145 miles an hour. The straight course fell just south of Linosa, which served as a navigation checkpoint. A dying gale, blowing from the northwest, buffeted the combinations into unpredictable altitudes and directions. Ordered to fly low to avoid detection by enemy radar, some planes flew so low that ocean spray lashed against plane and glider.

The sun set behind them as the leading pilots sighted Malta's flashing beacon. A few fighters swept overhead in the gloom, the only escort observed during the trip, and fortunately no enemy fighters appeared. Rounding the south-eastern corner of Malta, the pilots began the 70-mile leg north–north-east to a point five miles off Cape Passero, the south-eastern tip of Sicily. Although some sighted the Cape, many had to estimate their positions.

The dark mass of the Cape off to the north-west loomed into the view of some of the pilots at 2220, precisely the time the lead elements started the scheduled 18-mile leg to the north. Now the formation began to fly over the vast seaborne invasion fleet, warships and transports that were to discharge Montgomery's ground forces over the shores of Sicily at dawn. The ships held their fire, alerted to the over-flight of the airborne forces about to be launched at Syracuse.

It was now that the glider-and-tug combinations already seriously dispersed in the loosely-formed serials got into trouble. Those that had managed to hold formation began to overrun stragglers. Tug pilots tensely peered into the murky blackness, searching for a glimpse of exhaust flashes ahead, frequently veering violently, diving or throttling back, to avoid ploughing into a glider or plane that suddenly appeared from an unexpected direction. To avoid collision, some formations began to climb above the slower ones, and briefly flew layered one above another.

In a quick radio exchange, the leading tow pilots agreed to add 300 feet to the planned 1,500-feet release altitude. This new altitude was to give two additional miles of gliding range to the 'poor bastards' in tow; perhaps enough to buck the offshore winds, and leave them enough altitude to find the landing zone, or at least land. Except among some of the leading flights, order disappeared. A free-for-all ensued in the last ten critical minutes, while ahead the leaders started to climb to 1,800 feet and cut off.

In the dim light of the low half-moon, the first seven planes made their run exactly on schedule, undetected and undisturbed. Then the defenders awoke. Searchlights swept the sky, and from the beaches to the city anti-aircraft batteries began to fire. But only two searchlights probed from near the landing area, and the flak from the beaches was so light and scanty that no aircraft was seriously damaged. The wing commander later said that there was no flak within several thousand yards of the glider release point. However, the lights and flares dazzled the pilots, and the smoke of the firing, borne on the north-west wind, drifted over the shore and the release area. Confusion set in. The pilots found it increasingly difficult to judge their positions or even to see the shore. Several of them found that if they turned and ran west, the land was silhouetted beneath the moon. Others who had to swing around and repeat their runs flew through the formations behind them. Some pilots, anxious to allow for the wind, released CG-4As from as high as 3,000 feet so that they passed through, rather than under, the stream of traffic. Several formations had overrun each other and released simultaneously. The air was at times crowded with planes and gliders coming from all directions.

In this melee, teamwork between towing pilot and glider pilot proved inadequate. After all, they had never rehearsed releases under anything like combat conditions and none in near-gale winds. To add to their troubles, between twenty-five and thirty per cent of the intercom sets, supposed to provide telephone connections between plane and glider, worked badly or not at all. The gliders were supposed to cast off on oral or visual signals from the plane. Instead, about a dozen tows released their gliders and at least half a dozen glider crews cut loose without a proper signal. Winds blew fourteen combinations of the 28th Squadron well east of their course. Two became so completely lost that they turned back. One CG-4A was accidentally released en route, and one Horsa broke loose from its tow. Two others turned back because they could not orientate themselves after reaching Sicily. Some stragglers mistook distant parts of the coast for their objective and cut away. Five landed between Cape Passero and Avola, fifteen miles south of their objective. About a half dozen more, mistakenly released in that area, came down in the water. One glider was released near Augusta, 15 miles north of Syracuse.

Now those gliders still in what remained of the main serials were being released 3,000 yards from the shore. But either the extra 300 feet was not enough to fly the distance because the gliders had been too heavily loaded, or, as many cursing glider pilots asserted later, the planes had not been 3,000 yards, but twice that, or even miles, away. Even in daylight and the most ideal of circumstances, they could not have hoped to glide to shore.

Dennis E. McClendon, piloting an American C-47 towing a CG-4A with Sergeant Evans of the British Glider Regiment at the controls, was one of the 4-plane-glider combinations in his flight element. Looking for his landing zone, McClendon headed directly at a dim shape in the water a few miles south of Cape Passero; suddenly the 'shape' lighted up. Red lines of tracer shells flew toward them, and

then the blue-white orbs of star shells showed the outline of a merchant-
man. Now they could clearly see all the planes and gliders of their
four-plane formation. It flew alone.

Captain Johnny B. Blalock, one element leader, now turned into
the left-echeloned element, to avoid flying directly over the stacks of
Allied convoys. He nearly spun out of formation and into the drink, but
somehow managed to stay in number four position.

Five miles farther ahead another ship fired point-blank. Again
Blalock turned and flew into the echelon to avoid the fire. This time
he was just a shade too abrupt; the formation simply dissolved before
him. Somehow, he passed under the other three planes and gliders.
Since they were flying at 200 feet, McClendon knew very well that
what Blalock had done was impossible. But Blalock made it.

Once released, the glider pilots had trouble in finding their way.
Over half could not see the shore, and very few could recognize
inland landmarks by which to get a 'fix' on their landing zones. Of
forty-nine gliders that landed within ten miles of their goal, only two
CG-4As landed on LZ1. Twenty gliders landed within a mile of the

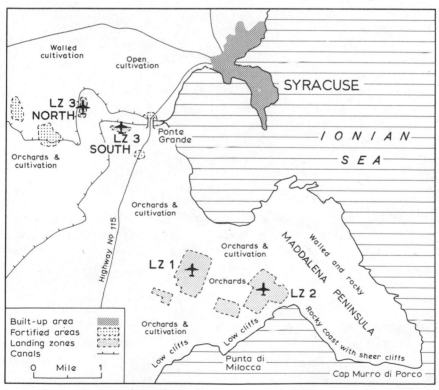

Operation Ladbroke (Sicily): (ii)

zone. Only one CG-4A managed to get to LZ2, and it hit a tree. The enemy hit a Horsa carrying a bangalore torpedo, and also carrying the commander of the mission, Major Ballinger. The glider blew up in mid-air.

In the case of gliders a miss is often as bad as a mile. The CG-4A could skid to a stop within 150 yards, but any obstacle on the landing area or in the last hundred yards of the approach generally caused a crash. In such cases the hinged cargo door in the nose of the glider usually jammed shut.

Orchards and vineyards chequered the land and, especially to the east, the fields were small and bounded by the stone walls that are characteristic of southern Italy. Seven CG-4As hit trees, and six CG-4As and two Horsas crashed into walls. Many others had rough landings. One Horsa flew head on into the canal bank that was almost on the edge of its landing zone and only 400 yards from the bridge.

Luckily McClendon found some unmistakable landmarks as he proceeded toward Syracuse during the next half hour. He came in forty minutes late, flew directly inland toward his assigned glider landing zone, and signalled 'go' to Sergeant Evans. Evans cut loose immediately to become one of four of the 137 glider pilots who landed where he was supposed to that night.

Lieutenant L. Withers, commander of the platoon riding in Galpin's glider, wasted no time awaiting the arrival of reinforcements from the gliders landing in widely outlying areas. He and five men swam the canal and made for the pillbox at the north end of the bridge. According to orders, the rest of his platoon attacked the enemy from the south. They took the bridge, removed the demolition charges and threw them in the river. Reinforcements arrived shortly from another Horsa which had landed about a half mile to the south. By early morning eight officers and sixty-five enlisted men were holding the bridge. They were joined at about 0730 by a small group, including an American glider pilot, who had fought their way northward from the vicinity of the CG-4A landing zones.

At 0800 enemy counter-attacks, one led by four armoured cars, began. Soon heavy and deadly accurate mortar fire began hitting the British positions. Short of ammunition for all weapons, the defenders could not fire back with an adequate volume of fire to silence the enemy mortars or machine guns. Now a big field gun began ranging in; and, finding the range, began to shell the position heavily. The enemy pressure began telling as soldier after soldier fell to shrapnel and bullets.

By 1500 the enemy had wiped out the small defending outposts and infiltrated the British position. At 1530 only fifteen men remained unwounded, and these were cornered at the point where the canal joins the Mediterranean, in an area devoid of trees, rock outcroppings or other protection. In a matter of a few minutes, the enemy swept over the position. A half-hour later, guided to the position by several glidermen who had evaded capture when the enemy re-took the bridge, a battalion of Scots Fusiliers attacked, and quickly won back everything that the gallant South Staffords had originally taken.

As the seesaw battle at the bridge was taking place, survivors of the outlying gliders, too far away to come to the assistance of those at the bridge, were nevertheless writing their own histories. A Waco carrying Colonel O. L. Jones, the deputy commander of the brigade, landed near an Italian coastal battery. He saw no other gliders. Colonel Jones made a hurried reconnaissance. From the barbed wire, and the number of enemy he could hear and glimpse, he assumed that an enemy battery too formidable to assault in the dark stood nearby. He therefore led his men to a nearby farmyard to await dawn.

At sun-up he made another reconnaissance and, as he had thought, found a well-dug-in enemy artillery position. Colonel Jones developed a thorough plan of attack. At 1115, leading a small force of staff officers, radio men and glider pilots, he attacked. Under the protection of withering small-arms fire from others in positions behind, one wave moved forward. Drawing close, they began hand-grenading the cowering defenders, who were soon overrun. Jones's party blew up five field guns and an ammunition dump.

Another unit deserted its glider, rapidly being swamped 250 yards offshore. With bullets and rounds of artillery spuming the sea, they swam for shore. Major Breman, two other line officers, one medical officer, the major's orderly, and a radio man managed to reach the pebbled beach. Now they had to snake through a 20-foot belt of barbed wire, somehow avoiding any major confrontation with the enemy. Managing to do so, they started on a ten-mile march spotted with adventures. After getting by the beach defences they attacked and captured two pillboxes. Later they fought several minor enemy units, and by the time they reached their unit, they had taken twenty-one prisoners, three machine guns and an anti-tank gun.

And it happened with so many others. Chatterton's glider, which also carried Brigadier Hicks, commander of the Airborne Brigade, released too far from shore. Chatterton realized he could not make the shore, and so steered for a black patch which loomed ahead, hoping that it was a small island. He had almost reached it when a stream of tracer bullets came from its summit; a searchlight was turned on, and he perceived he was approaching a steep cliff. He put the glider into a right-handed stalling turn and plunged seawards. At that moment a shell hit his starboard wing and the glider, damaged, struck the waves. Its occupants began to claw their way out. Only one was injured, but they were in a sorry plight, a mile from shore, illuminated by a searchlight, and under intermittent but heavy machine-gun fire.

'All is not well, Bill!' Brigadier Hicks murmured to his Brigade-Major as he crawled on to the undamaged wing.

The pilots and their passengers lay or crouched on the wing watching other gliders making for the shore. Many did not reach it, but like their own fell into the sea. Soon they heard the crackle of fire on the coast, accompanied by the flash of tracer. Chatterton, Hicks and the rest decided to swim for it. Leaving the wrecked and water-logged glider, they struck out for the beach, reached it eventually and there, falling in with a party who had been more fortunate than themselves and were on their way to dispose of a coastal battery, at length arrived at the Headquarters of the Airborne Force.

After releasing their gliders, the troop carriers dropped their tow ropes, turned south, and beat it for home at full throttle. Most of them followed orders to keep above 6,000 feet until past Malta, to avoid meeting seagoing convoys. Several planes did encounter convoys, but because they were at high altitudes and the timing of the flight coincided with information of the airborne attack, the ships held their fire.

Malta blazed with searchlights. Beyond Malta the troop carriers descended to 2,500 feet. Icing soon forced some to other levels. They then headed straight for Tunisia. The first plane of the 60th Group got home at 0015, and the first from the 62nd at 0055. Five pilots went astray, presumably because of erroneous information on direction of beams, one landing as far away as Tripoli. Nevertheless, before dawn every one of the 137 planes which had left Africa on the 'Ladbroke' mission had landed safely in friendly territory.

Despite some misgivings, tow pilots' initial reports indicated that ninety-five per cent of the gliders had been released at approximately the proper point. By 11th July the staff of the 51st Wing had calculated that over seventy gliders had landed in Sicily. Even this figure seems larger by four than the evidence warrants. In fact, at least sixty-nine CG-4As came down at sea, and an average of three men in each of these gliders were drowned. Seven CG-4As and three Horsas that were missing with all on board probably shared their fate.

The mercurial General Hopkinson, originator of the attack, burst into vituperative oaths. On the morning of the 9th he had glowingly commended the members of the 51st Wing for their efficiency and co-operation. When picked up that night from his waterlogged, wrecked glider, he cursed the Wing with every breath he could muster. His men did not hesitate to accuse the troop carriers of flinching from enemy anti-aircraft fire, and the charge was later to bring about brawls between British troop-carrier and airborne men in many an English tavern.

Troop-carrier pilots accused their flight element leaders of leading them too far offshore. This is borne out by the fact that of the first seven planes which released without any disturbance by enemy action, only two gliders reached land.

Some tug pilots may have been rattled by their first exposure to flak. Others, tense and over eager, released too soon. Most misjudged their position in the darkness and confusion. Glider operations with release over water were known to be very difficult, and doubly difficult in darkness. The makers of airborne doctrine in the United States and in England would have held that a mission involving both features was unsound; and so it proved.

Even if all the pilots had had nerves of steel and eyes like owls, many would have failed through an error in the planning. The altitudes prescribed for the gliders were not sufficient to enable them to reach their landing zones against the strong wind. The CG-4A pilots presumably did not minimise their achievements, but few of them claimed to have glided more than two and a half miles, and their average free flight seems to have been barely two miles. On that basis, if orders for the release had been followed exactly, a large percentage of the CG-4As would not have reached the landing zones.

Of the 137 gliders that started out, only forty-nine CG-4As and five Horsas landed in Sicily. Tow planes released all but one of these gliders at higher than 3,000 feet. About twenty-five of the forty-nine CG-4As were reportedly released within a mile of the shore, and three others that reached land had been given added range by being released at altitudes of over 1,000 feet more than that prescribed; facts accounting for their being able to reach Sicily successfully. Only nine of the forty-nine were released at approximately the planned altitude and distance from their LZs.

The conclusion to be drawn from these facts was clearly seen and frankly stated by American Generals Paul L. Williams and Raymond A. Dunn. The fault lay in the planning, and particularly in the release point set for the CG-4As. If that point had been over the shore, few pilots could have mistaken it. Also, if it had been 1,000 feet higher, the troop-carrier pilots could have adjusted their positions and the glider pilots could have compensated for the strong head wind. As it was, the glider pilots had to make the best of a bad situation.

Because so many gliders either ditched at sea or vanished with all hands, it is impossible to say exactly how many were released in the proper area. Nevertheless, it is estimated that between 109 and 119 planes, towing a force of over 1,200 fighting men, released their gliders within what would, by daylight, have been full view of the landing zones and of Syracuse itself. Near as they were, not more than one out of the fifteen men each glider carried was able to reach the objective area that night.

General Montgomery later stated that the taking of Ponte Grande saved him seven days. In addition, local actions around the many widely scattered gliders undoubtedly damaged enemy communications and morale. But whatever might be said to its credit, 'Ladbroke' was costly and inefficient. A month later the casualties were reckoned at 605 officers and men, of whom 326 were missing, probably drowned; a total representing one-half of the assault force. In return for this sacrifice, only about five per cent of all the airborne troops that flew from Africa had gone into action at the Ponte Grande bridge and captured it.

On 12th July the 51st Wing began briefing for 'Fustian', Montgomery's bid to take the Primasole bridge over the Simeto River, about five miles south of the city of Catania. Then there came the disappointment of a postponement. The Eighth Army was slowing down and was not within striking distance. Next day, however, Montgomery decided on an all-out effort to break through into the Catania plain before the Germans could consolidate their defences. A swift crossing of the Simeto was essential to his plan.

At 1630 on 13th July the troop carriers got the alert for 'Fustian'. The final briefing took place at 1745.

'Fustian' was a 135-plane mission, manned mainly by paratroopers, reinforced by glider-borne artillery. The U.S. 51st Troop Carrier Wing assigned to the mission 105 C-47s, fifty-one each from the 60th and 62nd Groups, and three from the 64th Group. Reinforced by eleven Albemarles of the 38th Wing, these were to carry 1,856 troops from the British 1st Parachute Brigade, with some engineer and medical personnel accompanying them. Following them would be eight CG-4As and eleven Horsas, transporting seventy-seven artillerymen, ten six-pounder guns, and eighteen jeeps. Twelve Albemarles and seven Halifaxes of the 38th Wing were to do the towing.

Paratroop planes began taking off from two fields at 1920 on 13th July, ten minutes ahead of schedule; others began taking off from two other fields half an hour later. It took forty-five minutes to get each serial in the air. At 2200 gliders began taking off. This timing gave the paratroops about two hours to land and secure the glider-landing area before gliders arrived, a tactic in full accordance with Allied airborne doctrine.

One Halifax had to be replaced at the last minute by an Albemarle. A C-47 returned immediately with engine trouble and was replaced by a substitute. Take-off accidents and a case of faulty controls prevented two CG-4As and a Horsa glider from leaving Africa. One C-47 and an Albemarle carrying paratroops turned back with engine trouble before they reached Malta.

The planes assembled over Tunisia at below 1,000 feet, and headed out to sea over the 'Ladbroke' course. The paratroopers' C-47s flew at 140 miles an hour. The Albemarles towing gliders cruised at 125 and the Halifaxes at 145 miles an hour.

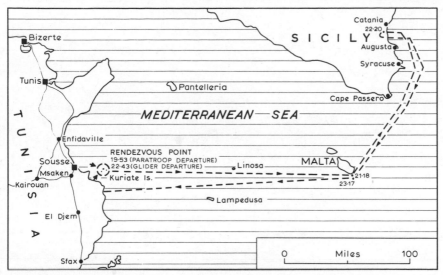

Operation Fustian (Sicily): (i)

The weather was clear and calm, as had been predicted. The sun set before Malta was reached, but a half-moon shone brightly through a slight haze, making navigation easier than in Operation Ladbroke. After rounding Malta, five miles to the south-east of Delimara Point, the troop-carriers set out on a senselessly complex 5-turn course, designed to keep them ten miles off the coast of Sicily until they were opposite the mouth of the Simeto River, yet out of the range of the guns of Allied convoys along the coast. Low-flying planes would be easy targets, and the airborne forces were given their course to avoid being shot at, as had happened so tragically several days earlier in parachute operation 'Husky'. The British naval commander had been notified of the route and the schedule for 'Fustian' and had approved them. For further safety the aircraft pilots had been briefed to fly at least six miles offshore until they approached their objective.

Somehow, however, the precautions taken to avoid convoys were not carried out. The C-47s found their complicated route passing over many ships. Pilots saw one convoy between Linosa and Malta; another, sighted north of Malta, fired on three Albemarles towing gliders.

The formations got into real trouble, however, in the 40-mile approach to Cape Passero, where the troop carrier route bordered the naval zone below. Thirty-three planes strafed above the ships; and naval guns, alerted and tensely awaiting an air attack by the Germans, mistakenly opened fire on the aeroplanes. Two planes dived into the sea. Nine others had been so torn through by the ship's fire, and so many pilots and passengers wounded, that they turned back to Africa. Two planes taking evasive action collided.

99

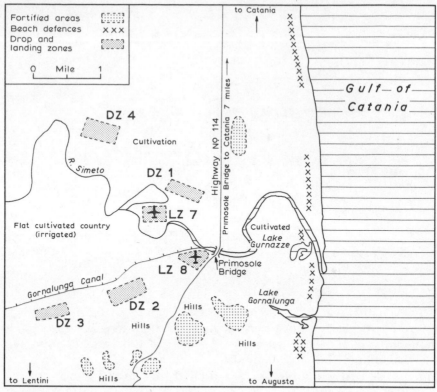

Operation Fustian (Sicily): (ii)

By the time the glider formation crossed the shore, one third had been lost. One glider released accidentally over the sea, and four were shot down. The Horsas had to reach LZ8, a 500-yard triangle touching the bridge at one point; the CG-4As aimed at LZ7.

Piloting a Horsa, Staff Sergeant White could see the landing zones clearly, since enemy batteries firing below and flaming tracers and explosions ahead were '. . . far brighter than the landing lights set out by the parachutist pathfinders'. One by one the pilots broke away from the tow planes in the intense flak. Riddled with flak, one landed north-east of Lentini, but only one man was wounded within. One crashed into the river, killing or maiming all except one airborne soldier. Another carrying the battery headquarters crashed and killed or injured everyone in it.

Sergeant White came over LZ8 twenty minutes behind schedule. He cut off, circled downward through the fire, and made a jarring landing a hundred yards south of Primasole bridge. He had no casualties, but the rough landing had shaken the jeep and gun about in the glider so that it took some time to get them out.

Lieutenant Thomas brought his Horsa down successfully, but seven miles from LZ8, too far to give White's force any early help. Three other Horsas had landed further away. The jeep could not be removed from one, but the troops, along with the parties from the other two with their jeeps, hauled three guns through the night towards the bridge. There they joined up with Thomas's and White's parties. Combined with paratroopers, the force at the bridge numbered 250; they had two mortars and three anti-tank guns. Major R. T. H. Lonsdale was in command.

At 0630 German forces, rushed by truck from Catania, attacked, and drove the airborne troops from the north end of the bridge. In the seesaw battle that ensued the airborne troops, supported by the pounding fire of the six-inch guns of an Allied cruiser lying offshore, finally seized the bridge. Thus the Navy, which had so nearly wrecked 'Fustian', played a part in saving it. Just before dark Eighth Army tanks appeared in the distance, and the Germans fell back.

'Ladbroke' taught the folly of releasing gliders in the dark over water. It showed the advisability of having large landing zones, and pointed up the weaknesses of the CG-4A glider—the inability to carry guns with prime movers for them, and a tendency for the cargo door in the nose to jam shut during landing.

In some respects the Allied airborne operations in Sicily bore similarities to the German airborne invasion of Crete. In each case the attacker considered the operation a disappointment, while the defender considered the operation a more or less spectacular success. Each operation was something of a turning point for the airborne effort in the respective military establishments. For the Germans, Crete was the end of major airborne operations. For the Allies, Sicily was only the beginning of airborne operations on an even larger scale.

To a large segment of American military opinion, the Sicilian operations seemed to demonstrate the costly futility of large airborne operations. Secretary of War Stimson leaned to that view, and Lieutenant General Lesley J. McNair, Commanding General of the Army Ground Forces, later wrote:

> After the airborne operations in Africa and Sicily, my staff and I had become convinced of the impracticability of handling large airborne units. I was prepared to recommend to the War Department that airborne divisions be abandoned in our scheme of organization and that the airborne effort be restricted to parachute units of battalion size or smaller.

CHAPTER VI

Sharpening the Eagle's Talons

Join the glider troops!
No flight pay
No jump pay
But never a dull moment.

The first U.S. Army air-landing unit (a troop formation that went into combat in either gliders or powered aircraft) was the 550th Infantry Airborne Battalion, activated in the Canal Zone in Panama in July 1941. Nevertheless, it was the 88th Airborne Battalion, activated in November 1942 at Fort Bragg, North Carolina, along with several parachute regiments and the Airborne Command, that became the nucleus of the greatest army to be transported by gliders and aeroplanes that the world has ever had. It was to grow to a force of five airborne divisions, a number of separate parachute regiments, many separate support units, topped by a U.S. corps headquarters, and an Allied airborne army headquarters to command joint U.S. and British operations.

But the inauguration of the airborne effort had more than its share of indecisions. At the time of the creation of the 88th, there was no indication of its future role as a glider unit. It was organized on an experimental basis and comprised a motorcycle company, some bicycle elements, light armour, and light military guns and equipment. This basis would enable planners to experiment with it in air transport operations; which they did on a meagre scale, calling for the unit to fly in any of several models of powered aircraft under various test conditions.

Experiments were conducted in loading and lashing equipment with several kinds of tie-down devices, that were later to be used in aeroplanes in world-wide parachute and glider operations. It was not an uncommon experience for a young lieutenant to find himself with a few men in the cargo compartment of a CG-4A glider or C-47 aeroplane wrestling with a jeep that had come loose from its lashing. Such a sobering experience is reminiscent of sea stories of old, when cannons came loose to wreak havoc in the holds of ships. Nor was the experience less harrowing when live rounds of mortar or artillery ammunition broke loose and floated around in the cabin, as the glider bounced in the turbulent air above the Carolinas where many of these tests took place.

The first proposals for an airborne organization came from the Office of the Chief of Infantry. On 6th May 1939, the executive in that office suggested to the Operations Office (G-3) of the War Department General Staff, that consideration be given to organizing a small detachment of air infantry. The initiation of a study on the subject led almost at once to differences of opinion over the control of the project. The Chief of Engineers contended that, inasmuch as para-chutists would be used primarily as demolition teams and saboteurs, the troops ought to be trained and employed by the Engineers. The Chief of the Army Air Corps held that logically the air infantry should be 'marines of the Air Corps'; therefore, he proposed that they be placed under the jurisdiction of the Air Corps and designated 'Air Grenadiers'. The Chief of Infantry maintained that parachute troops would fight on the ground as infantry and, to be effective, they would have to be trained as infantry, because 'Aircraft were to be regarded simply as a means of transporting them to the battlefield.'

The issue was not settled quickly. In June 1940 the G-3 Division of the War Department recommended that the programme be taken out of the hands of the Chief of Infantry and be placed directly under G-3. Shortly thereafter this division made a new proposal, that the project be placed under the Chief of the Air Corps Major General Henry J. Arnold. This proposal very soon had Arnold's strong support. But it met the vigorous objections of Brigadier General Lesley J. McNair, Chief of Staff of the newly organized General Headquarters (GHQ). He insisted, as had the Chief of the Infantry before him, that air trans-port was only another means of transportation, and that the primary mission of parachute troops was ground action. A later proposal—and it seemed a logical one because the airborne programme would cut across traditional Army branches—was that the project be placed directly under GHQ.

The matter came to a head with a prolonged discussion on 27th August 1940 in the office of Major General William Bryden, Deputy Chief of the War Department General Staff. At the conclusion of the discussion General Bryden announced that the project would continue under the supervision of the Chief of Infantry.

In May 1942 the War Department published *Tactics and Technique of Airborne Troops*. Although it was difficult to say that parachute troops 'generally' should perform in a certain way, when no American air-borne troops had as yet participated in any kind of an airborne opera-tion, much of what the publication presented remained valid in the test of combat. Also, much that was in the manual was retained in later statements of policy and doctrine.

The manual did state, however, that the concept of airborne warfare was that parachute troops should seize suitable landing areas, and then be reinforced by glider troops. American doctrine was thus, in the beginning, exactly the reverse of German doctrine. Its appearance at this early period lends credence to the idea that parachute-orientated leaders were already in the ascendancy, and prevailed, despite the evidence that German doctrine had been proven in combat.

Underlying the training programme of any military unit is the kind of employment planned for it. Since airborne troops had no traditional role in warfare and no top command decision had been made, a great deal of vagueness surrounded their possible employment at the time when organization began. As training began, the development of an airborne programme was based rather on the impression which the Germans had made in their airborne invasion of Crete than on any concrete notions about the probable employment of airborne divisions in some future invasion of Europe. In other words, there was simply a conviction that some airborne troops would be 'handy to have around'. Perhaps this is reason enough to justify a military organization, for hardly ever can military missions be defined very far in advance. But until strategic planning anticipated the employment of airborne units in specified theatres of operations, those units could not be expected to enjoy a very high priority in training and equipment.

As early as May 1942, the Operations Division of the GHQ in its preliminary forecast for the 1943 Troop Basis, allowed for seven airborne divisions. The troop basis as approved by the War Department reduced the allowance to five divisions. But in the initial stages of the mobilization there persisted in the minds of the GHQ staff a great deal of conflict and confusion, as to just when the divisions were to be combat-ready, where they were to be used, what their internal structure should be, and how many men within a division should be glidermen. The glider design and production and the airborne troop mobilization programmes were inextricably intertwined. As a matter of fact, there was no place in the early planning for the airborne division as such. This stemmed from the philosophy of a group of hard liners in the Army, who thought it a violation of the rule of economy of force to organize divisions solely for airborne operations. These planners assumed that specialized organizations (and their training) should be confined to parachute and special task and test-units. Concomitantly, all infantry divisions should, within the limitations of the availability of troop-carrier aircraft and gliders, be trained for airborne operations before their departure overseas. This philosophy was based on the concept of airborne operations being principally the action of troops landed either by aeroplane or by glider, in areas previously seized by parachutists. The magnitude of this confusion was illustrated on 28th May 1942 when Army Ground Forces (AGF) Fort Monroe, Virginia, indicated that airborne divisions should not be designated as such; they should be organized as infantry divisions and then trained for airborne operations. But within a month, AGF thinking had crystallized in favour of a specialized organization: the above policy should be ignored, and specifically-designated, specially-organized airborne divisions should be activated.

As the people who planned the invasion of Europe in 1943 contemplated the use of an American airborne division, General William C. Lee, commander of the 101st Airborne Division, who helped guide the U.S. airborne programme, was sent to Great Britain. He returned supporting the AGF viewpoint that special airborne divisions be organized and trained, and gave specific recommendations on its organization. His recommendations, together with those of Major William P. Yarborough, the Army Airborne Command intelligence officer, became the basis for a new division's organization. By 19th June 1942, General McNair was prepared to accept that the division should have two glider regiments and one parachute regiment and that training and equipment should be undertaken.

The idea that the airborne division should comprise two glider regiments and one parachute regiment was another manifestation of the earlier concept that the parachutists should be only the spearhead of air-landing troops. Whereas, on the basis of the British airborne organization, General Lee recommended two parachute regiments and one glider regiment, General McNair could find no valid reason for the British organization. Further inquiry suggested that it was born of necessity, rather than based on long-range plans. When intelligence information on German airborne activities was studied, no table of organization could be found that combined parachute and glider troops in one division. It seemed that the Germans had organized special task forces for each operation—the parachute troops were a part of the air force, and the glider troops were taken from the ground forces[1]. In view of plans for a European invasion within less than a year, General McNair then recommended that the training of standard infantry divisions to enable them to man planes and gliders be continued, and that two airborne divisions be formed. They were to be formed from the 82nd Motorized Division, then finishing its training. The resources of the 82nd were augmented by the necessary parachute units to give the division the paratrooper strength it needed.

Each new division was, in effect, a miniature infantry division consisting of 504 officers and 8,321 enlisted men. It was heavy in combat troops, and light in administrative, quartermaster, medical and other

[1] This was, of course, a mistaken viewpoint. German paratroopers had a dual role: either to jump or ride in gliders.

A CG-4A glider in tow just about to leave the ground

Douglas C-47s in flight, towing gliders

logistical elements. It was prepared to land, in combat, and strike a hard initial blow. No one expected it to fight for many days because it simply did not have the men and equipment to do so. It had one parachute regiment, two glider infantry regiments, several battalions of divisional artillery equipped with mountain howitzers, an engineer battalion, a medical company, a signal company, and a quartermaster company. It was suggested that the number of parachute and glider regiments might be altered as needed. The proposals won prompt approval in the War Department, and General Eisenhower, then commanding the European Theatre, expressed the hope that he might have airborne divisions in his forces by 1st April 1943.

Following this plan, the War Department activated the 82nd and the 101st Airborne Divisions at Fort Bragg, North Carolina, on 15th August 1942 under the respective commands of Generals Matthew B. Ridgway and Lee. General Headquarters initially planned to have them assigned to the Airborne Command for airborne training only, but General McNair felt that dividing training responsibility would lead to unsatisfactory results. Consequently they were placed under the Airborne Command for both basic and airborne training.

There was no great enthusiasm amongst the new glider troopers either. There is no indication that the mood ever really changed during the war even though officers were later given $100.00 per month glider pay and the enlisted men $50.00. General Ridgway, commander of the 82nd Division, sensed that the men weren't too keen about this glider business. The paratroopers wanted no part of it, naturally. They were volunteers. But they had volunteered to jump, not to ride down to a crash landing in one of these flimsy contraptions of steel tubing and thin canvas. The others were not volunteers. They were being put into gliders willy-nilly, and most of them didn't like it.

He figured he had to do something to boost their confidence, so he asked General Hap Arnold to send a glider down, piloted by a top pilot, so that the division could see what a fine, airworthy vehicle it was. Arnold sent Mike Murphy, an old stunt flyer, a magnificent pilot, with all the daring and dash in the world. They lined up the whole division for this demonstration that was to convert the sceptics. Ridgway felt that the division commander should go along on this first flight, so went out and crawled in beside Mike. As soon as he was well strapped in, Mike asked the general how he felt about doing a few loops. Ridgway told him he didn't see any sense in doing a few loops. Well, Mike said, if the general wanted the boys to see what a glider could do, he ought 'to really wring it out for them'. So Ridgway said that if Mike could stand it, the general guessed he could.

They went up to about 4,000 feet and cut loose and Mike did everything with the CG-4A glider that a powered plane could do. It was a big ship and Mike did a vertical bank with it, and a slow roll or two, and then he looped it three times, and when they came out of the last one the ground looked awfully close. Then Mike landed, pulling up short about three feet from a man he'd stationed on the runway, just to demonstrate how completely the thing could be controlled.

That demonstration convinced a lot of doubters that the glider wasn't the death trap they had heard it was.

The airborne programme continued to be buffeted by varying exigencies and unforeseen changes in plans—unforeseen at any rate to the Air Force and Army headquarters that were directly responsible for directing the programme. The glider segment continued to be hardest hit by these changes.

Then early in 1943 the glider proponents received their first serious blow. It came from an unexpected quarter. When the time came to plan for the overseas shipment of an airborne division, the War Department General Staff surprisingly swung around to the position that the ratio of parachute to glider regiments should be changed so that there would be two parachute regiments and one glider regiment in the division. The reason for this modification stemmed more from the problem of shipping gliders on freighters than from a change in the tactical employment of airborne divisions. No one had foreseen earlier what was to occur. One crated CG-4A weighed 20,000 pounds; but more distressing was the size of the crate used to ship the gliders. It came close to holding the record as the largest shipping container of World War II. The size and weight of gliders crated for overseas shipment was therefore a dominant factor in causing the War Department to cut down on glider shipments to overseas theatres; and the reduction in the number of glider regiments was the outcome.

The 82nd Airborne Division, in the throes of getting ready for shipment to Europe, was reorganized. The 326th Glider Infantry was withdrawn from the 82nd to become, for the time being, a part of the 1st Airborne Brigade—a 'catch-all' airborne unit—at Alliance, Nebraska, and a glider engineer company in the division was converted to a parachute company. A parachute regiment replaced the 326th.

Constant imbalances between the Air Force and the Army, in matters having to do with the stateside training and operations of the airborne elements, made the whole programme drag. They became a major factor in determining the training, and the nature of the operations that the airborne elements could perform and, ultimately, the success of the whole airborne effort during World War II.

The stateside performance was considerably less successful than desired. Experience to this date only forecast more of the same trouble. Was this to be the case? Would overseas collaboration and performance be any better?

There had always been differences in pay between parachute troops and glider troops, and these could only have resulted from overlooking the obvious implications for morale and *esprit de corps*. The low priority of the Troop Carrier Command in the Air Forces led to discrimination against it in the assignment of pilots and communications men, and in the withholding of such equipment as self-sealing gasoline tanks for troop-carrier aircraft. To fly heavily armed and armoured bombers at 300 miles an hour to drop bombs from an altitude of 20,000 feet—that was combat; but to fly an unarmed and unarmoured transport through heavy enemy anti-aircraft fire at 110 miles an hour, to drop men into a battle zone from an altitude of 500 feet—that was not combat. Further morale problems for troop-carrier units arose from the idleness of glider pilots caught in training bottlenecks, or shipped to the Pacific with no glider missions to fly.

Memory is usually kind in dimming some of the most unpleasant recollections of experience, and unattractive accompaniments of war have a way of fading, with the benefit of time and distance, into obscurity. Airborne war thus becomes only the sheer beauty of gliders flying stealthily through the thin clouds of a still moonlit night, or the glamour of hundreds of silken canopies drifting earthward from sunny, blue skies. But in the mind of a veteran trooper, the sound of roaring engines, the order to 'stand up and hoop up', the cry of 'Geronimo!' or 'Bill Lee!' or the feel of prop blast, would set racing through his consciousness deep-seated fears of jumping into the unknown, of facing heavy flak, of the depressing confusion of scattered drops in strange and hostile country. And he would know that plans for the future would have to recall the fears and shortcomings as well as the spectacle and the achievement.

A considerable part of the misfortunes of airborne operations in North Africa, Sicily and Normandy can be attributed to faulty training. In some cases training in the United States may have been adequate, but its effects were lost when the troop-carrier units were assigned to cargo-hauling missions for long periods of time. In other cases, the shortage of aircraft and the lack of co-ordination in the United States had left the training still unsatisfactory when units were sent overseas. General McNair was interested in seeing airborne divisions trained well for ground combat rather than in perfecting certain techniques peculiar to airborne operations at the expense of such training, and he had noted a tendency of 'trick outfits to over emphasize their tricks.'

CHAPTER VII

Orde Wingate's Glider Legacy

General Wingate had told me in Burma that without the gliders and the skill and courage of their pilots he could not have carried on that operation. From our experiences we learned a lot of lessons, which I took to England for use in the invasion of France.   Major William H. Taylor,
                                                          Commander, Glider Pilots

In February 1943 General Orde Charles Wingate led a brigade of Chindits on a long range penetration into Japanese controlled territory in Burma. Wingate, a student and protégé of T. E. Lawrence 'of Arabia', operated in the jungle until June. Under cover of the tangle of forests, and at times in the valley of the Irrawaddy, his brigade blew bridges, tore apart railway tracks, and blasted mountains to cause landslides that covered the roads. A force of five C-47s, two old Hudson bombers and some light aeroplanes sustained the operation by dropping to his several widely separated columns more than 300 tons of food and other supplies, in 178 sorties.

Although the operation served only to harass the Japanese, the experience proved invaluable to Wingate and his men. Leaders and troops got 'jungle wise'. Wingate spotted and made mental notes of clearings in the jungle that with some work could be converted to make landing strips, but most of all, he gained confidence that he could repeat the performance on a larger scale. The air-ground collaboration on this expedition was an Allied pioneering effort in the supply of ground troops by air.

Summoned to the Quebec conference to advise Western leaders on the Burma situation, Wingate managed to sell Winston Churchill on the idea of more extensive air support operations, as a way to break the stalemate in the China-Burma-India theatre. He proposed a grand scheme to strike with air landing forces in areas not held by the Japanese, establish landing fields, and then move to cut Japanese lines of communication to the north. Churchill—a great one for a daring plan—and President Roosevelt gave their support to the operation, particularly since it was the only offensive action that held some hope of giving the Allies sorely needed success in this theatre.

CG-4As of the 1st Air Commando Force ready for action, at Lalaghat in India

General Wingate and Colonel Cochran briefing British and American officers at Hailekandi

General Arnold carried Churchill's and Roosevelt's decision to Washington and there summoned two fighter pilots, Colonels Philip G. Cochran and John R. Alison. Arnold named Cochran to command Project 9, the unorthodox commando-support project which was to carry out the mission. Alison became Cochran's deputy. Seymour-Johnson Air Base in Goldsboro, North Carolina, became project headquarters. Close personal friends, Cochran and Alison had only a few months to collect aeroplanes, crate and ship them, train pilots, mechanics and crews, and transfer the whole outfit to Burma, where Wingate and Lord Louis Mountbatten anxiously awaited their arrival.

Given top priority and supported by Arnold's 'to hell with administration and paperwork, go out and fight' attitude, Cochran and Alison dived into their work. They called for volunteers from air transport units stationed at Seymour-Johnson and nearby bases. From an overwhelming number of volunteers they selected seventy-five glider pilots, a sizeable number of light plane pilots—chosen largely for their skill as mechanics—and a number of enlisted men. By October the first of the force of 523 officers and men were flying to India, where they landed in November 1943 and set up a base. Project 9 became the 5318th Provisional Air Unit, soon to go into action as the 1st Air Commando Force. Its airborne assault aircraft consisted of 150 CG-4A gliders; its liaison force of L-1s, L-5s and helicopters; its transport aircraft of C-47s and C-64s; and its fighter aircraft of P-47s and B-25s. It also had 75 TG-5 training gliders.

The glider elements moved to Barrackpore and used R.A.F. fields at Hailakandi and Lalaghat in Assam. Life was primitive, grimy and beardy.

After the force assembled from the States, Cochran set to the task of welding his heterogeneous group and training it for the missions ahead.

Mules imported from the States were playing an important part in hauling supplies through the jungle. It was foreseen that they would speed Wingate's operation considerably if they could be flown into forward areas, there to haul logs from across jungle paths or airstrips or to carry guns and ammunition packs. To solve the especially knotty problem of flying mules into operational areas, Cochran set up a series of experiments. Since mules had a reputation for cantankerousness long recognized in the U.S. military services as elsewhere, Cochran's men decided to restrain the mules so that the gliders, pilots and mule-handlers might survive flashing hoofs and gnashing teeth. Crews reinforced cargo floors and constructed three stalls of bamboo covered with coconut matting. For the first test flight crews constructed special platforms to which the mules could be tied and thus immobilized, and apprehensive veterinarians stood by to administer knockout shots. Before these ideas were put into practice, an apologetic private, who

A glider in tow at 8,000 feet over the China Hills

Mules inside a glider, protected by padded bamboo poles and straw matting. They proved excellent passengers

had civilian muleskinner experience, plausibly suggested that perhaps the mules could just be led into stalls and that the animals might readily comply.

This farmyard idea was tried while the nervous brass stood by, tongue in cheek. To their astonishment three mules calmly took their places in the stalls. Surprisingly mules became the most tranquil and adaptable glider riders in Burma. Colonel Cochran recalls that mules were naturals for the air age, leaning as a glider banked; taking turbulence and landing shock in their stride. They created no rumpus in flight, and it never became necessary for mule-handlers, standing at ready with rifle in hand, to pacify an animal with a lethal shot.

Wingate's mission, to cut Japanese communications in Central Burma and to force Jap withdrawal from all areas north of the 24th parallel, was part of a broad strategy to bring into co-ordination General Joseph Stilwell's forces and Colonel Merrill's marauders, and to cut Jap supply lines conclusively. Relying on air-support, on the deep-penetration principle, Wingate's strategy was to land troops by air in two open patches in the jungle between Chowringhee and Myirkyina dubbed Broadway and Piccadilly, which he had come across in his 1943 operations.

Brigadier Carter's 77th Indian Infantry Brigade moved to Haile-kandi and Lalaghat airfield and began preparations for a glider assault, the most enterprising part of Wingate's strategy.

Brigadier Walter D. A. Lentaigne, leading the 111th Indian Infantry Brigade, moved elements of his brigade to two fields, Lalaghat and

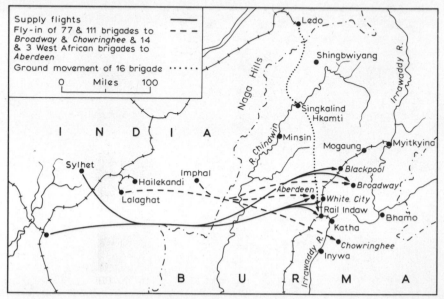

Airborne Assault Operation in Burma

Tulehal in the Imphal plain. There he prepared for a move by either gliders or transport aeroplanes to Aberdeen, another opening slashed out of the jungle.

On 5th February, a month before the planned airborne operation, Brigadier Bernard Fergusson, leading the 16th British Infantry Brigade, marched south on foot from Shingbwiyang, to be joined later by the airborne forces. The 16th left the road at Hamtung to break a way across some of the most difficult land imaginable, revetting each step into the hills with pick and shovel for men and animals to set foot. After they reached Hkalak Go, they set out towards Kanglai.

Here their route came close to Minsin, a Jap radio communication centre which could flash warnings of the Brigade's moves. Deciding to destroy the station, Fergusson called on the Commandos to liquidate the station. On 28th February a CG-4A took off from Lalaghat. It landed on a sandbank of the Chindwin, carrying seventeen troops (obviously overloaded), tore off landing gear and a wing, and injured three men in the process. Alerted by the accident, the Japs attacked; but the Chindits held them off for long enough for the pilots to evaporate into the jungle and start a 130-mile trek toward their base with the wounded, which they finally completed. Once the party with the wounded was on its way, the Chindits attacked and destroyed the station.

A day later two gliders carrying patrols took off to land on a sand bar located just south of where the 16th's march would meet the Chindwin River. Their mission was to booby-trap trails the Japanese might take, leading to the river, and to set up road blocks on key terrain to stop Jap thrusts towards the 16th's crossing-points.

By the 29th the 16th Brigade reached the Chindwin. Fergusson selected a crossing site near Singkalind Hkamti, where the Japs would not be likely to discover his presence. There Wingate, who had landed on a sand bar in an American U.C. 64 aeroplane, joined Fergusson. Fergusson requested boats and equipment to cross the river, and Wingate passed the request on to Colonel Alison's Commandos. Two gliders carrying two technicians, twelve folded boats, outboard motors and gasoline, took off at dusk. Coming in, ploughing through the sand, one glider lost its wheels. As soon as the crews could unload the two gliders, the tow-planes swept by and snatched the one flyable glider from the bar. It carried a litter case from the Brigade to hospital; making the first glider medical evacuation flight for the Allies.

Undetected by the Japs, on 5th March the 16th Brigade crossed the Chindwin, using powered pneumatic boats to push bamboo rafts loaded with men, mules and equipment.

On the late afternoon of the same day, at Lalaghat and Hailekandi, eighty CG-4 gliders parked in two parallel rows waited for tugs to taxi into position. Some men stood outside, smoking; others nervously entered the gliders and gave a final test pull at the lashings on jeeps, bulldozers and ammunition. It was now forty minutes before the gliders were to take off for Piccadilly and Broadway.

By chance, a fighter pilot seeking directions to Lalaghat landed at Hailekandi. There he was pressed into service as a courier. He flew on to Lalaghat, taking a vital photograph to Colonel Cochran, standing with General Wingate at the head of the column of gliders.

Colonel Cochran unrolled the photograph with General Wingate looking on. Taken two hours earlier by a B-25, it vividly showed Piccadilly, with white parallel lines obliquely across the clearing. The conclusion: the Japs had logged the clearing to create an anti-airlanding barrier, sure death to the gliders now set to take off and land there. Only two days earlier photos showed no trace of such obstacles. The Piccadilly landings had to be scrapped, and Wingate was now faced with developing a new course of action. He decided to start his campaign using Broadway alone. The matter settled, some shifting of troops took place among the gliders to adjust the forces to the single-field landing.

At 1812 the leading tow-plane roared down the runway, now thirty minutes behind schedule. One glider, then the other, followed in double tow. The plane struggled heroically at full throttle over the runway. The gliders were finally raised off the turf, the plane having used almost the whole field in the straining effort. Gliders built to carry no more than 3,750 pounds were carrying 4,500, or between twenty-five and thirty per cent overweight, far beyond established safety limits, a factor that was soon to produce tragic results.

It so happened that Wingate's supply officers had no interest in the technical limitations of gliders. Their goal was to deliver supplies, and they were not versed in the temperament of the glider. Area capacity in a glider, not weight, seemed to be their criterion.

In an attempt to meet the requirements of General Wingate's officers for greater loads than prescribed, Major William H. Taylor, the glider pilot commander, had initially agreed to accept 4,000-pound useful loads, or 250 pounds in excess of prescribed limits. The Wingate supply officers argued that they required more.

Major Taylor finally approved a 4,500-pound load maximum. But then load trouble came from an unexpected quarter. Gurkha and British troops, not disciplined to the danger that would be caused to a glider and its passengers by taking non-regulation articles, sneaked extra ammunition and food on board. Cumulatively, all weight added up to critical overloads. Yet, despite these technical violations, gliders were going into the mission *in double tow—at night*.[1]

---

[1] Apparently such practices were too frequent. One pilot complained, after another operation, that he had carried 6,400 pounds—a bulldozer, six heavy camouflage nets and many cans of gas. It took *two hours to reach 4,000 feet in double tow*.

Tow-ropes laid out ready to be hooked to gliders and planes for the take-off from Lalaghat

Last-minute reconnaissance photo of 'Piccadilly' showing that the Japanese had covered the airstrip with logs to prevent gliders from landing

Three more planes, each towing two gliders, followed in rapid succession. The combinations circled the field, sluggishly, monotonously, climbing slowly to get at least 8,ooo feet altitude to clear the 7,ooo-foot range to the east. The four combinations carried Colonel Alison, a path-finding team, and a protective force of the King's Regiment commanded by Colonel W. P. Scott.

Half an hour later the main echelon, carrying Brigadier Calvert and advance headquarters of the 77th Brigade, took off. Traffic control had been well organized beforehand, and hook-ups and take-offs went like clockwork.

At the moment of take-off all appeared to be going well. With the objective two-and-a-half hours distant, it would be at least another four to five hours before Lalaghat air base had positive news of how things were going. Except for a few necessary lights, the field was dark. Some thirty gliders stood parked along the strip, awaiting returning planes to tow them to Broadway.

It was perhaps fifteen minutes before word reached Colonel Cochran at the field that two gliders had broken loose before crossing the mountains. One landed somewhere beyond the field. Soon a plane came in, far ahead of schedule. Its gliders had been lost halfway. Then more pilots returned, all with dismal reports of having lost their gliders. Tow ropes, apparently deteriorated by months of rain and hot sun, had broken. Some gliders loads were seriously off centre, and caused pilot fatigue or fear, making them release their gliders prematurely. Turbulence forced others to break away.

Cochran and Wingate stood hopelessly by, now only able to await developments, and completely uncertain of how many, *if any*, gliders had reached Broadway. Tension broke when a faint 'Soyalink', a code word, cracked over the air. It meant 'send no more gliders'. General Wingate abided by the request, although Cochran urged crowding a glider rescue force into the restricted Broadway field come hell or high water.

Colonel Alison and the leading gliders had an almost uneventful flight until the landing. Major Taylor came in first, touched ground, neatly 'leapt' an elephant watering hole, lost a wheel when he hit the ground on the other side again, and stopped fifty yards from the place where he was scheduled to land, by the advance plans. Several gliders carrying Chindits came in and ground to a halt; the soldiers scrambled into the darkness and evaporated into the further blackness on their way to defend the strip.

The glider with Colonel Oley Olsen, who was to command at Broadway, did not appear. Nor did the one carrying the regular lighting equipment. After a 16-hour struggle to get through the jungle, a rescue crew got to the glider carrying the lighting equipment, which had crashed not far from Broadway. All on board were dead.

Aerial photographs had not revealed how poor a field Broadway was for landing. Some old teak logs lay hidden in the tall grass. Deep scars from logs hauled over the area rutted the field. Six of the eight advance-party gliders had made the harrowing landings, but all suffered minor to serious damage. The radio was inoperable.

When the main flight started to land, Alison had no way of warning the incoming gliders of the perils in their path. He and his men tried shouting, to no avail. Gliders piled into, onto, skipped over, and crashing headlong into, other gliders. Alison desperately wanted to tell Cochran at Lalaghat *'no more gliders!'* He could not.

Yet gliders kept piling in. The glider carrying the only bulldozer whistled by. All heard a terrifying crash. All knew then that they would never be able to hold Broadway; their only means of converting it into a landing strip was gone! Men ran over to count the dead. They found the glider fuselage among tall trees, its nose in the air, the wings ripped away. Miraculously the bulldozer sat in front of the glider almost undamaged. Thrust forward by the impact, the bulldozer had pulled the pilot and co-pilot up into the nose, safely out of its way, as it plunged out of the glider.

At 0227 the radio finally operated for long enough for Alison to signal, 'Soyalink'. Eight gliders of the second wave now on their way were recalled, a ninth carrying another bulldozer continued. Cochran had sent these gliders up in single tow in view of the mishaps to those in double tow. No more accidental or other releases in flight occurred.

Major Taylor's action report showed that fifty-four gliders carrying 839 men, forty-one tons of equipment, and six mules took off to Broadway. In addition to the three that broke loose near Lalaghat, a tug-plane having fuel trouble cut off two; another having electrical trouble cut off two. Eight gliders landed east of the Chindwin River. The personnel from two of these got back to friendly bases along the Chindwin; those of another kept on through the jungle to Broadway. Those of another two fell into Japanese hands, and two gliders and their personnel were never found. Among premature releases over Broadway two gliders crashed, killing all but two soldiers. Checking the gliders after the landing, Taylor found only three still flyable.

Suspicious of the cause, and remembering his own unexplainably rapid landing speed, Major Taylor checked his load the morning after. He found he had 6,000 pounds, almost twice as much as the glider was meant to carry. No wonder the cost in gliders was so high!

Brigadier Calvert did what he could to create some order and organization out of the chaos. He had 478 men left. Three mules arrived safely. Fortunately no Japs attacked, and Calvert's patrols discovered none the next day, probing as far as five miles into the jungle. Wingate got what he wanted, a landing unmolested by the Japs. Thank God!

By evening, engineers had cleared wreckage and built a 5,000-foot runway. The field was secure.

Four R.A.F. squadrons, with some assistance from the U.S. 27th and 315th Troop Carrier Squadrons and the 1st Air Commando Group, some sixty planes in all, flew the remainder of the 77th and 111th Indian Brigades, and supplies, into Broadway from Lalaghat and Imphal, using the improvised strip without difficulty.

The fly-in continued at full speed through the night of 10th March, and to complete the movement four more flights landed at Broadway the next night.

On the same night that the first troop transports landed at Broadway, twelve gliders landed at Chowringhee fifty miles to the south. Soaring over the mountains, the gliders swayed and dipped like flying surfboards when caught in sudden up and down-draughts. Japanese ack-ack guns opened up on them when they passed over the Chindwin River, but all got through. Flight Officer Jackie Coogan, former Hollywood child-actor, piloted the first glider. Major William T. Cherry, Jr., piloted his tow plane.

Coogan cut his glider loose at 1,000 feet, did a 360° turn, and landed at 120 miles an hour on the unlighted field, which was covered with four-foot high grass. He immediately started laying out smudge pots to guide in the other gliders. Meanwhile, his load of Gurkha troops fanned out to defend the field.

In another glider on the same mission, pilot Charles Turner, flying over the mountains at 7,000 feet, turned around to see a Gurkha lurching to the rear of the glider, unsteady in the turbulent air. The uncomfortable Gurkha was heeding nature's call. Invasion gliders have no facilities for such human frailties. That didn't deter the Gurkha. He simply stepped onto the frail fabric covering the tubing, the only flooring in that section of the glider, and made his own facilities. Turner almost fainted when he saw the Gurkha standing unconcerned on the fabric which ordinarily supported no more than a five pound weight. How it held his hobnailed boots is still a major mystery. But the pilot showed Major Taylor the Gurkha's footprints to prove it.

All but one glider landed safely. This one overshot the field and crashed, killing the pilot and two engineers and destroying the tractor it carried. Without a tractor the engineers from the other gliders could make little progress in building an airstrip, the first night. All the next day everybody kept out of sight, so as not to arouse Jap curiosity or risk an attack.

The troops holding Chowringhee radioed their plight to Broadway. Through the next day they got no response. In order to make a landing field of a sort, at sundown the Gurkhas went to work slashing at the four-foot grass with their kukri knives, and proceeded to clear twelve acres of land. At 2100 all heard the sound of aircraft engines. Coogan

At the Chowringhee airstrip gliders were moved to the edge of the field and screened under trees

Men recently landed at 'Broadway', behind the Japanese lines, wait beside their glider for further orders

and others had already set out working beacons. A glider piloted by Flight Officer William Mohr, carrying a 'dozer' and its operator, Corporal Walter Hybarger, arrived from Broadway. Four more gliders came in from Lalaghat about fifteen minutes later with more equipment. By the next morning enough of a strip had been prepared for C-47s to start landing.

Chowringhee was abandoned after receiving a total of 125 landings through the night of 9th March. Of the seventeen gliders landed at Chowringhee, the Commandos recovered fifteen by snatch take-offs.

This field was much more exposed than Broadway. Troops landing there had to cross the Irrawaddy River from east to west before they could unite with the main body of Chindits; and by the night of 9th March it was evident that Broadway could without serious difficulty accommodate the flights remaining to be flown. Japanese aircraft attacked Chowringhee, shortly after two crippled C-47s had been flown out, and just after the last ground troops had left the area.

From the night of 5th March through to the end of Operation Thursday the Air Commandos flew seventy-four glider sorties.

For the Broadway operation the enemy had no warning of Wingate's plans, nor had Wingate planned deceptive missions; but the forced landing of nine gliders near enemy positions provided 'an impromptu deception'. Two of these came down in the immediate vicinity of a Japanese divisional headquarters, and three near a regimental headquarters. The enemy concluded that an assault on some installations was under way, and alerted his landing fields to that effect. Perhaps the deception was more effective because of the long-planned counter-airforce activity of the Air Commandos—attacks by P-52s and B-25s on nearby airfields. In any event, enemy ignorance of Wingate's airborne operation afforded him time to establish his forces.

By 9th March the leading elements of the 16th Brigade reached the Irrawaddy River near Inywa. Brigadier Fergusson again called upon the Commandos for pneumatic boats and outboard motors. Four gliders took off on the afternoon of the 11th, loaded down with the equipment. They got over the sand bar, in the river on which they were to land, just at dark. John Masters in *The Road Past Mandalay* vividly describes the landings.

Fires built by R.A.F. liaison officers with the brigade vaguely outlined the area. The first glider *whooshed* in, overshot the runway, and disappeared. Liaison officers tried to redirect the others, by frantically radioing a warning to the tow-plane pilots to correct their courses to avoid a similar incident. Apparently the word never reached the glider pilots. The three came down still too high to come into the area outlined, overshot it, and landed a thousand yards down the sand bar from the fires. There were no trees in the way, and plenty of sand stretching down the river. All came in safely.

Unloading parties dashed after the gliders. Men and mules dragged the boats, life jackets, motors, and fuel to the crossing area nearby, as glider pilots got together and shifted the gliders into position for the night snatch take-off. Pilots inserted two tall poles topped by blue lights into the ground, fifty feet apart. Atop the poles spread the looped end of the tow rope, to be caught by the suspended hook of the tow planes. At 0200 tow planes could be heard, and shortly after were seen overhead, their red recognition lights flashing.

The word went up by radio that all was ready for the first snatch. The first C-47 came in, flaps down, propellers at full pitch, skimming the bar. A deft manoeuvre to accomplish even in daytime under ideal conditions, the C-47 pilot misjudged his course and missed the 'clothes line' on the first pass. He made it on the third, and in a few seconds the first glider, soon to be followed by two others, flew into the night. The fourth, which was the first to land, had been so badly damaged it could not be flown out. Accounts of this operation vary, but either five Jap prisoners, four Burmese traitors, or two ill Gurkhas were snatched up in one of the gliders.

On 18th March Wingate sent a five-glider mission, code named 'Bladet', twenty-five miles south of Katha. The gliders carried a task force of sixty-five officers and men, and three mules to haul the three tons of weapons, food and ammunition necessary to supply them. This was a special mission to drive towards Mandalay cutting railway lines, blowing bridges and doing what it could to disrupt Japanese communications throughout the Kawlin Wuntho area; and then it could direct the 1st Commando bombers to targets.

Again R.A.F. liaison officers reconnoitred for a suitable glider landing area. They found one on dry rice paddies near Shwemaunggan, along the Meza River, with no Japs reported nearby. They set to levelling the low earth banks that rimmed the paddies, and on the night of the 17th–18th built fires to mark the landing area.

Describing the incident, Masters reported that the first glider made a beautiful approach and touch-down—but exactly ninety degrees in the wrong direction—and stopped with a rending crash. Another came in, landing right on the centre of the strip in the right direction, but racing at such speed that it ended in the thicket rimming the paddies, and virtually vanished in the tangle of bamboo and vines. A third hit a giant clump of bamboo that caught it and held it hanging nose down.

The R.A.F. liaison officers, with the assistance of the task force that gradually came to their assistance, recovered most of the weapons, ammunition and equipment, and dragged out two of the three mules from the bush. The remaining three gliders fared little better. Major Blain, the task force commander, sent out patrols over the next few days. A number of men were wounded in sporadic encounters with the Japs. Burdened by those injured at landing, and the wounded, the force could not effectively undertake the eleven-day mission, and within seven days light liaison aeroplanes started to evacuate it.

On the 21st and 22nd March, six gliders towed to Mahnton on the Meza River delivered twenty-one glider and airborne aviation engineers, plus ten tons of equipment. With the aid of a hundred native troops they cleared the Aberdeen landing strip in twenty-four hours. Soon planes, loaded with supplies for the 77th Brigade, now fending off Japanese at Heno, started landing.

On the 25th the shocking news seeped out that Wingate had been killed in a plane crash in the Naga Hills, while en route from Broadway to Imphal. Shortly before the crash, Wingate was airing his greatest dream, a massive glider operation to take the Jap stronghold at Indaw. Reaction was mixed, and many were those who drew sighs of combined relief and sorrow at his death. With his death, glider warfare as a new method in war had lost its staunchest senior advocate in the Allied ranks.

General Lentaign succeeded Wingate, a staunch supporter of Wingate's tactics and strategy, as the campaign was drawing to a close.

Glider operations did not cease completely. The Japs were pressing the 77th hard, around Henu. Jap tanks attacked on the 26th March, and made serious penetrations into the 77th's positions. The Brigade had no anti-tank guns. Taking prompt cognizance of the unit's position, Lentaign ordered the Commandos to fly in anti-tank guns. Two gliders arrived on the 27th carrying guns which soon drove away the Jap tanks.

About 30th March two gliders landed near a road block at Henu delivering four men and four tons of weapons, chiefly bazookas and ammunition. Enemy fire prevented recovery of the gliders.

On 3rd April five gliders delivered sixteen men, ammunition, and eight tons of equipment to Henu, to build a landing strip later known as White-City; a new forward air base. The Japs attacked, and captured and destroyed the craft, but the men escaped with the equipment. Later the glider pilots joined the British, and the force re-took the strip. Early in May three gliders landed at Mohnyin, delivering six men and six tons of equipment, chiefly scout cars. Later in the month, five gliders delivered sixteen men and eight tons of equipment to Pinbaw, to build a landing strip. Two glider pilots were killed by ground fire. The fate of their gliders was never determined.

Early in the morning on 9th May four gliders carrying bulldozers began descents over rough ground in Burma, given the code name 'Blackpool'. The first tug and glider appeared just as dawn was breaking. The Japanese spotted the combination, and the stutter of guns began. The glider pilot cut off, banked easily, and started his descent. He levelled out and appeared to be coming in for a perfect landing; when just short of the field the glider suddenly went into a vertical dive, disintegrating in what Masters describes as 'a throaty rumble'. The R.A.F. ground control team radioed instructions to the aeroplane pilots to pass on to the glider pilots, correcting the course. The next three glider pilots heard and heeded, for each in turn landed safely. Unscathed, two bulldozers drove out from as many gliders and started work on the strip. Ground control took over one glider as a control tower. The next day five Dakotas landed. 'Blackpool' became the eleventh glider operation for Wingate's forces.

As April 1944 drew to an end, forces under General Stilwell, operating to the north, held the initiative in North Burma. Thanks to air supply the Allies had cleared the Hukawng Valley, and it was evident that in due time Kamaing and Mogaung must fall, opening the way toward Myitkyina. Only the greatly weakened Japanese 18th Division stood in the way; other Japanese units were busy in Manipur, on the Salween, in the Arakan, and around a road-block established by the second Wingate expedition at Mawlu. Some elements of the 18th Division were engaged north of Myitkyina, fighting British-led Kachins and Gurkhas who were advancing south from Sumprabum, which they had captured earlier.

Despite these advantages, the success of Stilwell's Burma effort was in serious jeopardy. The entire campaign had been directed toward the capture of Myitkyina, and by late April it was evident that the monsoon would arrive before Kamaing and Mogaung could be cleared. The coming of the rains would make the long march to Myitkyina impossible if the Japanese offered significant resistance. Furthermore, the Chinese units already in Burma would have their hands full completing the Mogaung operation, and Merrill's Marauders had been so exhausted and depleted by their long marches and hard fighting that their combat effectiveness was greatly reduced.

In these circumstances, it was evident that a quick stroke was required to attain the campaign's objective, and Stilwell had little choice but to ask one more effort of the tired Marauders. Reinforced with Chinese troops and a detachment of Kachin guerillas, Merrill's command was divided into three combat teams, and sent on a long flanking movement across the 6,000-foot Kumon Range. The Marauders traversed the mountains over almost-forgotten Kachin trails, so perilous that a score of mules lost their footing and plunged down precipices to destruction. After a seven-day march the Marauders emerged into the Irrawaddy Valley near Ritpong, a village some forty miles north of Myitkyina.

One of Merrill's combat teams marched south straight toward Myitkyina. This group encountered only scattered enemy patrols, and on the night of 16th May the Marauder team bivouacked south of the

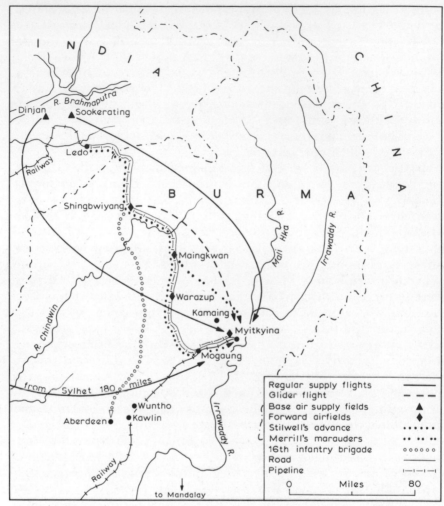

Myitkina Air Supply Operations

Mandalay-Myitkyina Railroad, and only four miles from Myitkyina South Airfield, which really lay about three miles west of the town. At 1000 on the morning of 17th May the Marauders swept over the field attaining complete tactical surprise. A message had already been sent alerting headquarters to have reinforcements ready, and as soon as the field was taken a prearranged signal was transmitted, to announce that the field was ready for the reception of reinforcements.

Taking the airfield was the culmination of the still-progressing drive down the Hukawng-Mogaung Valleys, and opened the way to Bhamo and a junction with the Burma Road. More important, Allied possession of the airfield made possible a more southerly air route to China.

Transports could fly at a lower altitude, and lower altitudes permitted them to carry less fuel and greater pay loads. Also, possession of the airfield made possible rapid reinforcement of the small body of troops which had effected its capture.

Plans for the fly-in of troops and equipment were completed on 15th May 1944. The crews that were to take part were briefed, and ten gliders, loaded with engineering equipment for repairing the runway, were made ready to be lifted from Shingbwiyand.

When the message that the airfield had been taken was broadcast, several C-47s of the 2nd Troop Carrier Squadron had arrived in the Myitkyina area to drop supplies to the Marauders. Four of these aircraft landed on the strip at about 1600, despite Japanese fire which knocked out the hydraulic system of the first one down. The next aircraft to arrive was an L-5 from Shaduzup, carrying panels for visual direction of glider pilots, and an SCR 284 radio for control of aircraft. Before the panels could be laid out, the gliders appeared overhead and began landing.

The first glider landed safely, but the pilot failed to carry out his instructions to act as a 'T' for the guidance of following pilots. The remaining gliders came into the field from all points of the compass under no ground control whatsoever. Four pilots deliberately landed at right angles to the runway, taking very seriously a warning given at briefing that the strip might be mined. Eight of the ten gliders were wrecked, but there were only three casualties to personnel aboard, and most of the engineering equipment remained operable. One of the tow-planes landed and evacuated the casualties. The engineers immediately began work on improving the runway.

Air transport operations into Myitkyina continued from 17th May 1944 to the end of the war, but the operations of the first three days, 17th to 19th May, during which gliders flew-in critically needed heavy equipment, may be considered as the fly-in phase, because it was during this period that the troops necessary to hold the airfield, and the equipment necessary for the emergency repair of it, were landed.

In all, the Air Commandos flew seventy-four glider sorties for General Wingate's forces, and a total of ninety-six by the end of the Myitkyina operation. This is not a significant number when compared to those flown later in Europe, but the sorties were certainly first rate for daring and accomplishment, as was Wingate's campaign plan itself. Fifty-four gliders were lost in the operations, but the many sorties had delivered 1,059 men to their objectives. Some indication of the magnitude of the accomplishment was given by a Burma correspondent of the London *News Chronicle*, writing in 1944:

> Flying over mountains 6,000 feet high, American glider pilots are evacuating British wounded from a strip cut out of jungle swamp.
> In five days they have taken out 298 severely wounded and sick men,

many of whom would have almost certainly died if they had been driven by road to the nearest base hospital.

The journey by glider takes one hour and ten minutes—by road it takes 11 days or more by elephant, mule or lorry with broken springs.

Wingate had used gliders with great imagination for reconnaissance, to spearhead an invasion, and to bring in supplies and equipment to his marching columns. The Commandos gave him willing and dedicated support, and in so doing developed a new aircraft into full stature as a weapon of war. After Burma, there could no longer be doubt that the glider had earned its way into the ranks of qualified war materiel. The question remained, however, would the lessons learned through harsh experience in Burma, under the tutelage of a great soldier, be taken seriously for the remainder of the war.

As the glider forays grew in number, and as Alison and Cochran gained further confidence and experience, their thoughts turned to future operations in which gliders would play a major role. They dreamed of a massive glider invasion of China, to drive the Japs northward or cut them off from Japan. According to their concept of operations, airborne armadas, consisting principally of glider echelons, were to make a series of 500-mile hops along the China coast; not unlike the jungle-hopping tactics they had tried and proved, and not unlike the Marines' idea of island-hopping, to close in on Japan from the Pacific side. General Stratemeyer was for the idea, but it would have taken huge resources which the theatre as yet did not have, and months of build-up. Perhaps this was the reason the plan never matured. More likely it died because Wingate, one of the greatest advocates of glider operations, had died.

Shortly, Colonel Alison received a message. When he opened it, he found it came from General Arnold. General Eisenhower had heard of General Wingate's use of gliders, and he wanted someone from 'that outfit' to come over and give him and his staff some pointers. The message ordered him to proceed immediately to Europe. Later, many of his experts and technicians left to give a hand in the Normandy invasion. Wingate had given them the opportunity, and gliders had earned their way into the ranks of Allied weapons of war. It was now up to the Allies to use what Wingate had left as a heritage.

CHAPTER VIII

U.S. Glider Pilots—The Bastards No One Wanted

A division lift requires 800 glider pilots. Based on testimony, the training of glider pilots has been far below that of power pilots . . . . Obviously corrective action must be taken to assure the successful use of this vehicle to contribute its proper share to airborne operations.   The Airborne Board

In terms of numbers to be trained, and the speed at which they were to be trained, the glider pilot training programme was more ambitious even than the fighter or bomber pilot training programmes. The A.A.F. programme demanded 12,000 pilots for the first year (one short-lived planners' phantasy had this figure at more than 36,000). The figure was unquestionably unrealistic and irresponsible. At the time this figure was being bandied around by heady men, the U.S. did not yet have *one* fully developed, flying, military combat glider and only had a few 2-place training gliders.

Moreover, the timing was hardly auspicious; and before long events were to confront the originators of this plan with hard facts and lead to drastic modifications. But before this took place, severe damage to morale was wrought in the ranks of the commissioned, non-commissioned, and student pilots, the men who would shortly issue from this paranoic planning to perform one of the most distasteful combat missions in the Air Corps—piloting a motorless, defenceless, aircraft, through flak-laden skies to an unknown destiny.

The formal initiation of the glider programme occurred in February 1941 when Major General Arnold, deputy Chief of Staff for Air, directed Major General Brett, acting Chief of the Air Corps, to implement the development of the glider. Based on proposals already received, the Air Corps negotiated two contracts for the training, at airborne flying schools, of twelve Air Corps officers, on courses of approximately three weeks' duration at a cost of less than 400.00 dollars a student.

In June 1941, at the Elmira Gliding Area Soaring Corporation, Harris Hill, Elmira, New York, and the Lewis School of Aeronautics, Lockport, Illinois, the first experimental training of Air Corps officers

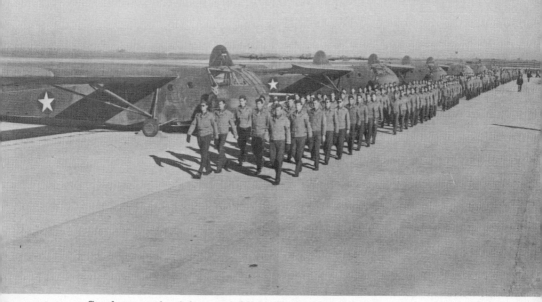

Students at the Advanced Glider Flying School at Stuttgart, Arkansas

Sailplanes used in glider training at Seven Palms, California

in glider piloting took place. The training was similar to the course these institutions had been giving to their civilian students. Initial instruction was given in single-place Franklin Utility gliders, towed by an automobile. The glider was towed across the field at 50 m.p.h. and the pilot required to keep it on the ground, although he had sufficient speed to fly. Successive series of tows permitted the pilot to fly an increasing distance off the ground, and then, after releasing the tow-rope, the pilot could practise approaches and spot landings.

After approximately eight hours, this instruction was shifted to 2-place Schweizer sailplanes, continuing with winch, automobile, and aeroplane tows. When possible, the student would 'slope soar' or seek thermal activity to prolong his flight. After demonstrating proficiency, students flew these sailplanes solo from the front cockpit. Each student completed eight hours of dual tow-work, that is a tow in which a plane towed two gliders. The last part of the instruction programme consisted of a cross-country tow-flight. All students made at least one cross-country flight, that terminated at an airport at least forty miles away.[1]

Early in July arrangements were made for a second class of officers to receive glider pilot training at Elmira. Arrangements at first indicated that ten officers were to take this course; but it appears to have been given to twelve instructors from the training centres who, it was contemplated, would later be used as instructors or supervisors, upon the further expansion of glider pilot training. The training, conducted in two classes of six students each, was completed on September 20th.

At this time, the Office Chief of Air Corps prepared the first programme of instruction for glider pilots. This programme was naturally tentative, and subject to change as the techniques of military glider flying were developed. The duration of the course was not to exceed four weeks, and its objective was to qualify the officer-pilot at the degree of proficiency necessary for an instructor or supervisor of glider-flying training. The programme included glider flying, to include winch, auto, and airplane tow; thermal soaring, with particular emphasis on spot landing proficiency and dual airplane towing practice; the duties of a ground supervisor, to include use and care of equipment; and the duties of an air instructor, and pilot of the tow plane. Actual flying instruction was to last twenty-five to thirty hours, with one hour of familiarization; nine hours of winch and auto tow; two and a half hours of single aeroplane tow and five of double; one two-hour cross-country flight of at least thirty miles; and five and a half to fifteen and a half hours of ridge and thermal soaring.

The ground school course, which was to be 'given in the classroom or on the flying field in conjunction with daily flying activities', was

[1] For additional information as to how such training is done see *Sailplanes and Soaring* by James E. Mrazek (Stackpole; Harrisburg, Pa. 1973).

to include aerodynamics pertaining to sailplanes and gliders, description of types of gliders and sailplanes with emphasis on efficiency, take-off technique methods, landing techniques, soaring meteorology, instruments and their uses, slope soaring, and thermal soaring.

However in spite of the training activity up to this time, no definite doctrine had been formulated on the military employment of gliders; the units to be formed, the size of these units, and the number of men to be transported by the glider echelon. It was therefore impossible for the Air Corps to determine the overall number of glider pilots to be trained. Nonetheless, on 21st August 1941 the Chief of the Air Staff directed the Chief of the Air Corps to make the necessary plans for the instruction of 150 officer-pilots in glider flying.

Twenty-nine Palms Air Academy, Twenty-nine Palms, California, was next selected as a major glider training centre. An Advanced School was not considered necessary at this time, but sites were being investigated.

Instruction was similar to that at Elmira, and included thirty hours of flying. The curriculum for glider training was still in the experimental stage since the procurement of military gliders was only just getting under way, and no one really knew what a military transport glider looked like. The men familiar with the technique of glider-flying were the civilian soaring enthusiasts who had been developing the art of thermal soaring over the past ten years. Consequently, at Twenty-nine Palms, where many civilians taught, and which had only sailplanes, the instruction was principally in soaring, *a flying skill that later proved of little value in military glider piloting.*

One of the reasons for the early confusion and indecision which characterized the glider programme was the fact that gliders, and the training of glider pilots, was entirely foreign to Air Corps personnel. There also seems to have existed then—and throughout the entire programme—a disinclination on the part of various Air Force agencies to take proper responsibility for getting the training done. The cause of this can probably be found in the ever-present antipathy of the power-pilot for any other aircraft. Another difficulty was perhaps that the glider programme was a borderline project, a case of divided responsibility between the Ground and Air Arms.

This early confusion was alleviated considerably in October 1941 when General Arnold personally summoned Lewin B. Barringer to Washington to act, in a civilian capacity, as co-ordinator of the glider programme. Barringer was one of the outstanding authorities on the art of gliding and soaring in the United States. He was commissioned a major in May 1942, and assigned to the Office of the Director of Air Support, in full charge of all matters pertaining to gliders. Barringer continued in this position until January 1943, when the plane in which he was flying was lost over the Caribbean. To him must go much of the credit for the achievement of a new and tremendous project. Not only did he play a large part in the development of the glider production and training programmes, but he also 'made possible the practical application of a device which enabled an airplane in flight to pick up a tow-glider on the ground'.

In rapid succession, and without serious forethought, the Air Force started three different and overlapping glider-pilot training programmes, causing untold confusion and problems of morale.

The 1,000-pilot programme of 20th December 1941 was predicated in the belief that sufficient transport planes would be available as tow-planes for testing, pilot-training and operational training. The programme called for the training of qualified aeroplane pilots only, preferably graduates of Air Corps flying schools. It was clearly apparent at that time (but overlooked conveniently later) that a large amount of skill was believed necessary to pilot a glider.

The primary course of training, which was to last four weeks, compared with that given at Elmira to the first trainees. Graduates were to receive the rating of Glider Pilot. An advanced course called for night flying and the actual carrying of troops under simulated combat conditions, using large gliders. Training was to include a preliminary course of approximately thirty hours in 2-place training gliders at Twenty-nine Palms, California, and a further course in transport gliders at an advanced school yet to be selected. The minimum requirements for this training were that applicants should be power-plane pilots who had taken the CAA[1] primary or secondary course, or civilian glider pilots who had at least fifty hours gliding time; this was later changed to thirty hours gliding time or 200 flights. The physical requirements were to be the same as those for aircrew training. The trainees were to start as enlisted men who upon graduation would be promoted to Staff Sergeant.

While the first of the 150 officer-pilots had hardly matriculated at Twenty-nine Palms, in March 1942, General Arnold initiated a study to triple the pilot programme. Not only was the objective greatly increased, but the time allotted to its achievement was decreased.

In order that this mammoth training effort could be put in operation as soon as possible, a directive dated 1st April 1942, over the signature of the Commanding General, Air Forces, ordered the Flying Training Command to train 4,200 glider-pilots by 1st July 1943; 2,000 of them were to have graduated by 1st January. This entailed an increase of 3,200 over the previous programme, as the 1,000 formerly directed were included in this figure. In conflict with the procurement policy of the 1,000 programme, as many as possible of these trainees were to be graduates of the twin-engine Advanced Pilot course, of Flight Officer or commissioned grade.

[1] Civil Aviation Administration.

Two days later, however, the indecision which characterized this period again caused a change in policy. All glider trainees were now to be enlisted graduates of the Air Forces advanced flying schools. Advanced pilot graduates were considered essential for the following reasons: 15-place troop gliders, now on procurement, were roughly equivalent in size to a B-18 aeroplane. 30-place gliders with wing spans longer than the B-17 bomber were under development. Formation, night and instrument flying requirements were to be commensurate to those required for aeroplane pilots. It was also planned that glider pilots at all stations must be prepared to fly as tug-pilots; therefore glider-pilots with the dual background could be used in this capacity.

It was soon realized, however, that the transfer of 4,200 enlisted pilots to the programme would seriously impair established pilot priorities for fighter and bomber aircraft. On 11th April, therefore, the minimum requirements for glider-pilot training were again revised. Candidates were to be between the ages of eighteen and thirty-two inclusive, and be graduates of a secondary pilot training course, or hold, or have held, a private Airman Certificate or higher, with power pilot ratings, or be glider-pilots having thirty hours or 200 flights.

The programme of instruction for enlisted personnel went into effect on 15th April 1942.

On 8th May, exactly thirty-eight days after the initiation of the 4,200 programme, the Chief of Air Staff directed that 3,000 pilots must be trained by 1st September, and a total of 6,000 by 31st December 1942. An entirely new programme now ensued. During six weeks, trainees would now get thirty hours in cub aircraft, eight in 2-place gliders, and eight in 9 and 15-place gliders, and qualifications were changed so that a trainee must be either a male command pilot training graduate, holder of a CAA Certificate, or a former CAA pilot whose licence had not been invalidated for more than two years, and must be between eighteen and thirty-five years of age.

Eighteen gliding schools sprang into existence around the country, each geared to train 80 to 212 student pilots.

Up to this time the glider-pilot training programme may be said to have been in its first formative stage.

Now that the 6,000-pilot programme was under way the first definition of the glider-pilot's role as a member of the combat team was transmitted to the training centres. It provided that primary attention would be given to their training as pilots. The pilot would receive the majority of his ground combat training in conjunction with the mass training of airborne troops in gliders which was to come after his assignment to a transport unit. Ground combat training during glider-pilot training would not interfere with his training as a pilot. In combat the glider pilot understood his job to be to land his glider safely, get his passengers and cargo out quickly, and secure his glider. He understood he would fight after landing only in exceptional circumstances.

A directive sent to the training centres, on ground combat training, went out to the schools. However, the contract schools did not have the instructors, materials, or incentive to teach student glider-pilots to fight as infantry; a situation that differed markedly from what took place in the training of glider pilots in both Germany and England.

The Air Forces called upon the Army for assistance in giving infantry training to glider pilots. Actually the action did not grow out of a desire to ensure that the glider-pilots would be able to play an effective role in ground combat after landing. Its more direct origin lay in the search for a solution to the rapidly deteriorating morale among idle glider-pilots who, having completed glider training, were awaiting assignment to advanced training schools. In December 1942, 2,754 such candidates were awaiting assignment to four schools in Texas and Arkansas, whose joint capacity was 600 students a month. This meant that, even if no more students completed basic training, some of those in the pool would have to wait as long as five months to pass that bottleneck. The director of glider training hoped that an active ground training programme would alleviate the state of low morale and discontent, the natural consequence of such a stalemate.

Willing to see what could be done, the Army directed the Airborne Command to furnish the necessary instructors and to work out the details with the Flying Training Command. General Chapman sent Lieutenant Colonel M. A. Quinto, of the 88th Glider Infantry, to the Flying Training Command headquarters to get further information. His report was that obstacles were practically insurmountable. The programme would require an estimated thirty officers and 150 enlisted men as instructors, but worst of all, they would have no training aids with which to work—no ranges, bayonet or grenade courses, not even infantry weapons. The Airborne Command felt it could not do the job, that such training in fact might well fall within the province of the Army Replacement and School Commands. Moreover, current doctrine did not contemplate the active employment of glider-pilots with airborne troops in tactical operations following landings in hostile territory.

Thus the situation stood. Many glider-pilots went overseas with the transport groups to which they were assigned having little or no knowledge of how to fire infantry weapons, and rudimentary knowledge, or none, about how to fight as an infantryman. At some overseas stations there was time to correct this deficiency, and some commanders seeing a responsibility corrected it. On the whole the U.S. glider-pilots were deplorably deficient in the combat knowledge and training that would have enabled them to fight on the ground, and also to protect themselves adequately once a glider had landed.

CHAPTER IX

Gliders Assault Normandy— U.S. Phase

In the darkness, early on 6th June 1944, three roaring streams of an airborne armada began releasing gliders and discharging paratroopers; the vanguard of Operation Overlord, the largest combined airborne and seaborne invasion in history. By 0400 elements of the American 82nd and 101st and the British 6th airborne divisions had pierced the northern walls of Hitler's vaunted European fortress. Operation Neptune, the airborne spear of General Dwight D. Eisenhower's armies, had been launched.

American airborne divisions had orders to protect the west flank of the Allied forces. The British 6th were to seize two important bridges, and the terrain east of Caen, and protect the east flank from what intelligence had predicted would be the main German counter-thrust. If 'Neptune' succeeded, Eisenhower's assault across the beaches would be less costly to the Allies, Generals Montgomery and Bradley would be able to consolidate their gains and organize their forces with less harassment from the Germans, and the expanding of an Allied foothold on the Continent would be speeded. That success would attend the airborne onslaught was anything but certain during the first hours of dawn.

'Neptune' called for six glider missions from the 82nd and the 101st Airborne Divisions, and a number of parachute drops. The 82nd was to descend on landing zone west (LZW) in pre-dawn darkness on D day. This mission was dubbed Operation Detroit. Mission Elmira, scheduled for sunset that day, was to reinforce the division, and two more such missions, 'Galveston' and 'Hackensack', were scheduled for D plus one. In Mission Chicago the 101st was to hit landing zone east (LZE), also during the pre-dawn hours on D day. 'Keokuk', scheduled for pre-sunset on D day, carried the division's ordnance company and other tactical support units.

Late in May, the time that the 'Detroit' and 'Chicago' missions were to take place was changed from twilight to before daybreak, to

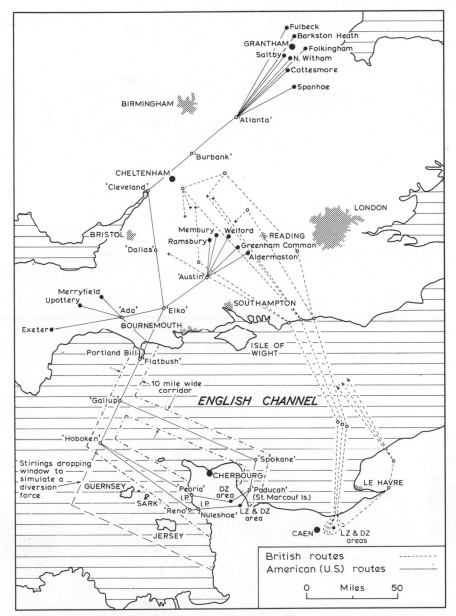

Cross-Channel Airborne Assault: (i) Approach

give the glidermen greater safety from ground fire. Release time for 'Chicago' was to be 0400 and that for Detroit 0407. Both the troop carrier and airborne commanders protested in vain that they were once more being committed to night landings, and that such landings on the small fields of the Cotentin Peninsula might cost half the force in crashes alone. Fear of the accuracy of German guns during daylight flights outweighed their objections, and the decision stood. As a concession, however, about two days before D day the IX Troop Transport Command was authorized to use Waco gliders exclusively in those two missions in place of the heavier, less manoeuvrable and less familiar Horsas. The change entailed a hasty revision of loading plans and a substantial reduction in the amount carried. Since the two serials were to approach under cover of darkness, they could safely follow the same routes as the paratroops. All glider operations in the Normandy invasion were carried out at single tow.

The first tow-plane in the 'Chicago' mission, piloted by Colonel William B. Whitacre, roared down the runway at 0119. Lieutenant Colonel Michael 'Mike' Murphy piloted the glider, *Fighting Falcon*. Murphy, a devil-may-care barnstormer of pre-war days, had gained fame in the United States with all who participated in the wartime glider programme. He was noted for stunting a CG-4A gracefully and dexterously in the fashion of a sailplane. At that time in charge of glider training at Stout Field, Indianapolis, Indiana, and in England ostensibly only to observe glider operations, with no obligation to participate in combat, he had wangled his way into the mission to get a first-hand look at how gliders operated in combat. General Donald Pratt, Assistant Division Commander of the 101st Airborne Division, occupied the co-pilot's seat.

Strung out behind was a procession of 52 gliders in formations of four, each towed by a Dakota . . . . High on the nose of Pratt's glider a big No. 1 was painted. A huge 'Screaming Eagle', insignia of the 101st, and a United States flag adorned the canvas on either side of the pilot's compartment. In the same formation Surgical Technician Emile Natalle looked down on shell bursts and burning vehicles below and saw a 'wall of fire coming up to greet us'. Still hitched to their planes, the gliders lurched from side to side, scudding through 'flak thick enough to land on'.

Unlike the paratroopers' planes, the gliders came in from the Channel and approached the peninsula from the east. They were only seconds past the coast when they saw the lights of the landing zone at Hiesville, four miles from Sainte-Mère-Église. One by one the 300-yard-long nylon tow ropes parted and the gliders came sloughing down. Natalle's glider overshot the zone and crashed into a field studded with 'Rommel's asparagus'— lines of heavy posts embedded in the ground as anti-glider obstacles. Sitting in a jeep inside the glider, Natalle gazed out through one of the small windows and watched with horrified fascination as the wings sheared off and the posts whizzed past. Then there was a ripping sound and the glider broke in two—directly behind the jeep in which Natalle was sitting. 'It made it very easy to get out', he recalls.[1]

Close by, Natalle came upon Murphy's glider, a total shambles. Its brakes were unable to halt its mad 100 mile an hour run, and it

---

[1] Cornelius Ryan, *The Longest Day*, New York: Simon and Schuster, 1956, p. 138.

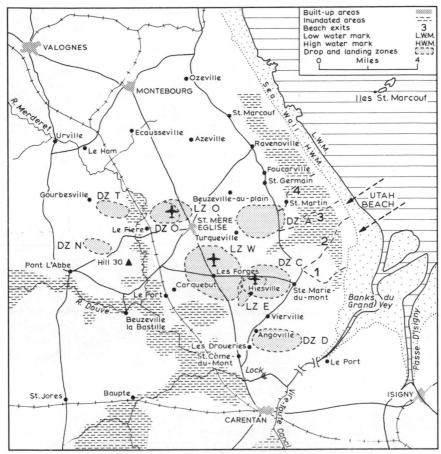

Built-up areas	
Inundated areas	
Beach exits	3
Low water mark	L.W.M.
High water mark	H.W.M.
Drop and landing zones	
0 Miles 4	

Cross-Channel Airborne Assault: (ii) American Operations

smashed head-on into a hedgerow. Natalle found Murphy thrown from the cockpit with both legs mangled, lying in the brush of the hedgerow. The crumpling of the steel tubing around the cockpit crushed and killed the General; the first general on either side to be killed on D day. Ironically his being in the mission was the result of a hurried change, since he was originally assigned to command the troops of the 101st that came across the Channel by boat.

General Pratt was one of two American airborne generals to land in combat by glider. A superb soldier, nevertheless, he had no taste for such an adventure, but being a good soldier he stoically did as he was ordered. Someone of general rank had to make a show in a glider operation, and apparently he was the one 'selected', much against his wishes. As a concession to him and to allay his concerns, his co-pilot's seat in the glider had armour plate under it; and to his great relief, Mike Murphy, the most experienced pilot, was assigned to fly him

Preparations for invasion: in the foreground, crated gliders; in the centre, fuselages; at the top, assembled gliders

Tow-planes alongside Horsa gliders ready for take-off to Normandy

into Normandy. Although Mike Murphy asserts to the contrary, there is a possibility that the extra weight caused by the armour plating in the nose of the glider changed the centre of gravity, and altered the flight characteristics of the glider sufficiently to challenge the skill even of Mike Murphy. This may have been responsible for the excessive landing speed. There is also one report that had there been no armour the general might have survived. The armour caused the seat to buckle and the general's head was fractured by the steel framework overhead.

Several others in the glider had also been killed. Somehow Murphy managed to reach American paratroops that had been dropped the night before, and was soon evacuated across the Channel by boat to a hospital in England. He became one of the first officers to arrive in the United States as a result of wounds received on D day.

Batteries A and B of the 81st Airborne AA Battalion occupied forty-four of the other gliders. Medical personnel, engineers, signals men and a few staff personnel occupied seven of the other gliders. In all, the serial carried 155 glidermen, sixteen 57-mm anti-tank guns, twenty-five jeeps (including a small bulldozer for the engineers), two and a half tons of ammunition and eleven tons of miscellaneous equipment.

Like the rest of that region LZE was flat, and divided into a checker-board of pastureland. Most fields were between 300 and 400 yards long, in the St Marie-du-Mont, Les Forges, Hiesville area; outside the zone the average field was considerably shorter, many being only 200 yards in length. Intelligence reports cautioned that trees averaging forty feet in height bordered the fields. These trees had not shown up well on reconnaissance photographs, and unwary glider pilots had not been told about them in briefings. They assumed that only hedges bordered the fields.

With its gliders in tow, the 434th Troop Carrier Group took off like clockwork from Aldermaston, and with bright moonlight to assist it, readily assembled into columns of four in echelon to the right. Shortly, a glider broke loose and landed four miles from the base. As luck would have it, it carried the SCR-499 radio for the 101st Division, which was to send vital messages to headquarters telling the much needed news of the division's progress, and of enemy resistance. The equipment was retrieved, and sent that evening in 'Keokuk' mission, but this accident prevented the division from communicating with invasion headquarters in the critical hours of dawn.

The rest of the serial of C-47 tugs and gliders reached the Normandy beaches without incident, but encountered sporadic rifle and machine-gun fire while crossing the peninsula. The enemy shot down one plane and glider near Pont l'Abbé and inflicted minor damage on seven planes. Gliders also took slight damage. The weather over the Cotentin Peninsula was cloudy, but except for one pilot who straggled, the planes were able to maintain formation. The straggler released his glider south of Carentan, about eight miles from the landing zone. For the last twenty miles, a Eureka radio beacon system set up by pathfinders guided pilots toward flashing green lights placed in the form of a T in the landing zone. After releasing their gliders, C-47 pilots headed out over the St. Marcouf Islands, just off the east coast of Normandy, to arrive at Aldermaston in Berkshire, soon after 0530. The C-47 pilots had done their job well.

But the glider pilots, groping in the black sky after release, ran into difficulties. Most of them swept in the prescribed 270° left turn, and somehow in the process many apparently lost sight of the T on the ground. Without it, in the dim light of a setting moon and with broken clouds that prevented moonlight illumination, most could not recognize their landing zone.

Soon the dark forms of high trees began flashing underneath and by windows and wings, seriously unnerving the glider pilots as they tensely peered ahead into the blackness and sped into landings. The hedgerowed fields, rimmed by poplars, some seventy feet tall, became death traps. The trees began to sever wings, bringing gliders into awkward crashes. Farmhouse roofs abruptly became small landing fields, and hedgerows braked gliders to rending halts from which no person stirred. Only a few gliders came out whole from the carnage of those minutes of terror.

It was determined upon later investigation that the T that was to guide the gliders was not at the location set up in the original plans. This was one of the basic reasons why most pilots landed in the wrong fields. *Only six landed on the zone.* Fifteen landed within about half a mile of it; ten were neatly concentrated near les Forges, one mile west of LZE, and the other eighteen were scattered east and south-east of the zone, all but one landing within two miles of it.

Despite these misfortunes the glider operation succeeded. Fortunately it was so dark during the descent that the enemy had trouble sighting on the gliders, so there were no crashes caused by enemy fire. All but a handful of glider pilots managed to stop without harming the passengers and contents, even though the gliders ended crumpled, torn and worthless.

Besides mortally wounding General Pratt, crashes killed four glidermen and injured seventeen. Seven were missing. With occasional interruptions by rifle fire or mortar shell, in strange territory it took time to pry equipment out of smashed gliders and more time for the glidermen to find, and assemble into, their platoons and companies. The 101st Division sent out a detachment at dawn to meet the troops from the glider mission at the landing zone and guide them to Hiesville. It did not return until noon, however. When it came back, it brought with it three jeeps, six anti-tank guns, 115 glidermen, and thirty-five prisoners to boot. Because of the bad drop of the 377th Parachute FA Battalion, that had preceded the 'Chicago' glider mission, the division had only one 75-mm pack howitzer on the northern perimeter near Foucarville, and one captured German gun at the headquarters of the 506th at Culoville. The gliderborne anti-tank guns were therefore particularly welcomed. On D plus one and D plus two, these guns lent their fire to an attack led by Colonel Robert F. Sink, which thrust southward against the Germans at St. Côme-du-Mont. Although badly shaken in the landing, the 'Chicago' mission had succeeded.

The first of the glider elements of the 82nd Airborne Division, consisting of fifty-two CG-4A gliders, took off on the 'Detroit' missions from Ramsbury, towed by fifty-two C-47 aeroplanes of the 437th Group. They departed ten minutes after the 'Chicago' serial of the 101st Division. The same Eureka beacon, and T of green lights, that guided the paratroopers to the 'Detroit' zone were to be used by the glider pilots. The gliders carried Batteries A and B of the 82nd Airborne Anti-aircraft Battalion, part of the divisional staff, and a signal detachment—220 troops in all. Twenty-two jeeps, five trailers, sixteen 57-mm anti-tank guns, and ten tons of other equipment jammed the gliders.

The first plane of the 437th with a CG-4A in tow lifted off the runway, and the last of the fifty-two teams left twenty-four minutes later. In other words, two teams left the airport every minute. One glider broke its tow close to the take-off field. The plane's pilot swung around, returned for a substitute and delivered it to the landing zone only half an hour late.

The Channel weather was good, with ten miles visibility at most points. The 437th found smooth going until, almost without forewarning, the point of its skytrain came upon a cloudbank which extended from 800 to 1,400 feet altitude.

The leader and many others independently climbed to 1,500 feet, flew over the clouds, and in two or three minutes were able to descend through breaks in the overcast. They emerged somewhat scattered and slightly north of course. These were the most fortunate of the serial. The other pilots plunged into clouds so dense that the glider pilots completely lost sight of their tow-planes. In desperation they had to rely on dimly-lit instruments. Inevitably that part of the formation broke, and all pilots flew virtually by 'the seat of their pants'. Most of them did remain approximately on course, however.

In the cloudbank seven gliders broke away, released either by nervous C-47 pilots or by dubious glider pilots. Some had their tow-ropes severed by enemy fire. Two were later located in western Normandy. Five were still unaccounted for a month later.[1]

---

[1] After diligent search through archives, the author was not able to find information disclosing what happened to these gliders.

Further inland the clouds became thinner and more broken, but visibility was still bad enough to cause the premature release of seven more gliders on the west side of the Merderet River. It appears that one or two pilots, catching a glimpse of the flooded valley ahead, mistook it for the sea and hastily gave the signal for release. Others behind them saw the gliders descending, assumed that the zone had been reached, and likewise released their gliders.

German rifle and machine-gun fire sprayed the C-47s mercilessly once they were out of the clouds, and one crashed. The fire so tore up thirteen C-47s that when they finally limped back to England, they had to be extensively repaired. Twenty-five others carried spatterings of bullets and shrapnel scars. The gliders also took hits while still in the air. Many glidermen were wounded before the gliders landed.

About thirty-seven pilots of the original fifty-two surmounted all difficulties and reached the vicinity of LZW between 0401 and 0410. The Eureka, which was established by pathfinder paratroopers who landed at LZO (the major glider landing area) early in the night, and which was intended to guide parachute and glider echelons, was functioning and had been picked up by the leaders of what remained of the serial at a distance of fifteen miles. The T was not in operation, and certain glider pilots who reported seeing a green T south of Sainte-Mère-Eglise had probably sighted the one on LZE.

Loose and disorganized though it was, part of the serial made a concerted release in two columns, with the left-hand column some 200 yards north of the landing zone and the right-hand one heading over the centre of the zone, at altitudes between 400 and 500 feet. Most of the stragglers that came in at odd intervals thereafter released in that general area and at roughly the same altitude. When free, the C-47s dived hurriedly to 100 feet to give the enemy less opportunity to observe them through the trees and brush. They skimmed out over the coast through a spatter of small-arms fire and headed home. The first C-47 reached the runway at Ramsbury at 0522, three hours after the last of the serial left England en route for Normandy. The last straggler was back by 0610.

While the descent of the gliders in 'Detroit' was marked by no such confusion as had marred the British glider assault in Sicily, certainly things did not go well. Instead of circling smoothly into their appointed fields, gliders came down by ones and by twos, with each pilot following the pattern that seemed best to him. Several were under fire on their way down, and one glider pilot claimed to have been attacked by an enemy fighter (probably another glider); but the main difficulty was the inability of glider pilots to identify their proper fields or, in some cases, to orientate themselves at all. The railway and town of Sainte-Mère-Eglise seem to have been the only landmarks that most could recognize in the dim light. Nevertheless, between

Gliders and tow-planes circle over the Cherbourg Peninsula. Some craft have already landed

D-Day. Gliders lying in the French fields where they landed

seventeen and twenty-three managed to land on or near LZO.

Five pilots of the 84th Troop Carrier Squadron landed their Wacos in adjoining fields at the western end of the landing zone, there making the greatest concentration. Nine gliders, including two which crash-landed in Sainte-Mère-Eglise, were within two miles of the zone. Three, which came down near Hiesville, may have followed directional aids set out on LZE for 'Chicago'. In all, this was a pretty dismal performance.

As in Mission Chicago most of the gliders got a severe battering on landing. Twenty-two of the mission's fifty-two gliders were destroyed, and all but about a dozen were badly smashed. Again, the principal cause of crashes was that the fields were too short for the gliders to land on; and had high trees around them. Swamps and other hazards, such as rows of posts known as 'Rommel's asparagus', accounted for nearly half the crack-ups. One glider collided with a frantic herd of cattle. The rough landings produced fewer casualties than might have been expected, however. Crashes killed three and injured twenty-three. Several jeeps broke loose during the landings, making a shambles of the interiors. Eleven of the twenty-two jeeps flown in were inoperable on arrival. The howitzers proved more durable. The U.S. paratroops, many who had landed earlier nearby, raced to the gliders coming in pell mell about them, to give their buddies whatever help they could. It was not entirely a humanitarian gesture, however, since they needed artillery. They were of great assistance in unloading the howitzers. Paratroops blasted an ancient wall, to get one gun out of an orchard close of Sainte-Mère-Eglise, and struggled furiously with another gun snared in a CG-4A that was wrapped grotesquely around a tree. By noon, glider artillerymen at La Fière, and two or three crews with the newly-arrived guns on the outskirts of Sainte-Mère-Eglise, were blasting away at the Germans. The artillery was now giving the airborne troops some badly needed firepower. The significant fact was that U.S. gliderborne artillery were in position miles inland from the Allied forces struggling to capture the Channel beaches, where no American artillery was yet in action.

From dawn to early evening on D day the American Air Force flew no more airborne missions. About 2100, two hours before sunset, the next great airborne action started, and soon 'Keokuk' and 'Elmira' forces arrived over Normandy. Allied fighters now lent a hand giving cover, and diving in to strafe enemy positions. Exposure to German anti-aircraft fire was reduced when the course flown by the serials was changed to enable them to approach their objectives from the east coast over the Utah beachhead.

'Keokuk' and the 101st Division took off from Aldermaston in Berkshire with thirty-two planes of the 434th Group, each towing a Horsa. The big gliders carried 157 signals, medical and staff personnel, forty vehicles, six guns and nineteen tons of other equipment. The gliders were to be released at 2100 over LZE. At 1830 take-off began on what proved to be an incredibly easy mission, as far as the aircraft crews were concerned. With good weather and daylight all the way, everyone kept on course and in formation. No enemy fighters showed up, and virtually no ground fire was met with. Battle damage consisted of a few nicks from flak in one plane. A detachment of glider pilots from earlier landings busily cleared LZE, cutting down trees, and the pathfinders marked it with a yellow panel T and green smoke.

The serial arrived ahead of schedule, and the gliders started cutting off at 2053. The glider pilots had a harder time than the plane crews, however. Many German fighting units were still around Turqueville, two miles north of LZE, and St Côme, two miles south of the zone, and other German groups between the forces were troublesome. After holding fire as the planes passed over, they concentrated it on slowly circling and descending gliders, but fortunately for the Americans, the range was too great, and the German weapons did not do much harm. Since it was daylight and visibility excellent, most of the glider pilots landed the Horsas with no more than moderate damage, a fact worth noting in view of what happened later to the 'Elmira' mission at sunset. However, bullets and accidents combined to kill fourteen men and cause thirty casualties. Ten glidermen, in two gliders that landed within the German lines near Les Droueries, were missing.

The distribution of the landings indicates that most of the serial had released its gliders at least a mile short of the proper point. Fourteen gliders were concentrated in a few fields about two and a half miles northeast of LZE; five were at points several hundred yards further east; eight were scattered south-east of the zone at distances up to two miles from it; and only five landed on the landing zone itself.

'Keokuk' was helpful rather than essential to the operations of the 101st Division. However it was important, being the Allies' first tactical glider operation in daylight. It shows that gliders, when not exposed to fire at close range, could be landed in daytime without excessive losses.

'Elmira' carried reinforcements for the 82nd Division. In order to limit the glider columns so that they could be protected by fighters, and to reduce congestion during the glider landings, staff planners split the mission in two. One, towing seventy-six gliders, was to be ten minutes behind the 101s. 'Keokuk', the other, towing a hundred gliders, would leave England two hours later.

LZW (landing zone west) was the goal, an oval about 2,800 yards long from north to south, and over 2,000 yards wide, on terrain much like that of LZE. The northern tip of the oval was about a mile south of Sainte-Mère-Eglise, and the highway from that town to Carentan ran through the middle of the zone. About 1,000 yards inside the southern end of the landing zone, the highway was intersected at Les Forges by the east-west road from Sainte-Marie-du-Mont.

The first echelon contained two serials, one of twenty-six planes of the 437th Group, towing eight Wacos and eighteen Horsas, and a second of fifty from the 438th Group with fourteen Wacos and thirty-six Horsas. In each flight the Wacos were segregated, to reduce the problem of flying two types of glider with different towing speeds in one formation. Within the gliders of the first echelon were Battery C of the 80th Airborne Battalion, contingents of medical, signals, and divisional headquarters personnel, a reconnaissance platoon and an air support party; 437 men in all. The cargo comprised sixty-four vehicles, mostly jeeps, thirteen 57-mm anti-tank guns, and twenty-four tons of equipment. Air transports took off from Greenham Common, Membury and Welford.

The 437th took off from Ramsbury between 1907 and 1921, and the 438th from Greenham Common between 1848 and 1916. Climbing with the heavily laden Horsas was a slow business, but all planes succeeded in assembling and setting out in formation. Over England, squally weather made the gliders hard to handle; they veered and pitched on their long ropes. From then on the weather was excellent, with unlimited visibility and scattered clouds overhead at 3,000 feet. At Portland Bill the fighter escort appeared. The sky seemed full of protective P-47s, P-51s and P-38s, a truly impressive array. Besides 'delousing' patrols ahead of the column, fighters flew close cover on both sides and high cover at between 3,000 and 5,000 feet. No German challengers appeared, and the columns flew in serenely and in a deceptive enemy silence over Utah Beach.

Suddenly, at the release point, a stream of enemy bullets streaked up. The crescendo increased, riddling planes and gliders. Fortunately, because the column flew through the worst quickly, and because the weapons employed were small arms and machine-guns with a little 20-mm flak, casualties were not high. Nevertheless, enemy troops were close to the line of flight, and the mission had neither surprise nor darkness to protect it; two aircraft were shot down after releasing their gliders. One of the planes, its engines dead, dived between two trees, stripping off both wings and engines, yet skidded safely to rest. Some thirty-seven planes returned to England with slight or moderate damage. Two had dead engines, one was decorated with sixty-five bullet holes, and one limped in with the crew chief holding its shattered feed lines together. Three men had been slightly wounded.

LZW, a short six miles from the coast, should have been easy to locate. The landscape was still plainly visible, and some pilots saw a panel T and green smoke, near which a Eureka beacon was sending out signals clearly received on the Rebecca sets in the planes. However, because of a still unknown emergency the T, the smoke and the radar were all not on LZW but two miles north-west of it. The potential source of confusion was that the panel T and green smoke had been set up for the 'Keokuk' mission in the vicinity of LZE, two miles east of Les Forges.

Guided by Gee[1], and by visual identification of the terrain, the leader of the 437th Group headed straight for LZW and released his glider there at 2104, followed by almost all his serial. Ten minutes later, planes of the 438th Group appeared over the zone and made their release, but part of the serial had erroneously loosed their gliders over LZE. Release altitudes were generally between 500 and 750 feet. From such heights a Waco could glide more than two miles, a Horsa less than a mile. After releasing their gliders, the troop carrier pilots swung their planes into a 180° left turn, thereby exposing themselves to fire from the Germans around Saint-Côme-du-Mont, and scooted over Utah Beach to England.

No one who knew the situation on LZW at that moment would have recommended landing gliders on it. The wedge of the German resistance between Turqueville and Carquebut extended across the northern part of the zone, and isolated it from the territory taken by the 505th Parachute Regiment. The paratroops around Sainte-Mère-Eglise could not get through the belt of German territory to reconnoitre LZW, let alone to set up beacons there, and until late in the day General Ridgway had every reason to believe that the entire zone was in German hands. This was why he had decided to place the beacons and markers in the vicinity of LZO. He had attempted to get word of the situation to IX Troop Carrier Command, first by radio and later by panels laid out for a reconnaissance plane, but the message was not received, and the panels were not observed.

During the afternoon of the 6th, two battalions of the 8th U.S. Infantry Regiment that had landed on the invasion beaches, had driven the enemy from the southern portion of LZW. Small seaborne elements of the 82nd Division under Colonel Edson D. Raff made two unsuccessful attempts later to push the Nazis from the rest of the zone. However, when the gliders arrived, the Germans still held approximately the northern quarter. From their lines, southward almost to Les Forges, the zone was a no-man's land, full of snipers, traversed by German patrols, and under observed fire from mortars and an 88-mm gun on high ground near Fauville. Raff's men did their best to steer the gliders to safety by waving yellow flags and making an F of orange smoke, but the glider pilots either did not see them or did not know what to make of the unexpected signals.

Raff describes the alarming situation to which he now was a helpless bystander:

[1] A ground pulsing beacon

At approximately 1,500 feet, headed directly for LZW, was a serial of approximately 60 C-47s towing Horsas with CG-4As following. The troop carriers released their gliders directly over what proved to be an enemy position in the woods. As soon as the troop carriers approached, the whole hill on the opposite side opened up with small arms, Schmeissers, and even anti-tank guns, firing at the C-47s and gliders. Despite this fact, the gliders were released right over the landing zone, and many of them landed there, although others obviously realized that something was wrong and landed between our forward tank line and Le Port. Almost all the gliders were forced to make crash landings, and here it was noted that the Horsa glider seemed to break into many pieces, while the CG-4As' framework was more or less intact. The difference between the two upon impact was visible to me as an eye witness. The Horsa seemed to fall apart. One or two gliders, not making their turn, landed on the hill occupied by the enemy. One of them landed beside what we believed was a pillbox. At least one glider landed beside our still burning tanks, and after its passengers had fled, it burned on the spot. The C-47s then proceeded east and came back low over the landing zone, although some of them scattered and flew back behind our own positions.

I ordered Major Ingersoll to gather up and assemble all officers and men of the Division, including the glider pilots, near the crossroads, with the hope and intention of collecting enough men to make the breakthrough to Sainte-Mère-Église. By next morning I had perhaps in excess of 200 men, but not more than about 150 of them were trained infantry soldiers. The medical detachment, which evidently had come in on some of the gliders, established an aid station at the crossroads at Le Port, where many of the gliders were assembled. We saw other gliders come in later, and this time I noted that the Germans held their fire until the gliders got in very low and very close.

As a final hazard, landings had to be made in the face of obstacles greater than those on the other zones. Not only were there 'postage stamp' fields 200 yards long, bordered by fifty-foot trees, but also some of the designated fields turned out to be flooded. Others were studded with poles more than five inches thick and ten feet or more in height. Trip-wires for mines had been attached to many of the poles; but fortunately the mines themselves had not been installed.

A Horsa, carrying Captain William W. Bates of the 53rd Wing, made a fairly typical landing. Unable to reach a large field, the pilot picked a small one, lowered his flaps, and landed at about seventy miles an hour. The glider bounced twice. When about ten feet off the ground on its second bounce, it crashed through a row of trees, which stripped it of its wings and landing gear. The craft scraped to a stop ten yards behind Raff's forward positions. There were plenty of bullet holes in the tail, but the only casualty was a soldier who suffered a broken leg as a result of leaving his safety belt unbuckled during the landing. The cargo, an ammunition trailer, was intact, and was unloaded in twenty minutes.

All things considered, the glider pilots did fairly well under difficult circumstances. Only two gliders in the first serial landed on LZW but twelve came within a mile, and all but one or two were within two miles of it. In the second serial all but one of the fourteen Wacos flown by the 88th Troop Carrier Squadron, landed on or very near the zone, nine Horsas hit the zone and six came within a mile of it. On the other hand, a dozen Horsas in that serial landed near LZE, and four missed the zone by about three miles. Few, if any, followed the path-finder aids to LZO, and the 82nd Division therefore considered the release inaccurate.

Thanks to greater durability and longer gliding range, the Wacos made a much better safety record than the Horsas. Over half of them landed intact, while only about twenty per cent of the Horsas were undamaged. Three Wacos and twenty-one Horsas were destroyed; a large number by enemy fire.

Glidermen altered their tactics against enemy anti-airborne defences as gliders continued to pour into Normandy. Particularly in the case of landings north of Les Forges, glidermen jumped out of gliders and into the nearest ditch before the Germans could range in with artillery, mortars or machine guns. Unloading waited until night, or until it was clear the glider was not a target. However, in spite of any delays, in just a few hours most of the men and material which had landed in friendly territory on or near the landing zone had filtered through to Colonel Raff's command post on the north side of Les Forges. Five glider pilots were killed, four missing and seventeen wounded or injured; five glidermen were killed and eighteen injured or wounded, but none were missing.

The second echelon of 'Elmira' contained one fifty-plane serial from the 436th Group at Membury with two Wacos and forty-eight Horsas, and another from the 435th Group at Welford with twelve Wacos and thirty-eight Horsas. With them went a paratroop plane of the 435th which had failed to drop its troops the night before. The greater capacity of the Horsas enabled these serials to carry much more than those in the morning missions. The first serial carried the 319th Glider Field Artillery Battalion and a few other artillerymen, medical units and engineers, a total of 418 airborne troops. It lifted thirty-one jeeps, twelve 75-mm howitzers, twenty-six tons of ammunition and twenty-five tons of other equipment. The second serial was occupied exclusively by the 320th Field Artillery Battalion with 319 glider artillerymen, twelve 105-mm howitzers, twenty-eight jeeps, thirty-three tons of ammunition and twenty-three tons of supplies.

The troop carriers set out unaware that the 82nd Division was marking LZO instead of LZW. They did receive a last-minute phone call from the 53rd Wing, directing them to make a 180° right turn after releasing their gliders instead of the left turn prescribed in their orders. Presumably it had been learned that the Germans still held the St. Côme area in strength.

The lead plane of the 436th took off at 2037 and that of the 435th about 2040. As the 435th circled upward to form its column of fours, one Horsa broke loose, and one plane turned back, its generators burned out. (Both loads joined the 437th Group on the 'Galveston' mission.) Good weather and swarms of Allied fighters made for an uneventful flight but, presumably because of the impending darkness the fighters turned back at the St. Marcouf Islands.

The sun set a few minutes before the serials reached Utah Beach, and as they passed over Normandy, the landscape lay in deepening shadow. The pathfinder troops on LZE had long since ceased operations. Undistracted by landmarks or rival beacons, the second installment of 'Elmira' headed for the Eureka and the visual aids set up by the 82nd Division in the vicinity of LZO.

To their surprise, about three miles inland the serials ran into fire bad enough to make earlier flights seem like a milk run. Long sloping streams of deadly flak looped towards the armada, brilliantly lighting the darkness. The fire grew hotter as the gliders started releasing. It poured at them as planes made a 180° turn to the right. Some planes caught enemy fire all the way back to the coast. German marksmanship was aided by the white-hot flame dampeners on the C-47's glowing brightly in the semi darkness.

Flight Officer Fowler peeled away from the formation on release, and somehow made a safe landing. He joined the troops from his glider, and for several days they fought it out with the Germans. He killed nine of them, before he and several others were captured. Then American fighters strafed the German captors and their prisoners, and he barely missed being hit; during the attack he managed to escape, after killing a German colonel and several German soldiers. He finally made his way back to the 435th Troop Transport Group wearing the dead colonel's binoculars.

Fortunately the enemy barrage took a less deadly toll on planes and gliders than first feared. The damage it caused aboard the planes was proportionately about the same as to the previous echelon. In the first serial the Germans hit thirty-three planes, and two troop-carrier men were wounded. In the other serial, three C-47s ditched in the English Channel because enemy hits caused engine and fuel system failures. Naval ships rescued the crews. Two planes had to make emergency landings in England; twenty more were damaged but their crews repaired them in a few days. One member of the 435th Group was killed and one wounded. Planes of both transport groups had scattered and returned in driblets, some landing as late as 0300 next morning.

The initial glider release in this part of 'Elmira' occurred at 2255, five minutes ahead of schedule. The second serial loosed its first glider at 2305. Most of the lead serial released their gliders over a mile short of LZO, and six gliders were released at least five miles east of the zone. The main body of the second serial was quite accurate, but five of its pilots flew to LZW by mistake. Undoubtedly they failed to use the Rebecca directional beacon.

Once again, small fields and enemy fire played havoc with the glider landings. The fire in some places was intense and killed or wounded many glider troops in the one or two minutes immediately before the gliders landed. Despite strict orders to land at a slow speed, some pilots brought their Horsas in at 100 miles an hour. Since the fields were short, some only 100 yards long, and since the twilight made a precise approach over the hedgerows increasingly difficult, even the most careful pilots were lucky to escape a crash.

Counting some damage done by enemy fire after landing, *only thirteen out of eighty-four Horsas were left intact, and fifty-six were totally destroyed.* Despite widespread feeling among the glider pilots that the Wacos, with their gentler glide and tougher frames, would have done better than the Horsas in this particular landing operation, oddly enough none of the fourteen Wacos on the mission survived intact, and eight were destroyed. Of 196 glider pilots, ten were killed, twenty-nine or more were wounded or injured, and seven were still missing at the end of the month. Twenty-eight glidermen died, and 106 were wounded or injured. All those missing turned up within two days.

Once again glidermen scrambled from the gliders and streaked for cover to get out of enemy artillery fire. Unloading was postponed until after dark. The cargoes had come through surprisingly well. The 435th Group estimated that thirty-nine of its forty-eight glider loads were usable, and this is confirmed by estimates from glider units that forty-two out of fifty-nine jeeps, twenty-eight out of thirty-nine trailers and fifteen out of twenty-four howitzers were serviceable. However, because of enemy fire, the material could not be collected or used immediately.

The focal point for landing of gliders in the first serial was almost two miles north-east of LZO. This put them near to, and in some cases within, the German positions. A member of the divisional artillery staff, who had come with the serial, gathered about 200 men of the 319th and led them during the night into the lines of the American 4th Division east of Sainte-Mère-Eglise. Other groups made their way back with more or less difficulty, and at 1715 on 8th June the 319th Field Artillery went into action near Chef-du-Pont with almost all its men, and six howitzers.

From the second serial, carrying the 320th Field Artillery Battalion, all gliders but the five released near LZW, and one or two released a few seconds too soon north-east of Sainte-Mère-Eglise, landed within a mile of LZO. Major Robert M. Silvey of the 320th, who had landed in 'Detroit' mission that morning, waited beside the pathfinders on the zone, and had soon gathered about half the battalion and two howitzers. These began firing at 0930 on the 7th from positions 400 yards west of Sainte-Mère-Eglise. Thereafter, patrols guided party after party of glider troopers with equipment from gliders in outlying areas, and by the evening of 8th June the battalion had eight of its howitzers in action, including two landed in the vicinity of LZW, and had gathered practically all glidermen.

Reports of the hazards and confusion which plagued 'Elmira' prompted the 53rd Wing to make certain changes in 'Galveston'. This was the first glider mission scheduled for D plus one, and carried artillery, jeeps and glider infantry for General Ridgway's 82nd Division. Landfall was to be made four miles south of Utah Beach on the north side of the Douve estuary. Instead of using LZW, the pilots were to release their gliders in the vicinity of LZE, about a mile west of Ste-Marie-du-Mont, and their homeward turn after release would be made to the left, instead of the right. These changes would keep the serials out of range of the enemy, north of Sainte-Mère-Eglise and in the Tourqueville enclave.

Fifty C-47s of the 437th Group took off from Ramsbury on 'Galveston', towing thirty-two Wacos and eighteen Horsas. The 1st Battalion of the 325th Glider Infantry and part of an engineering company, a total of 717 troops with seventeen vehicles, nine pieces of artillery and twenty tons of equipment, rode the gliders. A second serial, the 434th Group from Aldermaston, had fifty planes and fifty Wacos transporting the headquarters of the 325th Glider Infantry, the Reconnaissance Platoon of the 82nd Division and sundry engineers and artillerymen, in all 251 men. In addition it carried twenty-four vehicles, eleven guns, five tons of ammunition and one and a half tons of other material. With the mission went two planes of the 435th Group towing Horsas that had aborted the 'Elmira' mission.

Take-offs at the two fields began at 0439 and 0432 respectively, more than half an hour before dawn, in poor visibility, rain, and gusty wind. The plane towing one Horsa of the 437th with a 1,000-pound overload could not get the glider moving fast enough for the combination to get off the ground, and had to release the glider. The pilot brought it to a stop on the end of the strip. Another was accidentally released during assembly of the sky train and landed near Portland Bill.

One glider combination after another roared down the field. Now it was Lieutenant Rendelman's turn. The rope of his glider tightened. As it did so, the glider nose pulled downward. Rendelman pulled back on the controls, and a fraction of a second later the glider was on its way down the runway with roller-coaster sound and speed. Sergeant Edward H. Shimko and his mortar squad sat tensely in the fuselage behind with twenty-two boxes of anti-tank rifle grenades, an 81-mm mortar and thirty-six rounds of mortar ammunition lashed tightly to the floor.

No more than seventy-five feet into the take-off, when tension on the tow system was greatest, all heard an explosion back of Lieutenant Rendelman. Momentarily none knew what happened. Rendelman took little notice—his eyes glued ahead in those critical moments of take-off.

In a few moments, as he went faster, wind started to blow in behind him. He turned around, and saw runway pavement speeding by underneath. Then he realized that the nose latch had broken under the pull. He was now airborne. The glider nose opened at the base, looking like a tremendous whale taking a gulp of air. Wind shrieked into the opening.

Sergeant Shimko threw off his seat belt and jumped to the opening. He grabbed the steel framework of the nose, struggling to pull it closed. By now several of his men had joined the effort, and Rendelman cut loose. The glidermen managed to get some rope around the nose tubing, and through some of the lashing rings on the floor of the glider, pulled at the nose until it closed and tied it.

Rendelman landed the glider back at Ramsbury. There he found an empty glider, Shimko transferred the load and got ready to go. Now Rendelman was at a loss, because he was not certain where to land. Colonel Donald French, the deputy group commander, told Rendelman he would tow the glider with a spare plane that was available, but with the main column far ahead now, he could not tell them exactly where to cut off. Shimko, not one to be left behind, assured Rendelman he knew where the glider should cut off and would give him the signal. Soon they were again on their way.

Meanwhile, as the flight continued far ahead, pilots found the Channel and Normandy weather better. The rain had given way to thin, high, broken clouds and the visibility became excellent. Since the sun was up and the Normandy coast plainly visible, navigation was not difficult. The serials passed over or near many Allied ships, but by daylight the glider formations with their identifying strips were recognized in all cases. Some of the gliders, sluggish because of overloads, were hard to manage, and some formations became scrambled. One glider pilot got understandably squeamish seeing C-47s directly above and beneath him.

Between the coast and the landing zone both serials flew into rifle and machine-gun fire from Germans who had been pushed south from the Utah beach area on the previous day and had not yet been mopped up. The 437th also got caught in anti-aircraft fire after a turn which probably brought them over the German salient around St. Côme.

The 437th Group arrived at 0655, five minutes ahead of schedule. Its serial came in low and released most of its gliders at between 200 and 300 feet, and a few of them even lower. Release at such altitudes meant that the gliders could not glide much more than half a mile or stay in the air over half a minute. It decreased exposure to enemy fire but increased the chance of accidents. All but five or six of the gliders were released too soon and landed between the two southern causeways and LZE, the greatest concentration being a mile north-east of Sainte-Marie-du-Mont.

The gliders landing east of LZE had only an occasional sniper or mortar shell to harass them, but suffered many accidents. Of the eighteen that started, ten Horsas were destroyed and seven damaged, with seventeen troops killed and sixty-three injured. Nine Wacos were destroyed and fifteen damaged, but only twenty-two of their passengers were injured and none killed. The glider pilots apparently had no deaths and few injuries. The lone combination carrying Shimko found the going rough. It came in over the coast of France from north to south at an air speed of about 160 miles per hour, skimming the tree tops. German fire concentrated on the single glider all the way from the coast to the landing area.

They landed at 0718 in a mined field three miles north of Caen, but fortunately no mines went off. The glider cut through some barbed wire, however, on landing, ripping the fuselage and wings.

Immediately, Shimko and his men scattered, and stayed still for a few minutes to see what would happen. After that they made a reconnaissance of the immediate vicinity and found no Germans; they had left when the glider came in. There were trenches all around, about six or eight feet deep, and underground living quarters about every 500 yards. Having found no Germans in the immediate vicinity, they unloaded the glider, put the equipment and ammunition in hedgerows in the area, and took up a defensive position. After a brief encounter with retreating Germans, Shimko and his men tried to locate their position. Deciding to march westward, they encountered British troops and finally located their unit one week later. Rendelman, who had remained near the glider, was captured and sent to Buchtenwald. Fortunately he survived.

The 434th Group, flying second in 'Galveston', reached its release area at 0701, nine minutes ahead of time. Unlike the first serial, it appears to have released over LZW and, despite lack of beacons and markers, to have done so very accurately. The 82nd Division credited it with twenty gliders landed on the zone, nineteen within a mile of it, and eight within two miles. One was two and a half miles off, and one four and a half miles away. Accidents destroyed sixteen Wacos and damaged twenty-six, but killed no troops and injured only thirteen. Moreover, at least nineteen jeeps, six trailers and seven guns came through satisfactorily. The enemy around Turqueville still kept LZW under fire, but in spite of them the gliders were unloaded in fairly good time, and the glider troops assembled near Les Forges. Eight of the 437th's aeroplanes returned damaged from enemy shellfire, and eighteen of the 434th's were also damaged.

The last glider mission in Operation Neptune was 'Hackensack', which was flown to LZW two hours after 'Galveston'. Its lead serial, fifty planes towing thirty Horsas and twenty Wacos, was provided by the 439th Group at Upottery. This carried the 2nd Battalion, 325th Glider Infantry and most of the 2nd Battalion, 401st Glider Infantry, which was attached to the 325th and acted as its third battalion. These numbered 968 troops of which Horsas carried over 800. The cargo included five vehicles, eleven tons of ammunition and ten tons of other supplies. The other serial consisted of fifty planes and fifty Wacos of the 441st Group from Merryfield. They carried 363 troops, mostly service personnel of the 325th and 401st, and eighteen tons of equipment, including thirteen 81-mm mortars, twenty jeeps, nine trailers and six tons of ammunition. A pathfinder aircraft, piloted by Colonel Julian M. Chappell, commander of the 50th Wing, and Lieutenant Colonel Kershaw of the 441st, accompanied the serial to guide it to the zone.

Take-off, from static hook-up, began at 0647 from Upottery, and about 0717 from Merryfield. Some of the troop carriers complained that the airborne troops had seriously overloaded their gliders, making them difficult for pilots to handle. The sky was leaden and the air so rough that spectators on the ground could easily see the gliders pitching. After the gliders left England, conditions improved. The ceiling rose from 2,000 to 8,000 feet and the clouds thinned out. Over France clouds were scattered, at over 3,000 feet, and visibility was excellent. Like the daylight missions of the day before, Hackensack had many fighters to protect it, from the English coast onward, thus reassuring all in the skytrains. They approached via the east coast over the St. Marcouf Islands and Utah Beach, to LZW. No enemy fighters appeared, and enemy ground fire was negligible until the landing zone was reached. There, gliders became the primary targets. The lead serial began releasing gliders at 0851, nine minutes ahead of schedule, and the other released its first gliders at 0859, eleven minutes early. Serials then banked to the right, and went home as they had come. Meagre small-arms fire during and after the homeward turn scored some hits. Three planes in the 439th, and eight in the 441st were damaged, but none was lost. Between about 1000 and 1038 all pilots arrived at their bases, except one who landed at Warmwell; his detour caused by one dead engine.

Glider release had been made from about 600 feet. The 439th Group seems to have released by squadron, rather than as a unit, and since there was no marking on the zone to guide them, the glider pilots headed wherever they saw a promising spot. A dozen gliders from one squadron came down near the northern end of the zone under intense fire, killing several of the glider troops. Most of the gliders in another squadron landed about a mile west of the zone, while from a third squadron several landed about two and a half miles east of it. The last squadron's gliders were released over the south-west side of LZW with the result that some came down in the flooded area, which at that point extended very close to the zone, if not actually into it. Of twenty-nine Horsas accounted for, twelve landed within a mile of the zone, seven more within two miles of it, nine from two to four miles away, and one nine miles off. Of the Wacos, seven were within a mile, six more within two miles and six between two and four miles away.

Small fields, high trees, flooded marshland, poles and wires set up by the Germans, debris from previous glider landings, and enemy fire, caused numerous accidents. No less than sixteen Horsas were destroyed and ten damaged in landing, fifteen of the troops aboard them being killed and fifty-nine injured. Of the Wacos only four were destroyed and ten damaged, apparently without casualties. Two glider pilots in the serial were killed and ten or eleven injured.

For no obvious reason, the comparatively inexperienced 441st Group did vastly better than the three preceding serials. It made a concerted release over the northern part of LZW, and its gliders started down in the approved spiral pattern. The hazards and obstacles already described forced many glider pilots to zig-zag about, looking for a safe landing place, but by daylight, in Wacos released above 600 feet, they could pick and choose in an area of several square miles. At least twenty-five gliders in this serial hit the zone, another nineteen were within about a mile of it, and the remaining six were probably not far off. Although eight Wacos were destroyed and twenty-eight damaged, only one of the airborne occupants was killed and fifteen injured; while eighteen out of twenty jeeps, and eight out of nine trailers, came through unscathed. One glider pilot was killed and five injured. Highly accurate, with few casualties and with cargoes almost intact, this one serial reached the standard that glider enthusiasts had dreamed of.

By about 1015 all battalions of the 325th Glider Regiment had reported in. A glider battalion instantly struck westward to Carquebut, to eliminate Germans who had held out stubbornly there on the previous night against the 8th Infantry Regiment (which had come in by sea). The battalion arrived at its objective early in the afternoon only to find that the Germans had fled. It then followed the rest of the 325th Glider Infantry Regiment to Chef-du-Pont where the regiment was to report for duty as the 82nd division reserve. That evening the 1st Battalion reported 545 officers and men fit for duty, the 2nd Battalion 624, and the 3rd, 550. Only fifty-seven glidermen were missing from the regiment, all but one of those being from the 1st Battalion. Despite the death or injury of seven and a half per cent of its men, from enemy anti-aircraft fire or crashes, and the fact many had been severely shaken and bruised, about ninety per cent of the glider regiment was ready to fight.

In all, U.S. glider landings and troop and equipment readiness satisfied the invasion planners, and to some the results vastly exceeded expectations. The pre-dawn missions had demonstrated that gliders could deliver artillery to difficult terrain in bad weather and in semi-darkness, and put forty to fifty per cent of it in usable condition within two miles of a given point. The missions on D plus one had shown that by day infantry units could be landed within artillery range of an enemy, and have ninety per cent of their men assembled and ready for action within a couple of hours. While some felt that the 'Chicago' and 'Detroit' missions proved the feasibility of flying glider missions at night, the general consensus was that landing in daytime, or at least about sun-up, had proven to be much more accurate and much less subject to accidents, and that the vulnerability of gliders to ground fire had been overrated.

American experience in Normandy indicated that the Waco was easier to fly, much easier to land, and very much more durable than the Horsa. Such a conclusion was not entirely warranted, since the unfamiliarity to their American pilots, the low release altitudes of the American missions, and the use of fields of minimum size for landings, had combined to show the Horsas in an unfavourable light. In Normandy and in other operations later the British got good results with the big gliders.

General James Gavin rued the fact that glidermen did not have at least some rudimentary skill in piloting a glider. As he pointed out, some glidermen found themselves seated beside a wounded glider pilot, suddenly faced with getting the hurtling, heavily-loaded glider safely to the ground. As he stated, fortunately the CG-4A was not too hard to fly. 'But having to do it for the first time in combat was a chastening experience; it really gave a man religion'.

In the hope of recovering a substantial proportion of the gliders used in 'Neptune', 108 sets of glider pick-up equipment had been sent to England. Although IX Troop Carrier Command had put half its pick-up sets in storage, damaged twenty others, and had only a limited number of crews qualified for pick-up operations, its resources proved to be more than sufficient. The American Horsas in Normandy were practically all unflyable. All but about forty of the Wacos were also found to be unserviceable, or inaccessible to pick-up planes. Many of the remainder were damaged by vandals before they could be picked up. Some gliders in marginal condition might have been repaired on the spot, or after a short flight to some base in Normandy. However, the troop carriers did not and could not have guards, bases or repair units in Normandy for many weeks after 'Neptune'. The ground forces, hard put to sustain their fighting men, opposed the landing of any non-essential personnel, and the few bases in the beachhead were jammed to capacity with fighters. Bad weather and the combat situation combined to delay recovery operations until 23rd June. After that, fifteen gliders were picked up and flown back to England. The technique worked well. *However, ninety-seven per cent of the gliders used by American forces in Normandy were no longer combat-worthy and were left to rot in the narrow pastures in which they landed.*

The status of the glider pilots after landing was anomalous. They were Air Corps troop-carrier personnel and, while they had been given some training in infantry tactics, it had been short and relatively sketchy. Yet they constituted twenty per cent of approximately 5,000 men brought into the battle area by glider. Plans called for them to assist in the unloading of the gliders and the clearing of the landing area, to assemble under the senior glider pilot in their vicinity, and to report to the headquarters of the airborne division for such duties as might be required of them. It was contemplated that they would guard command posts and prisoners until a firm link-up with the amphibious forces was made, and then be evacuated as soon as possible.

A majority of the glider pilots followed this pattern, and on the whole did very well. About 300 gathered at Raff's headquarters near Les Forges, and 270 of them were evacuated to the beaches on the afternoon of the 7th. About 170 others, who had been guarding the headquarters and prisoners of the 82nd Division west of Sainte-Mère-Eglise, departed for the beaches with 362 prisoners at noon on 8th June—after General Ridgway had addressed them in a speech, later embodied in a commendation, which thanked them warmly for their good service in Normandy. Most of the rest were collected and evacuated within three days after they landed.

While many glider pilots, particularly those landed in outlying areas, fought alongside the soldiers from the airborne units for a day or two, combat participation by the great majority was limited to a short period during unloading and assembly. There are few cases in which glider pilots were killed or wounded after leaving the vicinity of their gliders.

Out of 1,030 American glider pilots reaching Normandy, all but 197 had been accounted for by 13th June. What had happened to most of those missing at that time is indicated by a rise in known casualties from twenty-eight on 13th June to 147 on 23rd July. Of the latter total, twenty-five were dead, thirty-one wounded, and ninety-one injured. An additional thirty-three who were still missing were probably prisoners.

The discipline and ground combat training of the glider pilots was criticized by the airborne, and by some of their own members. However, the policy of quick evacuation had worked well in Normandy and had won general acceptance. As long as it was assumed that glider pilots could and should be quickly evacuated, there was no justification for giving them extensive infantry training. It seemed much more important to improve their proficiency in tactical landings.

The 82nd Airborne after-action narrative stated that the chance of becoming a casualty in a Horsa were 16 per cent in darkness and 11 in daylight, or fifty per cent more than CG-4A rates.

Colonel Harry L. Lewis, commander of the 325th Glider Infantry Regiment, reported that thirty-five of his men flying in Horsas had been killed, and one in the CG-4As. Thirty-one men in Horsas had been wounded; twelve in CG-4As. His regiment flew in forty-eight Horsas and 148 CG-4As.

Operation Neptune proved that gliders could do their part in an airborne operation. They had carried ninety-five howitzers and anti-tank guns, 290 vehicles, and 238 tons of other cargo, in addition to 4,021 men. 222 Horsas and 295 Wacos had taken off from airfields in England. Somewhere en route, four of each had aborted their missions. Among the landing casualties 123 came from among the troops who flew in the CG-4As, 340 from those in Horsas; or some eleven per cent of the whole glider force; a substantial cost for an invasion foothold, but a cost that might have been tripled if the same number of troops had had to come over the beaches from landing craft, and struggle overland to objectives taken in minutes by glidermen coming in by air.

Perhaps a better solution than Neptune would have been one Generals Marshall and Arnold endorsed. Arnold complained bitterly, in his book *Global Mission* (published by Harper and Row):

It was obvious that General Eisenhower's staff had no intention of using airborne troops except for tactical missions directly in rear of the enemy lines. The Air Force wanted to use these troops strategically, i.e. take a mass—four or five divisions—drop them down in a specially selected transportation centre, for example—an area where there were several aviation fields, a locality that would be astride the German lines of communication, a position, the holding of which would make it impossible for the German troops to advance reinforcements and supplies, but definitely an area some distance behind the actual battlefield and beyond the area in which reserves were normally located.

For instance, the spot we had selected in connection with the Battle of Normandy was an area somewhere around Paris, where we believed the dropping of four, five, or six airborne divisions would make it impossible for the Germans to hold out for any length of time against our troops which were then on the beachheads. And the site we had tentatively selected for strategic paratroop operations when our troops reached a position approximately along the Rhine was an area far to the rear of the German lines, about halfway between the Rhine and Berlin—a zone far removed from any German reserves, which contained airdromes that we could use for supply, reinforcements, and such operations as were deemed necessary.

We presented these ideas to General Marshall, and he in turn asked us to send our planning team to Europe to sell the proposal to General Eisenhower and his staff. We sent them, but we didn't sell the idea to the SHAEF Staff. We felt one of the advantages of these operations would be that the troops would drop in localities where there was no assembly of enemy reserves. We knew that every time we dropped airborne troops directly in the rear of the German lines, the paratroopers came down right in the midst of the reserve German divisions, and the landings of our airborne and glider troops following them in had to be made under the most difficult conditions. The Germans, anticipating this close-in drop, usually set up stakes and wires in the open fields.

General Marshall stated in his letter to General Eisenhower, of 10th February 1944, that if he (Marshall) were in command of operation Overlord, this was exactly the sort of thing (dropping near Paris) he would do. The minds of General Eisenhower and his staff, however, were fixed on the necessity of obtaining the port of Cherbourg as quickly as possible; moreover airborne commanders were apprehensive about an armoured counter-attack against an airhead. To the first objection it could be replied that a port would have been less necessary if supplies were going in by air.

82ND AIRBORNE DIVISION GLIDER MOVEMENT TABLE

Serial	Airborne Unit	Carrier Unit	No. C-47s	CG 4A	Hor-sa	Takeoff Airfield	LZ	LZ Time
	Mission 'Detroit' (D-Day)							
28	Btys A & B 80 Abn AA Bn	437 Gp	52	42		Ramsbury	0	0400
	Hq 82 Abn Div (–)			6				
	ASP (Glider)			1				
	82 Abn Div Arty			1				
	82 Abn Sig Co			2				
	Mission 'Elmira' (D-Day)							
30	Bty C 80 Abn AA Bn	437 Gp	26		13	Ramsbury	W	2110
	Hq 82 Abn Div				4			
	Cmd Veh, Div Hq			3				
	82 Abn Sig Co			1				
	ASP (Glider)			1				
	82 Abn Div Arty			1	1			
	Hq 80 Abn AA Bn			2				
31	307 Abn Med Co	438 Gp	50		18	Greenham Common	W	2120
	82 Ron Plat			11				
	82 Abn Sig Co			1	9			
	Hq 82 Abn Div				9			
	ASP Vehicles (Prcht)			2				

Serial	Airborne Unit	Carrier Unit	No. C-47s	CG 4A	Hor-sa	Takeoff Airfield	LZ	LZ Time
32	319 Gli FA Bn	436 Gp	50		40	Membury	W	2300
	320 Gli FA Bn				4			
	82 Abn Div Arty			1	2			
	307 Abn Med Co			1	1			
	Co A 307 Abn Engr Bn (–)				1			
33	320 Gli FA Bn	435 Gp	50	12	38	Welford	W	2310

Mission 'Galveston' (D-Plus-One)

Serial	Airborne Unit	Carrier Unit	No. C-47s	CG 4A	Hor-sa	Takeoff Airfield	LZ	LZ Time
34	1 Bn 325 Gli Inf	437 Gp	50	28	15	Ramsbury	W	0700
	Co A 307 Abn Engr Bn			4	3			
35	Hq & Hq Co 325 Gli Inf	434 Gp	50	40		Aldermaston	W	0710
	82 Abn Div Arty			5				
	Co A 307 Abn Engr Bn			2				
	82 Abn Ron Plat			2				
	Cmd Veh 508 Prcht Inf			1				

Mission 'Hackensack' (D-Plus-One)

Serial	Airborne Unit	Carrier Unit	No. C-47s	CG 4A	Hor-sa	Takeoff Airfield	LZ	LZ Time
56	2 Bn 325 Gli Inf	439 Gp	50	10	15	Uppottery	W	0900
	2 Bn 401 Gli Inf			10	15			
37	2 Bn 325 Gli Inf Sply	441 Gp	50	18				0910
	2 Bn 401 Gli Inf Sply			18				
	Scrv Co 325 Gli Inf			3				
	Cmd Veh 505, 507, 508 Prcht Infs			11				
	Totals		428	240	188			

Equipment Damaged in Landings
Daylight

	Jeeps			Trailers			Guns		
	No.	%	No. carried	No.	%	No. carried	No.	%	No. carried
Horsas	5	12·1	41	3	9·3	32	2	25	8
CG-4A	14	20	70	5	20	25	2	22·2	9

Darkness

	Jeeps			Trailers			Guns		
	No.	%	No. carried	No.	%	No. carried	No.	%	No. carried
Horsas	19	31·6	60	11	28	39	7	58	12
CG-4A	11	47·8	23	1	20	5	7	25	28

CHAPTER X

Gliders Assault Normandy— British Phase

At about 2200 hours on 6 June 1944, three Horsas towed by Albemarles one after another lifted off the Tarrant-Rushton Airfield in Dorset, their mission to destroy a major German coastal gun battery at Merville, sited to sweep the Normandy beaches and sea with deadly fire. The four 6-inch guns protruded from under a six-foot-thick concrete roof. Mines and barbed wire ringed the monster emplacement. If the glider force failed in its mission, fire from the Merville guns would later reach ships while yet at sea, carrying the 3rd British Infantry Division, and also rake troops as they landed and crossed the beaches.

Major General R. N. Gale, Commander of the 6th Division, ordered the fifty-eight-man force of volunteers to crash land in the heart of the German position, relying on the concrete emplacement to tear off glider wings, and to arrest the progress of the fuselages.

A parachute battalion went ahead to be dropped in advance. It would assemble, breach the battery's defences from without, and assist the glider force. A five-glider support force was also en route carrying anti-tank guns, jeeps loaded with ammunition, and scaling ladders for the paratroopers.

Right at the start the combinations hit rough weather. Barely away from the airfield one rope broke, and to the chagrin of its passengers and crew they had to land. The other combinations forged into the murk, finally climbed above it, but then found dense cloud masses ahead. The Albemarle pilots wove around clouds when they could, and ploughed through many others. Glider pilots gamely kept on, although buffeted severely.

Halfway over the Channel the passengers and crew in the glider piloted by Staff Sergeant S. G. Bone felt a sudden heart-stopping deceleration. The arrester parachute, deployed to brake the glider when landing, had unaccountably broken open. The combination quickly began losing altitude. Bone realized what had happened and jettisoned the parachute seconds later, but the damage was done.

164

Horsa being loaded by men of the 6th Airborne Division with a
6-pounder anti-tank gun

A jeep being pushed up the loading-ramp into a Horsa

Fortunately, the glider was still in one piece, but the tremendous jerk had severely strained the rear of its fuselage at the tail junction. How this would affect the landing was yet to be seen.

Hardly had things been sorted out, when tracers started reaching for the glider and tow-plane. They were over the French coast, not more than 1,000 feet up, with heavy cloud directly above. Pilot Officer Garnett at the controls of the Albemarle did not flinch but pushed through increasing flak to just above where he believed the objective was. But he was not sure, and began to circle. The Germans now had the combination in their sights and kept firing, while Garnett circled the area four times. In agreement with Garnett that the objective was close, realizing his luck was dwindling, and so as not to risk being shot down, Bone cut away from the Albemarle. He started towards what he thought was the battery. At only 500 feet altitude, he realized his mistake. It was the town he saw. He turned away, but now had to get landing attitude. He levelled off and brought the glider into a safe landing; but more than a half mile from the battery.

The remaining glider, piloted by Staff Sergeant L. D. F. Kerr, had better luck getting to the French coast, but then started taking flak. In short order two men were hit. He circled the objective area four times, but not before two more men were shot. He released, saw what he thought to be the battery, aimed for it, streamed his parachute, heard the slap of orchard tree tops against the fuselage, and mushroomed headlong into them, making a rending stop fifty yards from the battery. Outside, the glider was a torn shambles, but the fuselage, though scarred by rocks and trees, was intact. Inside, all was a jumble of groaning wounded, whole but dazed survivors, and equipment. Hardly had the first man left the glider when he spotted a German platoon advancing on it, where it rested between the platoon and the battery.

The glidermen quickly opened fire felling the foremost of the Germans who, it was now realized, were reinforcements trying to get through to the battery. The glidermen drove the Germans back, and then took up defensive positions among the trees and held off German assaults for five hours. No Germans broke through the British line.

Although they had not landed where planned, their efforts were proving invaluable. Lieutenant Colonel T. B. H. Otway, leading the 150 paratroopers (all he could collect of his badly scattered 600-man battalion), attacked the battery while the glidermen held off the German reserves. Paratroopers crawled forward and managed to push bangalore torpedoes under the wire. They blew two gaps, and parachutists streamed through. Sweating, grimy paratroopers threw themselves at the Germans in dugouts and trenches rimming the emplacement, fighting hand to hand. The Germans determinedly fought back until one, seeing the paratroopers' badges somehow through

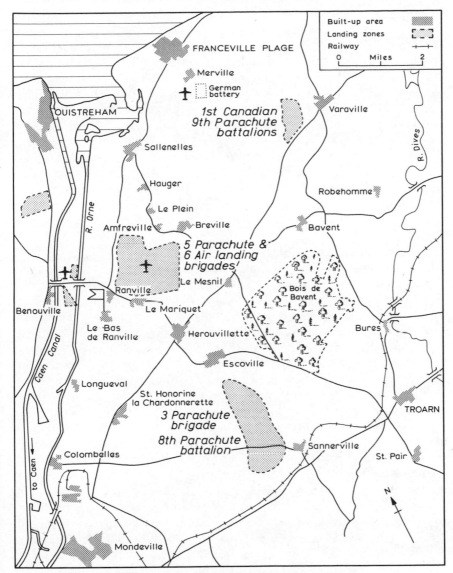

Cross-Channel Airborne Assault: (iii) British Operation

the dark, screamed 'Paratruppar!' and all those Germans left, some twenty-two, surrendered. Otway's men threw explosives down the tubes of the guns, found to be 75-mm calibre. Otway had lost five officers and sixty-five men.

Meanwhile another force in six gliders was on the way to capture two vital bridges. One was a swing bridge across the Caen Canal connecting Caen and the English Channel. The other crossed the

River Orne, a few hundred yards away, running parallel to the canal. Three gliders had orders to land within fifty yards of the east end of the canal bridge, the other three fifty yards west of the river bridge. According to plan, the 7th Parachute Battalion, landing some 1,000 yards east of the Orne bridge, would reach the glider forces by capturing the bridge within half an hour of the glider landings. D-day, the 6th June, was nine minutes old when the first six combinations of Horsas and Halifax bombers crossed above the French coast, followed closely by four others.

At 5,000 feet, and just above the outline of the French coast, glider pilots cut away from their tow-planes far enough from the bridges for their towing aeroplanes to turn back unheard by the Germans; the gliders could sneak in like thieves in the night. It was so quiet and normal after crossing the coast that it seemed to some merely like another airborne exercise.

For the men in one glider, their chief worry was whether the obstruction poles they had seen in reconnaissance photographs would wreck the glider when it came in to land. They were ready to face this risk, but knew that it was serious. To guard against it as far as possible, they all linked arms in the glider and braced themselves; and their most vivid memory is of the long time that elapsed between the moment of release and the moment of landing, though it was only seven minutes. In fact what they had thought to be poles proved to be holes dug by the Hun a few days before. He had not had time to set up the wooden uprights.

The glider piloted by Staff Sergeants J. H. Wallwork and J. Ainsworth landed heavily, but safely. There was a loud crash as the wheels came off, and sparks flashed past. They thought they had 'bought' it because the sparks looked like tracer bullets; in fact, they were caused by striking a wire fence. They had thrust up the exit door during the glide, and as soon as they came to rest Ainsworth dived out and landed on his head. On getting to his feet his first impulse was to feel his limbs to see that they were all there. His glider landed precisely on target. Two more came in close behind, not far from the quaint Norman inn owned by Monsieur Georges Gondrée.

Madame Gondrée, who did not sleep well during the war, heard unusual rustling in the air outside the open bedroom window. She rushed to her husband's bedroom and shook him. At that time they slept in separate rooms, not because they wanted to, but because that was the best way of preventing German troops from being billeted in their house. She said, 'Get up! Don't you hear what's happening? Open the window.' Gondrée was sleepy and it took him some little time to grasp what she meant. She repeated, 'Get up! Listen! It sounds like wood breaking.' He opened the window and looked out.

The window which Gondrée opened was on the first floor of a café on the outskirts of Benouville, a village in Normandy. It is situated a few yards from the western end of the steel swing bridge which here crosses the Canal de Caen, and which by decree of the French Government will always be known as 'Pegasus Bridge', after the shoulder-patch of the 6th Division. It was moonlight, but he could see nothing, though he did hear snapping and crunching sounds. A German sentry stood at the bridgehead a few yards away, and Gondrée, whose wife was an Alsatian and spoke excellent German, suggested that she should ask him what was happening. She leant out of the window and did so, while her husband observed his face, clearly visible in the moonlight. His features were working, his eyes wide with fear. For a moment he did not speak, and then they saw that he was literally struck dumb by terror. At last he stammered out the one word *'parachutists'*.

'What a pity,' said Madame Gondrée to her husband, 'those English lads (*gars*) will be captured,' for they both thought at that moment that what the sentry had seen was the crew of a bomber baling out. Almost immediately firing broke out and tracers began to flash across the night sky. Having two small children, the Gondrées took refuge in the cellar, where they remained for some time listening to the spasmodic sounds of battle outside. Presently there was a knock on the front door, and a voice called on them in German to leave the café and walk in front of German troops. This German version of 'Dilly dally, come and be killed' did not appeal to them, and they remained where they were until Madame Gondrée, clad only in her nightdress and shivering with cold, urged her husband to go up and see what was happening. Gondrée did so. 'I am not a brave man,' he said later, 'and I did not want to be shot, so I went upstairs on all fours and crawled to the first-floor window. There I heard talk outside, but could not distinguish the words, so I pushed open the window and peeped out cautiously. . . . I saw in front of the café two soldiers sitting near my petrol pump with a corpse between them.'

Somewhat unnerved by this sight, Gondrée could not clearly understand the reply of the soldiers to his hail in French, but he thought one of them said: *Armée de l'air*,' and the other 'English *flieger*'. He still thought that they belonged to the crew of a crashed bomber, but was worried by the clothes they had on, and also by the fact that they seemed to be wearing black masks. This was scarcely reassuring, but the innkeeper, mindful of the danger in which he and his family appeared to stand, determined to continue his investigations.

He went to another window, this one looking on to the canal bank, which ran at right angles to the road crossing the bridge. Peering out, he saw two more soldiers who lifted their weapons and pointed them at him. By then there were a number of flares burning in the sky, so that he could see quite plainly. One of the soldiers said to him, *'Vous civile?'*

He replied, '*Oui, Oui,*' and added something else which he does not remember.

The soldier repeated, '*Vous civile?*', and after a moment the inn-keeper realized that these were the only words of French the soldier knew. Gondrée had been for twelve years a bank clerk in Lloyds Bank in Paris, and he therefore spoke good English, but did not wish to let that fact be known at that moment, for he was not sure who they were. One of the soldiers then put his finger to his lips and gestured with his hands to indicate that Gondrée should close the shutter. This he did and went back to the cellar.

Nothing more happened for some time till the Gondrées heard sounds of digging in their vegetable garden outside. They looked through a hole in the cellar and 'there was the wonderful air of dawn coming up over the land.' Vague figures moved about. They seemed peaceful enough, and to Gondrée's astonishment he could hear no guttural orders, which he always associated with a German working party. He turned to his wife and said: '*Ils ne guelent pas comme d'habitude.*' The light grew stronger, and he began to have serious doubts as to whether the people he could see were in fact the crew of a bomber; their behaviour seemed to him to be very strange. Gondrée told his wife to go to the hole in the cellar, listen and tell him if they were speaking German. She did so and presently said that she could not understand what they were saying. Then he in turn listened, and his heart began to beat quicker for he thought he heard the words, 'all right'.

Presently there were further sounds of knocking, and this time Gondrée opened the door, to be confronted by two men with coal-black faces. He then realized that it was paint, not masks, that they were wearing. They inquired in French whether there were any Germans in the house. He answered 'no' and brought them in to the bar, and thence, with some reluctance on their part which he over-came by smiles and gestures, to the cellar. Arriving there, he pointed to his wife and two children. For a moment there was silence; then one soldier turned to the other and said: 'It's all right, chum.' At last he knew that they were English, and burst into tears.

Madame Gondrée and her children at once kissed the soldiers, and as a result were immediately covered with black camouflage paint

Monsieur and Madame Gondrée were, in all probability, the first French civilians to see British airborne troops, harbingers of freedom and victory, when they landed by parachute and from gliders on the morning of the Allied invasion of Europe.

Whatever resistance the Germans made came mostly from a few non-commissioned officers, deserted by their men who had fled into the night.

Major R. J. Howard, in charge of the support gliders, ordered the glider pilots to unload the heavy weapons and to do so as quickly as possible, for the enemy was expected to counter-attack from Benouville at any moment.

'That's a funny sort of make-up. You look like a Red Indian,' said Howard to Sergeant Wallwork, the first pilot of his glider. Then he realized it was blood, for Wallwork had been badly cut by splinters of perspex and wood. The sergeant went on unloading the glider and then took his place in the defence. Howard rushed a Piat (projector, infantry, anti-tank) forward to cover the approaches to the bridge, and placed it in position near Gondrée's land. It opened fire and destroyed the first of three old French tanks sent in by the Germans as the vanguard of their expected counter-attack. Its ammunition continued to explode for more than an hour, giving the impression that a great battle was raging at the bridge.

Later Monsieur Gondrée opened the little café, tending the wounded and adding to the noise of battle a more convivial sound. He uncorked ninety-seven bottles of champagne, carefully hidden for just such a day as this: (the German occupying troops had been kept happy with a concoction made by his wife from rotting melons and half-fermented sugar; this the Germans bought at twenty-five francs the glass and drank with avidity).

After a brush with a German patrol, the sound of grinding gears in the darkness seemed to betoken the presence of another tank; which, however, proved to be a German staff-car with a motor-cyclist behind it. The first burst of fire checked but did not stop the car, and it roared over the bridge, only to be met by another and more accurate burst, which sent it reeling into the ditch. Out of it was taken the German officer in command of the bridge defences, two empty wine bottles, a number of dirty plates, and a quantity of rouge and face-powder. Declaring that he had lost his honour by his failure to maintain the defences of the bridge, the officer asked for death.

Meanwhile two gliders had landed to seize the Caen River bridge. One came in close, the other 400 yards away. The troops from the closest, led by Lieutenant D. B. Fox, quickly attacked, supported by men under Lieutenant T. J. Sweeney, from the second glider. They fought across the bridge.

Having crossed it, Sweeney found a small house on the other side occupied by a tiny old lady and her husband. In his best French he explained that he and his men had arrived '*pour la liberation de la France*'. The old couple were frightened; for they thought at first that he was a German carrying out an exercise for the purpose of deceiving the French inhabitants, who might thus be induced to give themselves away and provide new victims for the Gestapo. Such German ruses were greatly feared throughout the invasion area, and go far to explain the apparent indifference or covert hostility with which Allied troops were at first greeted. When dawn came, and with light on the situation, the little old lady, realizing what had happened, kissed Lieutenant Sweeney and made ready to rejoice. He, like Major Howard at the bridge over the canal, had been busy developing defences to hold his bridge. Glider engineers soon discovered that for some unaccountable reason the Germans had placed no explosives to blow up the bridges, to prevent them from falling to the Allied forces intact.

Soon the long column carrying the main glider force was on its way from England to France. Lieutenant Colonel Iain Murray could see the outline of the immense armada. His glider carried Brigadier the Hon. Hugh Kindersley, Commanding the 6th Air Landing Brigade, some of his staff, and Chester Wilmot, the writer, who was doing a running commentary into a recording machine.

Turning in from the coast the visibility became very poor. A combination of cloud, smoke, and dust caused by bombing, obscured the ground completely. This may have been a godsend, for it made the considerable ack-ack fire inaccurate. Nearing their objective, the glider pilots found the visibility improved, and soon they could see the flares put out by the Independent Parachute Company. The gliders cast off from their tugs. As aerial photos had shown, the Germans had anti-glider 'Rommel's asparagus', heavy logs set upright in countless holes over the glider landing areas. In the last few yards one post tore a wing-tip, and one collapsed when hit head-on by the cockpit. Murray thought this one must have been loosely placed by some patriotic Frenchman employed by the Germans.

Soon after landing he found that Chester Wilmot's recorder had been smashed by a piece of shell from an ack-ack gun, which was most unfortunate. However, Wilmot had a good picture in his mind, and the description he later gave in his book *Struggle for Europe*, gave a very clear account of events up to the time of landing.

Apart from occasional rifle and machine-gun fire there was no great opposition, and they soon gathered at the rendezvous to await the dawn. As soon as daylight came, they went down to the 'Pegasus' bridge to find that one glider had landed within a hundred feet of it. This was a remarkable feat on the part of the glider pilot. It had enabled the troops he carried to rush the bridge and capture it before it could be blown. This was a very vital task, for the use of the bridge was of great assistance to the Commandos and the main body of troops in crossing the river.

It was on this bridge that General Gale waited at midday to hand over control to Lord Lovat and his Commandos, having bet Lord Lovat a case of champagne that he would not be there at the appointed time. As the hour approached, there was no sign of him. But as the clock struck noon, a piper seemed to appear from nowhere, leading Lord Lovat and his Commandos to relieve General Gale and win his bet.

Landing-zone for the main force of the 6th Airborne Division

Eleven Horsas came in to the parachute landing zone carrying engineers, anti-tank guns for the paratroopers, and two bulldozers. Pilots found landing-control lights difficult to see, through the dust and smoke.

One pilot said goodbye to his tug pilot, heard a 'good luck' come back, and then there was the familiar jerk, with the noise of the wind gradually receding to the background and the speed dropping back to a modest eighty m.p.h. Paddy, his co-pilot, had handed over the controls and was intently watching an ack-ack battery on the right, whose tracer seemed to be a bit too near. Paddy motioned to it, and almost at once, as the pilot put on half flap, the flak turned and seemed to find another target. Then they saw the target, another Horsa, well below, flying towards the flak. Just a second afterwards the Horsa switched on its emergency lights and illuminated a small row of trees between the pilot's glider and the T along which the second Horsa was flying. It crashed.

Fortunately Paddy's glider was coming in just right. There came a little bump, and then another, something like a ditch. Then a wheel seemed to stick, and started to swing the glider round. With a deft touch on the opposite rudder and brake it straightened out and stopped. Paddy and his pilot heaved a sigh—and then immediately shot out of their seats; they were on the first light of the T and not in their correct position on the extreme left of the T. Having been forewarned by a training mishap that this might happen, they arranged that Paddy should jump out and wave his torch to show the rear of the glider. This he did, while with feverish haste, grabbing personal kits and rifles, the co-pilot jumped out, and they took up positions on either side of the glider.

All got ready to beat a hasty retreat if another glider started coming in on top of them, but there was not a sign of anything in the sky. It was like being at an appointed place at the right time, waiting for someone to arrive, and being 'stood up'; causing you to go away in disgust. All felt like that at first. Then a feeling of loneliness descended. Even the Germans did not greet them. Where were the independent parachutists who had put the T out? Not a soul, not a noise, nothing. Paddy stared towards the pilot in the blackness and said, 'Let's get the tail off.'

They went inside the glider and began to undo the nuts holding the tail. They had them off within a quarter of an hour, but the tail would not budge. They called the two drivers over; and then began the oddest tug-of-war. One Horsa Mark I versus four tired and sweating airborne types. The glider won, and while they sat back exhausted for a moment, it sat there quite contentedly, for all the world as if it were back in England. They thought of blowing the tail off but the noise it would make, and the type of equipment inside, decided them against it. Then, just as they had picked up the hand-saw, they heard the sound of approaching aircraft, and right above them the air blossomed with billowing parachutes. It was a wonderful sight, and they didn't feel lonely any more. For the next five minutes they busily dodged kit bags dangling from the feet of heavily-loaded paratroopers. One even landed on the Horsa's tail, but nothing happened; and when asked for help to get the tail off, the paratrooper simply grinned and vanished. An Albemarle on the left lit up in flames and brought them all back to earth with a jolt.

Gliders crossed other gliders' approach paths unknowingly; gliders whizzed past from opposite directions, seeing each other go by only when the distance closed to thirty feet or so; but with the Horsa's ability to absorb punishment, few men were hurt. One bulldozer broke through the floor as its Horsa careened over the earth, but stayed with the glider till it stopped. Seventy-nine Horsas were landing, their pilots having great difficulty because of the appalling conditions.

Staff Sergeant Leslie Foster saw a flaming British plane dive towards the ground. He kept looking for the church tower and other landmarks which marked turning and landing points. There was the tower! He spoke into the intercom, thanking the tow-pilot for the ride and got an 'O.K. Matchbox, best of luck.'

Foster reached for and pulled the release, the glider slowed, and flew alone over the fields of France. He put down half-flap and turned slowly to port, a full 180°, and there was the landing field stretched out before them. He increased to full flap and put the nose down. Everything seemed to be going extremely well, when a warning shout came from his co-pilot: 'Les—kite coming in from——.' It was too late to do anything but pull back hard on the stick as the other glider soared up under and across him. There was a terrible tearing, crashing sound, and he saw the other cabin hang for a split second under him and then fall away. The speed dropped alarmingly as they hovered with the nose up. He quickly brought up the flaps and pushed hard on the stick to try to get up some speed. It was obvious that the undercarriage must have gone in the crash, and he realized that it would have to be a 'belly-landing' if they were fortunate enough to reach the ground in one piece.

There was no sound from the men inside, but the roaring of the air increased as the needle moved faster and faster. It was no use letting up. He would have no brakes, and his safest bet was to hit the ground as soon as possible and pray that the good hard French soil would halt them before they hit the trees at the far end of the field. Ninety, ninety-five—the screaming of the air past the fuselage. One hundred—a hundred and ten—full flap on—up with the nose—and they were tearing through the high French corn, the red earth pouring through the broken floor—nothing but the long straight parting of the corn, and then, suddenly, the open patch before the trees. Hard kick on the right rudder—would it work?—and they slewed round in a great half-circle, the soil spurning high in the air. As they stopped, almost touching the trees, there was a tearing sound, and a very tired port wing fell to the ground. When they had extricated themselves from the remains, they found that one of their Thermos flasks was miraculously unbroken, and as they sat sipping the hot tea they examined themselves. A few scratches on the co-pilot. A few on Foster. No passenger casualties.

Others were not so fortunate. Many of their gliders landed far from the zone, others snapped off wings on the poles, or on the heavy cable which the Germans had strung between the poles, connecting them to fused artillery shells. These went off when shocked by a glider's impact.

Staff Sergeant A. Proctor was the last of a flight of Horsas to arrive over the landing zone and, in consequence, came in at the end of a long queue of gliders on the approach. Perhaps for this reason he presented the best target, and the German gunners gave him their undivided attention. Evasive action became essential, and as there was no room in the approach area, he dived away into-wind with the intention of pulling out at the last moment and making a cross-wind landing. The plan worked well until he pulled up to about 100 feet from the ground and turned cross-wind. The area he had chosen to land in was heavily studded with anti-invasion poles, but there was no alternative but to land there. In a rapid survey of the ground, he made an interesting discovery: the methodical Germans had erected the poles in a distinct pattern; and it was this that saved him. He man-oeuvred the glider until they were flying a few feet over the poles, then ordered full-flap, and as the next gap appeared he thrust the stick forward. Both wings struck poles simultaneously, and with a great rending of wood he landed heavily, but still on a straight course, coming to a halt before reaching the next alternating row of poles. Five trembling artillerymen emerged from the cockpit, and assured him that they had never doubted his ability. It seemed kinder, at the time, to believe them.

The second pilot, Sergeant Wright, took charge of the unloading; and while this was being done, Proctor thought it might be prudent to see what was going on outside. It was then that he heard the whine of bullets uncomfortably close, and realized with some alarm that they were probably being directed at him. He went to ground with speed and observed that the fire was coming from a church tower about 500 yards away. He shouted a message to this effect to the glider, to which Sergeant Wright replied, 'Come inside then, you silly ————.' Saving his rude remarks until later, Proctor asked for the Bren gun, and worming his way round the glider, sited the gun, and opened fire on the church tower. This silenced them. Unloading was then completed, farewells exchanged, and the Royal Artillery left at high speed

Sergeant Proctor and Sergeant Wright took a compass-bearing and set off in a direct line for their own rendezvous, coming upon another Horsa that in landing in the same area had struck a pole head on, killing both pilots in a horrible fashion.

Meanwhile the glider engineers, with their two bulldozers, hurriedly began to get launching strips ready for the arrival of the largest serial of the British 'Neptune' operation, consisting of sixty-eight Horsas and four Hamilcars. Both machines were at work on preparing landing strips within an hour of landing. In eight hours, well within the margin of time allotted, they had cleared the four strips of glider debris, and filled in the anti-glider post holes which had been dug by the enemy. The engineers worked without pause or intermission, all the time under sniper, mortar and shell fire. By the time the leading glider, carrying General Gale appeared, the sappers had cleared two 1,000-foot airstrips and lighted them with flares. Though the airstrips provided so much landing space, it was far from adequate for the forty-nine remaining enormous birds that had made it to their objective. A vicious cross wind made matters worse. The pilots crowded their Horsas into the strips where they could, but some could not avoid the poles fringing the strips, that the engineers had not had time to remove. Some piled into other gliders.

When he cast off Staff Sergeant T. W. Pearce found the air crowded with gliders, parachutes, and discarded tow-ropes. Without warning, the glider got a rending jolt. His glider and another had collided. He was 600 feet up. He struggled to get control and just barely managed to land sideways, coming to a juddering halt in tall corn. His first pilot turned to him and said: 'Time for a cup of char, Tom!' (They had two flasks strapped above their heads; one was still intact—as were the 'pin-ups' they had admired on the way over.) Chopping their way out of the wreckage they dashed over to the other glider, or rather to what was left of it. In the mid-air crash the tail unit had been destroyed and it had dived vertically from 600 feet. Pearce had lost two of his own flight, but all in the other glider had perished.

Huw Wheldon, of B.B.C. T.V.'s feature 'Monitor', came in in one of the gliders, escorted by a cloud of fighters. But nothing, absolutely nothing, about D-day was turning out as expected. There was no fierce fighter opposition, no signs of flak, no wrecked gliders in the fields below.

In his glider some of the 'Red Devils' about to penetrate the Atlantic Wall were sucking jujubes. Or they looked like jujubes . . . Looking again Wheldon saw that they had taken the barley sugar from the special airborne rations which were supposed to last for three days.

'Put them away,' he said sharply, before they devoured the compound cakes of porridge. 'Want to live on grass?'

'But, sor,' said one Irish rifleman, 'they're very good, them sweets.'

(*above*) Tank-carrying Hamilcars gliding into Normandy. (*below*) The scene after the landings. One has crashed in flames

They were not gliding in the accepted sense of the word. As always, it was as if they were 'in a very old railway carriage being yanked across the sky.' As always . . . for weeks and months they had rehearsed for this, landing on fields and roads and hills. Once they even turned over in the air and sitting upside down, strapped into his seat, the platoon sergeant, famed for his ferocity, had recited the Lord's Prayer seven times without pause or punctuation.

From the moment they crossed the French coastline sweat began to run down the back of the glider pilot's neck. There were two little runnels of it, 'like bacon fat'. He was working overtime.

'We're casting off,' he said, and Wheldon turned round to strap himself into his seat. At first he could not believe it—but Mullins, the company runner, was asleep. Mullins was a magnificent character, later to become a sergeant. He had been very good company all the way and had now apparently decided to have a quiet nap just before the towing-plane discarded them.

'Come on, Mullins,' Wheldon said, 'we're invading Europe.' Groaning, Mullins rubbed at his eyes and, looking bored, began to buckle up.

The glider came down with all the grace 'of an empty can', as Wheldon recounted. It made a perfectly smooth landing on a soft field on a glorious summer's night. Other gliders, quite undamaged, did the same. France. But it was pretty difficult to believe it. They had been warned and trained, trained and warned, that the dangerous time was the moment immediately after landing, when they would be disorganized and defenceless, relaxing in the relief of being down.

Like everybody else Wheldon had to leap out of this cardboard aeroplane and become part of an organized unit round the Bren gun. He leaped out and the grass smelled fine and sweet. All around there was action and machine-guns were hiccupping, but nobody seemed to be firing at them.

After two hours in the glider he wanted to relieve himself first, certain that the others would gather round the machine-gun. When he looked round to make sure that they were in what they were pleased to call all-round defences, he saw that all of them were following his example. Despite the rifles and the ammunition, despite the camouflaged smocks and parachute helmets, despite the blackened faces, they looked like small boys on a Sunday school treat. The absurdity of it dawned on them all, and they dived down behind the Bren gun as if their lives depended on it.

Their next job was to leave this area, which was not all that healthy, and rendezvous with the rest of 'C' Company, 1st Battalion Royal Ulster Rifles, in a wood. Thereafter 'C' Company as a whole would go to the battalion starting line for the attack. When they reached this little wood one of the riflemen from another glider was waiting.

As they crouched to talk Wheldon noticed that the man was feeling like the rest. He had this dreamy, slightly mystified, let's-try-to-take-it-seriously look.

'Sor,' he whispered, 'it's a miracle. Not a casualty. Not a single Anglo-Saxon man. Every Anglo-Saxon man's arrived unharmed. The whole Anglo-Saxon company's here. It's an Anglo-Saxon miracle.'

While they were cowering there, McCutcheon came out from the wood. He was the bravest man Wheldon ever knew; the best man he ever knew.

'Sir, come into Headquarters,' he said.

'Let's get on,' Wheldon said. 'We don't have to go into Company Headquarters. Got to get on.'

'Sir,' he said, and there was determination in his voice, 'I would like you to come into Company Headquarters.'

Through nettles and brambles they plunged into the wood. Right in the centre there was a lean-to hut and a small fire. They had been fifteen minutes on the soil of France, and the men had been ten minutes in that hut at the most. Nodding like a chummy canteen hostess, Rifleman Rimmer handed Wheldon a cup of tea.

Once on the ground the glider pilots began fighting as a unit, and were soon in action. By the evening, ninety-three pilots composing 'Force John', were dug in and defending their landing zone from the south-west. One of them, Captain B. Murdoch, presently found himself involved in a brisk action against tanks. He was acting as loader at the time to a six-pounder anti-tank gun, of which the layer (a member of the gun crew) was killed. Captain Murdoch took over, and he and the other gunners miraculously succeeded in destroying four out of five enemy tanks.

Although General Gale now had a substantial force available from the gliders that had started from England, he had them at substantial cost. In the serial with which he had taken off, forty-nine out of the seventy-two gliders that took off landed according to plan. Five made forced landings in the United Kingdom, three in the sea and fourteen were lost.

Of the fourteen gliders that failed to reach their destination, one, piloted by Major J. F. Lyne, was hit by flak in the tail when crossing the coast, and the tow-rope broke. The glider was in clouds and immediately began to descend. On coming out into clear air it was again hit, a shell bursting in the centre of the fuselage, damaging the jeep on board but hurting no one. Beneath, blinking gunfire and arching tracers broke the blackness. To choose a suitable spot for landing was a nerve-racking task for the pilot. The glider sailed remorselessly earthward, and at the last moment a pale patch, which 'seemed to be a little less dark than the rest of the countryside,' loomed up. It was an orchard, and into it Major Lyne crashed his glider, breaking his foot and cutting the face of his second pilot. These were the only mishaps.

The party of seven set off, their object being to find someone who could tell them where they were. They soon ran into Germans, and to avoid detection the party hid under nominal concealment in a field until dawn. They then found a farmer who directed them towards the River Dives. This they swam, and joined up with some Canadian parachute troops, isolated near Robehomme. By then they were entirely surrounded by the enemy, and it took them three days to break out and reach Ranville. Throughout that time the French inhabitants were of the greatest help, and their grapevine information service enabled Lyne and his men to know at all times the exact position of the enemy. During their wanderings they met with a farm labourer and his family who produced as evidence of their love of England 'a portrait of Queen Victoria tastefully executed in Nottingham lace' and provided them with a meal, a map torn from a school atlas and two pocket dictionaries.

Eventually Major Lyne and the rest entered the Bois de Bavent and there, exhausted by forty-eight hours of stumbling through swampy ground, hiding in ditches, swimming streams and thrusting their way through unyielding undergrowth, reached at long last a road running in the right direction. At that moment the enemy appeared. The weary men sprang into action. 'We managed to eliminate two lorry-loads of Germans, and a car with four officers in it,' reported Major Lyne, 'by the simple process of throwing hand grenades at them. They were all wiped out. By this time we were all very tired.' When they eventually reached the landing zone, after another fight, they had marched forty-five miles from the place where the glider had landed.

Men like these and their comrades, stubbornly holding the boundaries of the landing zones, made possible the mass landing of gliders on the evening of the first day, which had been watched so thankfully by Private Owen from his slit trench on the bank of the Caen Canal. In a manoeuvre as technically perfect as the changing of the guard at Buckingham Palace, every Hamilcar carrying tanks, and 112 out of the 114 Horsas, landed and poured out the 6th Air Landing Brigade and a number of other units, including the Armoured Reconnaissance Regiment; all under intense shelling.

Hamilcars and Tetrarchs engaged in their own unique and totally surprising, if not precarious, adventures. In one Tetrarch, Major Barnett heard his Hamilcar pilot saying over the intercom, 'the landing zone is in view, prepare to cast off from the tug.' Seconds later the tank crew felt the nose of the glider rise as though on the crest of a gentle wave as the rope was released. On full flaps it nosed into a steep dive towards the north–south landing lane on LZN. The Hamilcar cut

Men of the 6th Airborne Division beside the glider in which they landed

A Horsa which crashed into a wall near St. Mère Eglise killing two of its passengers

through young corn at nearly eighty miles an hour, lurching violently and sloughing away half a wing at an obstacle pole. Sensing touchdown, the tank driver started the engine; once the Hamilcar had come to rest the co-pilot 'pulled the plug out' to drain the oil from the shock-absorbers and allow the fuselage to sink wearily onto the ground. Spoiling for action, the tank driver threw off the tank's mooring ropes, and the Tetrarch nudged forward, striking the trip-wire to open the nose door.

Other Hamilcars jostling for position in the eager dive for fields in the landing zone, found little space left. One of them slammed into a Tetrarch that had suddenly appeared forty yards ahead, and the tank was knocked over. This was the only casualty among the Tetrarchs. Even at that, it was not long out of commission; the crew were unhurt and during the night, helped by another tank crew, with their tank, they righted it.

Some of the gliders were barely scratched. Even one that ripped a hedgerow would have flown again. One of the first fatal casualties was a Hamilcar pilot, Staff Sergeant C. B. Robinson, killed by mortar fire at landing. Pilots assembled in an orchard, trying unsuccessfully to dig defensive trenches with inadequate tools; a failure that thoroughly upset a platoon of tough paratroopers intending to position themselves there. It almost produced a state of civil war between the two factions.

Next day glider pilots proceeded to the beaches, past the crumpled Horsas and over one of the bridges which the troops they carried had captured and defended. There a ship took them to England and a de-briefing.

Rumbling out of the gliders, intent upon heading swiftly south-east through fields and hedgerows to their pre-arranged rendezvous near Breville, Tetrarchs found the ground littered with discarded para-chutes that had brought troops and supplies, dropped earlier in the day. The nylon canopies and rigging lines, winding around the sprockets, choked and immobilized half the tanks only 300 yards from their gliders. The coloured canopies of the parachutes were easy to see from a distance, and the drivers had a chance to steer around them; but the camouflaged paratrooper parachutes merged deceptively with the ground. Dusk made their perception doubly difficult. The tanks were trapped within an unyielding nylon net of snaking lines, there amid the crops. Most crews struggled desperately to get the spaghetti-like tangle unravelled. Mercifully the enemy did not harass the dis-gruntled crews.

By noon on D-day, ten anti-tank guns, together with the tanks brought in by the Hamilcar and the troops brought in by gliders, had joined in the overall effort of the 6th Division, to clear the east flank of the invasion of Germans; had effectively silenced the German battery at Neville; and were helping to drive off counter-attacks.

CHAPTER XI

Abandon Glider!

I said, 'I've heard a lot of wild reports in my life, but that's the wildest I *ever* heard! The Japs can't possibly tow gliders here from their nearest base, and certainly, they're not going to waste their precious carrier decks on any such nonsense. My God!'

Admiral William F. Halsey to Admiral Husband E. Kimmel
several days after the Japanese attack on Pearl Harbour.
(From: *Admiral Halsey's Story*)

In 1941 the U.S. Navy enthusiastically started a transport-glider programme independent of the Air Force; and abandoned it with an epithet in 1943, a dismal failure. It was one of the major endeavours of the military services that figuratively—and almost literally—never got off the ground. The Navy had more difficulty in developing and procuring its gliders, and more trouble with the contractors who were engaged to produce them, than the Air Force, if this indeed was possible.

In April 1941, one year after the Germans first used gliders, Captain Marc A. Mitscher, then the Assistant Chief of the Bureau of Naval Aeronautics, directed the production of a personnel and equipment-carrying Navy glider. The Navy quickly reacted to the German airborne invasion of Crete that month, and within a fortnight decided to produce enough gliders to transport a Marine battalion. Accordingly it quickly contracted to develop and build two float-wing gliders that could land upon water. One glider was to carry twelve, and the other twin-hull model twenty-four passengers.

So enthusiastic was the Marine Corps about the glider as a military weapon that it pressed the Navy's Bureau of Aeronautics for production, before an experimental glider had been built. The Marines wanted a hundred 12-place and fifty 24-place gliders, enough to transport two battalions. Although there was no strategic plan for the use of the amphibious gliders, the Marine Corps wanted to be prepared to use any weapon and any method of attack that could be developed, and they wanted it in their arsenal ready to go. However, conservative heads decided that until experimental gliders could be tested, and questions relating to the technique of towing settled, there should be no large-scale procurement.

In view of German sinkings of Allied shipping, glider enthusiasts argued that the demand for transport gliders would be enormous as soon as models were flying. The Germans had not only demonstrated the usefulness of these aircraft in the capture of Crete, but also, according to their latest information, the Germans were making extensive use of gliders to supply Rommel in Africa. This was Hitler's method of overcoming the problem of Allied control in the Mediterranean. The glider sponsors in the United States saw that U.S. military forces were faced with critical shortages of supplies, because of the growing number of ship sinkings, and saw in large cargo gliders a way to move critical supplies over-water quickly. They also wanted to solve the problem of jumping from island to island in the Pacific, over the head of the Japanese fleet.

In spite of the enthusiasm, success in the development of gliders was certainly less than desirable. The programme was in chaos, and major delays commonplace. The pressure to expand the programme was strong too, however. At this stage the Marine Corps had raised their sights, and asked for sufficient gliders to transport four battalions and enough replacement equipment for three successive operations; all too quickly the Navy upped requirements from 150 to 1,000 gliders. By June 1942 the programme looked toward 1,371 gliders, and 3,436 pilots and co-pilots flying 10,800 men—despite the evidence that gliders would be about as useful on the Pacific islands as pogo sticks. So contagious was the expansive attitude that one contractor proposed to the Navy the production of 12,000 12-place amphibious gliders.

Regardless of the optimism in certain quarters, delays in building test gliders continued to grow, so that it was not until October 1942 that the Navy got its first test glider, more than a year and a half after the programme was first visualized. This so dimmed the outlook for the Navy's 24-place development models yet to be built, that some planners recommended the British 25-place Horsa glider be used as a hedge against the failure of the former programme. Desperate for usable aircraft, the Navy strategists now looked to the Army's 15-place CG-4A to fill Marine Corps needs. The fly in the ointment was, however, that the Horsa and the CG-4A were not floatable, and were difficult to adapt to amphibious warfare, and the plan was dropped. The delays in the programme actually acted as a dissuading force on those who were intent on its development, and these delays served to enable the Navy and the Marine Corps to make a more thorough study of the glider as a weapon suitable to their needs in the Pacific. By September 1942 the services gradually took the viewpoint that gliders were a less efficient means of transport than powered aircraft, and that they were not practicable over great distances, particularly

The U.S. naval glider XLRQ-1, which also had retractable gear for landing on the ground

in weather that would make it necessary for glider pilots to fly by instruments. Already by the middle of October 1942, it became evident that the glider programme was 'satisfactory in no respect', although a review board suggested the continuance of certain parts of the programme.

Soon the Navy dropped two of the four major contractors.

The hopes of certain advocates in the Marine Corps for the extensive use of gliders in the Pacific dwindled. They realized they knew little regarding the abilities of the glider, and little experience was coming in from any other source to enable them to have a sound position in their debates. Although the Navy was seriously involved in deciding whether the Marine Corps would be able to use gliders in the Pacific, it too was making little headway in coming to a decision on the matter. Apparently the Navy was withholding a decision until experience could be obtained, even though as late as April 1943 General Thomas Holcomb, the Commandant of the Marine Corps, recommended that, in view of the number of adverse reports, the Marine Corps glider programme should be abandoned.

In May 1943 one of the contractors finally delivered the first flight-test glider. The delay in delivery was caused largely by difficulties in installing a retractable tricycle landing gear on the machine; but more accurately, it stemmed from inexperience in building gliders.

By 1943 the American fortunes in the Pacific were so remarkably improved that the need for gliders had become less urgent; and by now opinion had changed conclusively. Studies concluded that military gliders, whether amphibious or land-based, were of no value to the Marine Corps, and cited a year's study and observation of production and operations in the United States and abroad. The two services also concluded that the military glider as of that time was not a proven weapon and that the *Marine Corps had no use for unproven equipment*. Also, the funds and personnel involved in the programme had been of such magnitudes, and the results so dismal, that it was felt there had been an unnecessary and unjustifiable use of resources. No one wanted more of this unconscionable waste. One company charged the Navy 150,000 dollars for each of the fifteen gliders it built, or about five times the average cost of the Army's CG-4A. Another company brought costs down to 100,000 dollars for each glider.

Undismayed, supporters of the programme continued to push for its continuance, maintaining that the main trouble with the Marine Corps organization of glider troop battalions, and its operational planning, was that it had got going too early, far ahead of the production of gliders; and also that uninformed senior officers never divorced the fragile sailplane from the combat glider. Many people who returned from the South Pacific said that float-wing gliders would have been useful at Guadalcanal in bringing men, gasoline, and supplies to the beachhead. Sentiment for the glider persisted in some Navy quarters, despite growing Marine disenchantment. This segment thought the Navy should take charge of the programme and develop gliders for Naval supply operations, such as carrying gasoline and high priority cargo, although by the close of 1943 it appeared to everyone that the glider programme would thereafter have a low priority.

Exasperated with the way the programme was going, Mr Thomas S. Gates, Jr., the Assistant Secretary of the Navy for Air, sent a memorandum to one of his assistants, involved in the programme, on 4th September 1943, stating in effect that the production of one of the manufacturers '. . . looks like a mess, and that it has followed a course some predicted. Who wants these goddamed gliders? Why not cancel the whole damned contract right now, call it a day, save man-hours and money'. He tolled the death knell of the programme. Whatever residues then remained in actual gliders and materials were transferred to the Naval Aircraft Factory in Philadelphia and the Naval Aircraft Modification Unit at Johnsonville, Pennsylvania, by the end of 1943, and the programme ended. At its peak strength the Marines' glider organization had thirty-six officers, 246 men and twenty-one gliders.

The glider had come over the intellectual horizon of naval leaders a bit too unexpectedly. As with Air Force leaders, who knew too little about this maverick aeroplane, who could see no way to the stars through supporting it or flying in it, and whose time and materials were drawn to more glamorous aircraft, so it was with the Admirals. Admirals sail in ships; not in 'sailplanes', or anything coming close to this unknown weapon of war, which had no proven qualities.

CHAPTER XII

'Dragoon'—The Southern Pincer

If a glider should break loose at sea, the towing aircraft will circle the glider and send out normal distress signals stating glider down at sea!
62nd T. C. Gp. Ops Order, 13th Aug. 1944

At about 0630 on 15th August 1944, the first gliders of the final Allied invasion to strike Hitler's shrinking fortress in Europe began taking off from a cluster of airfields near Rome, and from other fields extending 150 miles down the Italian coast. They were to fly for some four hours, behind serials of hundreds of planes loaded with paratroopers. The force was on its way to 'Dragoon', a mission to drop troops in the Argens River Valley, well behind the Mediterranean coast of Southern France, and to cut off German units in the coastal area from German forces to the north.

The U.S. Seventh Army staffs began planning 'Dragoon' in February 1944. A shortage of airborne troops and air transports put the staff in a quandary as to who could be freed, from other critical commitments, for the job ahead. It was not until a month before D-day that the situation jelled and specific airborne units received orders forming them into the First Airborne Task Force, a provisional airborne division commanded by Major General Robert T. Frederick. Brigadier General Paul L. Williams took command of a Provisional Troop Carrier Air Division assigned to transport Frederick's Task Force.

U.S. airborne units, together with the British 2nd Parachute Brigade Group and special units activated for the mission, had been rapidly assembled near Rome to prepare for 'Dragoon'. The War Department sent thirty-six officers for General Frederick's staff. Most were from the 13th Airborne Division, a few from the Airborne Centre.

The British 2nd Air Landing Brigade, the U.S. 550th Glider Infantry Battalion and an assortment of signal and other support units made up the glider troop elements, totalling some 2,700 men. Horsas and Wacos, piloted by British and Americans respectively, were to bring in more than 220 jeeps, trailers, and guns, and the major portion of supplies and ammunition.

Nine pathfinder planes with 121 paratroopers took off at 0100 from Marcigliana in Italy, to mark the parachute dropping zones around Le Muy, lying on the Argens River in Southern France about twenty-five miles west of Cannes. Shortly after, the first aeroplanes, carrying the main parachute forces, followed. Some forecast of the problems that were to arise through the morning could be made from what befell the pathfinders. They reached France exactly on schedule and approximately on course. Over the Riviera they encountered a blanket of fog, through which they had to grope by dead reckoning supplemented by vague relief maps of the terrain. The nine-plane serial lost its way, circled back to the sea and made a second run. After about half an hour of circling, one plane dropped its troops and went home. Two other aircraft separated soon after that, and one dropped its team about 0400. The last team jumped at about 0415, on its sixth run.

All three teams of airborne troops landed in the same general area, a wooded and mountainous region between Frejus and Grasse from ten to fifteen miles east of DZ 'C'. Some peculiarity of the landscape may have deluded the navigators into thinking they were over the drop zone. Two were sure they had dropped in the right place. Lost in the woods and far from their objective, none of the three teams reached the Le Muy area in time to act as pathfinders or even to take part in the fighting there.

Without the pathfinders, although helped to some extent by the Eureka beacons operated by the French *maquis*, the parachute airplanes on the whole groped blindly for cues as to where to discharge their troops. Some of the ten serials carrying the 5,600 paratroop infantry and artillery did notably well, and by dead reckoning dropped their men right on target. Others dropped men as far as ten miles from Le Muy. The fog, and the uncertainty created, led to the wide dispersal of paratroopers, and had an adverse bearing on 'Bluebird', the morning glider mission now warming up.

At 0518 the first of thirty-five Horsa combinations, towed by C-47s of the 435th Troop Carrier Group, took off from Tarquinia, the others following at one-minute intervals. They crossed Cape D-Uomo at 0612, followed eight minutes later by the 436th, towing forty CG-4As. They were hardly off the coast when one Waco combination turned back, its C-47 engines heating up unduly.

The last Horsa had just passed over Corsica when General Williams radioed the serial commander to turn back. His instructions were that they should land at fields in Corsica if fuel was low, although this was a slight possibility, for the planes had been in the air only slightly over an hour. General Williams had foreseen trouble if the C-47s had

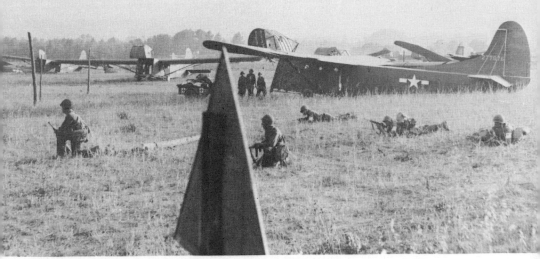

Men and gliders of the 1st Airborne Task Force, recently landed at La Motte

Posts set up near La Motte as an anti-glider device

to delay releasing the Horsas over the target because of the reported fog. Although the maximum Horsa load was only 6,900 pounds, about its normal rated cargo capacity, the heavy glider made a gross load that would tax the C-47 for the long flight under the best of conditions, leaving little fuel for emergencies towards the end of the plane's round trip.

General Williams pondered the wisdom of his decision. He now had to decide what to do about the returning Horsas. He had a hasty conference with Colonel Frank J. McNees, Commander of the 435th, and Colonel T. Beach of the Airborne Task Force staff. They decided for an afternoon mission.

Turning back somewhere near Corsica, one plane with engine trouble and another short of fuel released their Horsas. Both gliders landed safely on the island. The rest of the serial continued to Tarquinia, meeting en route the substitute C-47, towing the glider that had turned back from the earlier take-off. Seeing the returning Horsas, the C-47 pilot, thinking the whole airborne operation had been cancelled, also turned back. His glider pilot's relief at not having to go the whole way was to be short lived, however.

Next came the CG-4A combinations. As they passed the halfway point from Corsica to the release point, one glider either blew up or disintegrated from overstress, and its debris scattered over the Mediterranean, leaving no trace. Soon another's tow-rope parted, and it peeled off from the formation, circled downward, and landed on the water. An Allied Naval ship, witnessing the glider's descent, sped to the craft and got to it some minutes after it had landed on the water. Fortunately, the CG-4A had buoyancy to remain afloat for long enough for the ship to rescue the pilots and all the drenched passengers.

The serial approached the drop area at 0820 to find the still-impenetrable layer of fog hanging over the Argens valley. The group leader decided to risk waiting out the fog. He began a large lazy circling over Le Muy and kept this up for an hour. At about 0926, with his fuel dangerously low, the fog cleared enough for pilots to see ground features, and the leader flashed the red light, then the white, and the glider pilot cut away.

Thirty-seven gliders got down, bringing in the 64th Light Artillery, some headquarters personnel for the brigade, and ammunition and equipment. General Frederick, who was one of the few to have parachuted in close to the correct area during darkness, had his headquarters operating at the time of the glider landings, and he radioed the 436th that only thirty-three gliders had made it to the LZ. Four gliders must have landed well outside the LZ.

The British paratroopers quickly occupied the village of Le Mitan, on the eastern edge of their drop zone. They set up their headquarters in the village; and at 1000, after staff personnel had arrived in the

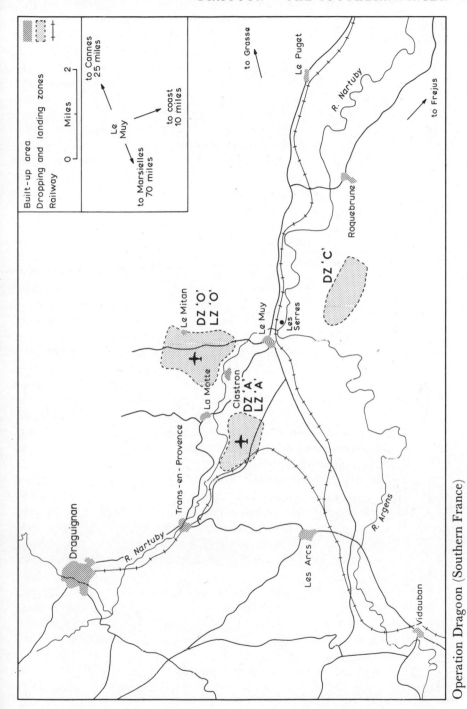

Operation Dragoon (Southern France)

first glider mission, the task force also set up its headquarters there. One battalion of the brigade moved west, seizing eighty prisoners in the hamlet of Clastron, a mile and a half north-west of Le Muy, and making contact with the 517th at La Motte. Another battalion pushed south, and before noon had taken the tiny village of Les Serres on the north bank of the Nartuby less than half a mile from Le Muy. Then it ran into difficulties. The enemy had strong positions around the bridge which spanned the Nartuby just outside Les Serres. Hampered, per-haps, by the absence of the artillery carried by the recalled Horsa serial, the British did not have the punch to take the bridge until late afternoon. By that time the reinforcements carried in the afternoon missions were overhead.

Troop carrier operations on the afternoon of D-day began at 1504, when the thirty-five Horsa-towing aircraft made their second start. The big gliders carried 233 troops, thirty-five jeeps, thirty guns, and 31,378 pounds of ammunition, a total load of 248,000 pounds. The Waco-towing substitute from the 436th Group, which had mistakenly returned with them in the morning, joined them in the assembly area. The 435th had sent a plane to Corsica to pick up one of the Horsas released there on the first trip. Glider and tug joined the for-mation at the first marker boat, north-west of Corsica.

The air was calm and slightly hazy. Over the battlefield the smoke was thickening, and the maximum visibility near Le Muy was five miles. The planes released thirty-seven gliders over LZ 'O' at 1749. Parachute serials followed the Horsas and dropped thousands of men.

After the parachute drop came the big glider mission 'Dove'. Seven serials, each forty-eight-combination strong, towed 332 Waco gliders carrying the 550th Glider Infantry Battalion, additional artillery, and support troops numbering about 2,250 men—and with them twenty-five howitzers and 166 vehicles. Course, formation, flight-procedure and navigational aids, were the same as those employed in the morning glider mission. The leading plane of each successive serial, except the last two, was eight or nine minutes behind the leading plane of the serial ahead. As it turned out, this spacing was a trifle tight.

The glider pilots had been briefed at 1300, and an hour before take-off time the planes and gliders were in position. The 442nd Group began its take-off from Follonica at 1535 in heavy dust. At the southern end of the line the 64th Group at Ciampino, mindful of the facts that it was more than an hour's flight from the command assembly point over Elba, had put its first plane in the air at 1510. Probably the last group aloft was the 440th which, delayed by dust at Ombrone, took from 1610 to 1646 to complete take-off. One glider was no sooner in the air than it had to make a forced landing. Its load was trucked back to the field and loaded on a substitute, which made a successful flight two hours later. An abortive take-off in the 438th Group was likewise followed by transfer of the load and dispatch of a substitute.

Trouble began as the 332nd crossed the coast. They claimed to have been impeded off Point Ala by the Horsa-towing planes. This is hard to believe, since the records show that the Horsas had passed Elba by 1610, while the 442nd Group was not due there until 1631. Possibly the parachute serials caused the delay, though it seems unlikely that a parachute mission could be mistaken for one towing gliders.

More serious was the delay caused when, after passing Corsica, the glider towed by the leading plane of the 442nd had to be ditched because of weakness in the tail. The group made a full turn to avoid a possible accident, and to keep in touch with its leader. All personnel aboard the glider were later rescued. Several gliders released prematurely and three or four came down at sea off the French coast. Most of the occupants were saved.

All groups found the landing zones and saw fluorescent Ts. The panels showed up well.

All serials, and about ninety-five per cent of the gliders, reached the landing area. Unfortunately, largely because of the delay encountered by the 442nd, the serials jammed up, so that at one moment four were over the area at the same time. At 1827, seventeen minutes late, the 442nd Group arrived, and took fifteen minutes to get rid of its gliders. The 441st arrived simultaneously with the 442nd. Though the 442nd was at LZ 'O' and the 441st split between 'O' and 'A', the congestion was considerable. The two zones were unusually close together; the route to LZ 'A' led along the southern edge of 'O'. The 440th Group, which arrived at 1840, made a 180° turn to avoid the congestion and the blinding western sun, and approached LZ 'A' from the west. The 439th arrived about 1848 to release twenty-one gliders on 'O' and twenty-six on 'A'. It found planes of the 441st still releasing at 'O', and planes and gliders of the 441st and 440th crisscrossing spectacularly over 'A'. One minute later the 438th Group arrived at LZ 'O' and released its gliders.

The 62nd Group cut loose its gliders over LZ 'O' between 1854 and 1900, and the 64th began its release over 'A' at 1905. Comparatively free from interference by groups ahead of them, the 62nd and 64th found that the 1,000-foot intervals between their own elements were insufficient. The rear elements climbed over the forward ones to make their release, with the result that several layers of gliders were in the air at once, and that many gliders were released at excessive heights. Some in the 62nd were released at over 2,000 feet and some in the 64th as high as 3,000 feet.

Dodging and diving with agility, the glider pilots managed to avoid colliding in mid-air. However, their first sight of the landing zones revealed something for which neither their briefing nor the available photographs had prepared them. The fields were studded with obstacles, which here consisted of 'Rommel's asparagus'—poles from four to six inches in diameter set in rows from fifteen to forty feet apart. Wires had been stretched between them, but the paratroops had cut the wires. Mines had been laid, but fortunately the Germans had not as yet been able to get fuses for them. Thus the glider pilots were able by adroit manoeuvring to set their gliders down between the rows of poles.

In the circumstances it was natural that they should land wherever they could. Even in the lead group, the 442nd, the pilots of the last twelve gliders found no room on their assigned fields, and coasted down south of La Motte about two miles away. Fortunately, their loads were principally vehicles and extra ammunition for which there was no immediate need. The glider detachments of the 62nd and 64th Groups found their fields completely filled with gliders and had to crash-land at average speeds of eighty to ninety miles an hour. Though they sheered off their wings on the poles and hit all kinds of obstacles, the pilots managed to get their passengers and cargoes to earth with an astonishing degree of safety.

The gliders, however, were a total loss. The 50th Wing reported two weeks later that only two gliders were serviceable, and that only twenty-six could be salvaged. Indications are that the gliders in the three rear serials, which arrived after the good landing grounds were pre-empted, fared even worse. In the hectic time following the invasion, such gliders as were salvagable were left unguarded. Weather and pillage combined to destroy them. Not one was ever recovered.

In making the landings, eleven glider pilots were killed and over thirty were injured. About 100 of the glider troops were seriously hurt. Very little damage was done to the cargoes, although as usual great difficulty was encountered in getting them out. (For example, the 62nd Group reported that all its gliders crashed but only one load was damaged.)

The relatively high casualties among the pilots were caused partly by the obstacles into which they crashed, and partly by heavy equipment in the gliders, which lunged forward against them at the moment of impact. Most of them felt that had the Griswold nose, a special protection for the pilot, been used, it would have greatly reduced the casualties. They also favoured use of parachute arrestors (general installation of which had been considered and given up due to lack of time), heavier lashing for the loads, and safety-belts for the troops. Some pilots suggested that jeeps or tractors should have been employed, to pull gliders that had landed in one wave out of the way, so that the next serial could land.

After leaving the release area, the troop-carriers dropped their tow-ropes at a designated point, turned right, and returned according to plan. One plane was hit by a burst of German anti-aircraft fire and forced to come down in the sea off the French coast. All aboard were saved. The destruction of this single C-47 was the only appreciable damage the Germans were able to inflict.

In general, anti-aircraft fire was even slighter than it had been in the morning. At no time during the day did enemy aircraft attack the airborne missions. The fighter escort left early by prior agreement in order to reach its base before dark, but no Nazi prowlers were on hand to attack the unprotected rear of the returning column. At 2138 the last plane of the 62nd Group hit the runway at Galera. The troop carriers had completed their mission.

The effort put forth on D-day may be summarized as follows:

Sorties Intended.	857
Sorties Accomplished	852
Glider Sorties, Waco	372
Glider Sorties, Horsa. . . .	36
Paratroop Sorties.	444
Troops Delivered	9,099
Paratroops	6,488
Glider Troops.	2,611
Glider Troops on or near LZ . .	90–95%
Paratroops on or near DZ . . .	50%
Drop Casualties	2%
Landing Casualties	4%
Artillery Pieces Delivered . . .	213
Vehicles Delivered	221
Other Supplies and Equipment .	500 tons

In achieving this record most planes and flying personnel had flown between 900 and 1,300 miles on two separate missions within a period of less than twenty hours. They had accomplished the dawn paratroop mission in the face of warnings that problems of take-off, assembly, formation flying and navigation at night might make it impracticable. They had carried out a large glider mission with a degree of success which put 'Ladbroke' to shame, and compared favourably with the glider missions in 'Neptune'.

CHAPTER XIII

Arnhem—Grasp for the Rhine

On 16th August 1944 General Eisenhower created the First Allied Airborne Army to manage his airborne operations. The premise upon which he formed the Army was that airborne and troop carrier units are theatre-of-operations forces, and plans for their combined employment must be prepared by the agency having authority to direct the necessary co-ordinated action of all land, sea and air forces in the area involved. Sorely needed, it was a tardy response to the inadequate co-ordination of airborne resources in past operations, and to the need for a single headquarters guided by a man of sufficient stature and rank to give direction and leadership. Eisenhower assigned Lieutenant General Lewis H. Brereton to command the Army, with General F. A. M. Browning as his deputy. Brereton created an XVIII Airborne Corps, subordinate to his headquarters, and placed it under the command of General Matthew B. Ridgway.

General Brereton had operational control over the IX Troop Carrier Command, the XVIII Corps consisting of the U.S. 17th, 82nd and 101st Airborne Divisions and smaller U.S. separate airborne units, all British Airborne Troops, and such Royal Air Force troop-carrier units as might be allocated from time to time.

General Brereton began training programmes; but these were hobbled on occasion, such as when two troop-carrier wings, urgently needed for glider-tow and parachute-jump training, were sent to participate in 'Dragoon', the airborne invasion of Southern France. When available, troop-carrier crews practised day and night flying, dual glider-tow and glider pick-ups. They operated with the 82nd and 101st Division, providing aircraft and gliders for practice loading and unloading drills, simulated airlandings, and practice tactical glider flights.

In the forty days after the formation of the Army, General Brereton had his staff work out plans for eighteen different operations; most of them were scrubbed because the ground armies moved too fast, forcing troop-carrier wings to supply the ground units by air. 'Transfigure', the first of a succession of plans, 'Boxer', 'Linnet', and others were all shelved. Glider pilots got briefings, re-briefings and more briefings. Gliders had been packed with their combat loads, and stood with ropes hitched to noses, parked in readiness for take-off. Glider troops usually waited nervously in barbed-wire-enclosed assembly areas, near or adjacent to airfields, prepared to fly the one-way trip in the gliders at short notice. On more than one occasion, the land tail (the trucks, tanks and impedimenta not normally carried in the air) had already put to sea to cross the Channel, expecting to link up with the airborne units, when a condition arose to make the proposed operations unfeasible.

Gliders were now gaining increased importance in Brereton's concept of airborne operations. 'Linnet' was a prime example of this. The 101st, the 82nd, and the British 1st, and the 1st Polish Parachute Brigade, were to fly two major airlifts a day on the first and second days to seize Tournai in France, to hold a bridgehead over the Escaut River, and to control the roads leading north-west through Tournai, Lille and Coutrai. Such was the intensity of the operation that the first lift had 120 aircraft towing two gliders each, 350 aircraft towing one glider each, and 1,055 parachute aircraft, and the total length of the flight column was more than two hours. The second lift, even more imposing in glider participation, comprised 880 tug aircraft with double glider tow, 307 aircraft with single glider tow, and 126 parachute aircraft. A lift of seventy-five tugs with two gliders each and 114 parachute aircraft, was scheduled for the morning of D plus 1, and 436 parachute aircraft were to fly a resupply lift that afternoon. On D plus 2 the British 52nd Division (airtransportable) was to begin airlanding operations. Each hour, from H to H-plus-11 hours, thirty-six aircraft were to land, unload, and depart at each of three airstrips. This operation was to be completed on D-plus-3. 'Linnet' was shelved for a new version, 'Linnet II', and this plan was also cancelled. Nonetheless, airborne muscles were now flexing for some championship encounters.

On 5th September 1944 General Eisenhower directed the Air Army to operate in support of Montgomery's 21st Army Group until after the Rhine had been crossed, and then to be prepared to operate on a large scale for the advance into Germany. This was the kind of support General Brereton, his staff and commanders had been awaiting. It now appeared that some of the doubts that had been built up within GHQ were to be dispelled, and all were only awaiting the favourable opportunity. It was not long in coming.

The same evening that 'Linnet II' was cancelled, Montgomery asked General Brereton to seize the Rhine bridges from Arnhem to Wesel in order to prepare for a ground advance by Montgomery's force to the north of the Ruhr. Later the plan, called 'Comet', was narrowed to the Nijmegen-Arnhem area. The British 1st Airborne

Division, with the 1st Polish Parachute Brigade, had to seize and hold bridges over the Maas at Grave, over the Waal at Nijmegen, and over the Lower Rhine at Arnhem. The U.S. 878th Airborne Engineer Battalion then was to prepare an airstrip for the airlanding of the British 52nd Division. D-day was set for 8th September. Postponed once because of the weather and twice because of the uncertain ground battle, Montgomery cancelled 'Comet' on 10th September.

Flight-readied since 2nd September, British and Polish troops stood by awaiting the next operational alert. In a mere day or two Montgomery settled on 'Market', an ambitious plan to cut off major German forces in Holland, and perhaps exploit the "attractive possibility' of the British turning both the Rhine and the German Siegfried Line. It called for Brereton's forces to seize bridges that would open the way for armour of the British Second Army to drive to the Zuider Zee in the co-ordinated ground follow-up operation, called 'Garden'. The 101st Airborne Division was ordered to seize bridges and roads along the route between Eindhoven and Grave; the 82nd Airborne Division had to capture the bridge over the Maas north of Grave, and the bridge over the Waal at Nijmegen; the British 1st Airborne Division, with the Polish Parachute Brigade, had to seize the bridge over the Lower Rhine at Arnhem. The British 52nd Division was to go into the Arnhem area by airlanding as soon as an airstrip could be prepared. The ground attack would be on a narrow front, northward from the British Second Army's line along the Albert and Escaut Canals in northern Belgium. For much of the distance only a single road would be available for the advance and supply route. Spearheading the ground attack would be the Guards Armoured Division of 30 Corps. Its time schedule called for it to reach Eindhoven (about fifteen miles north of the Escaut Canal) within eight hours; Nijmegen (more than forty miles, by highway, northeast of Eindhoven), by noon on D-plus-1; and Arnhem (eleven miles north of Nijmegen) by noon on D-plus-2.

The first question was whether 'Market' should follow the pattern of Sicily and Normandy in being another night operation, or whether an attempt should now be made to conduct a major airborne operation in daylight. Difficulties of navigation and of assembly of troops on the ground in darkness were well known, and this was to be a period of no moon. At the same time the German night-fighter force, relatively intact (it was estimated that 100 effective enemy night fighters were within range), might be more formidable than the day fighters—and it would be more difficult for escorting fighters to protect the column at night. Anti-aircraft fire could be expected at night as well as in daylight. Moreover, IX Troop Carrier Command had not been practising night glider assemblies in formation for the last three months, and therefore gliders should probably be taken in during daylight (the

Men of the 277th Parachute Field Artillery wait beside their gliders for the take-off to Arnhem

In a field in Holland, Dutch people help the troops to clear a glider

morning after a night parachute drop) in any case. On the other hand, enemy flak would doubtless be far more accurate in daylight. Flak was a primary concern for the slow, low-flying troop carriers. Overwhelming air support against flak positions and against enemy fighters seemed essential for a daylight airborne operation. General Brereton believed that sufficient air support was at hand, and he believed that the air force could knock out most flak positions in advance of the arrival of the airborne armada. Thus he decided on a daylight operation.

Another question to be decided was that of the routes which the troop carriers should follow to the target areas. Several factors, not always compatible, had to be taken into account. Aside from following prominent terrain features, which would simplify navigation, the route should be the shortest and most direct possible; it should respect traffic control patterns of IX Troop Carrier and R.A.F. units; it should avoid barrage balloon and anti-aircraft areas in Great Britain; it should avoid known and suspected enemy anti-aircraft batteries; it should avoid turns over water; it should make landfall over prominent, irregular coastline; it should proceed the shortest possible distance over hostile territory.

Preliminary studies suggested two possible routes. The most direct lay across the North Sea from Orford Ness in Suffolk, passed over the Dutch Islands, and turned north-east near Hertogenbosch; this route required a flight of some eighty miles over enemy-held territory. A more southerly route led from North Foreland in Kent, to Belgium, turned northward near Gheel, crossed the front line and passed over sixty-five miles of enemy-held territory.

General Williams recommended that both routes be used—the 101st Airborne Division to follow the southern, and the British 1st and U.S. 82nd to follow the northern. If only one route were used in the initial lift, the column would be so long that the enemy might be alerted in time to bring effective fire against the rear elements; or the aircraft would have to fly in parallel columns so broad that all could not avoid known flak locations. Another advantage in having two routes would be that on subsequent days, reinforcing and resupply lifts could be routed either way, if weather or enemy action ruled out one while the other remained open.

General Browning's original plan had called for the 101st Airborne Division to go into the Grave-Nijmegen area, and the 82nd into the Eindhoven-Uden area, but the use of two routes as outlined by General Williams, with respect to the location of the troops in England, made it desirable to transpose the objectives of the two divisions to avoid crossing routes. General Brereton accepted the recommendations and changed the divisions' missions accordingly.

No problem was more important from the point of view of airborne commanders than the selection of drop zones (DZs) for the parachute

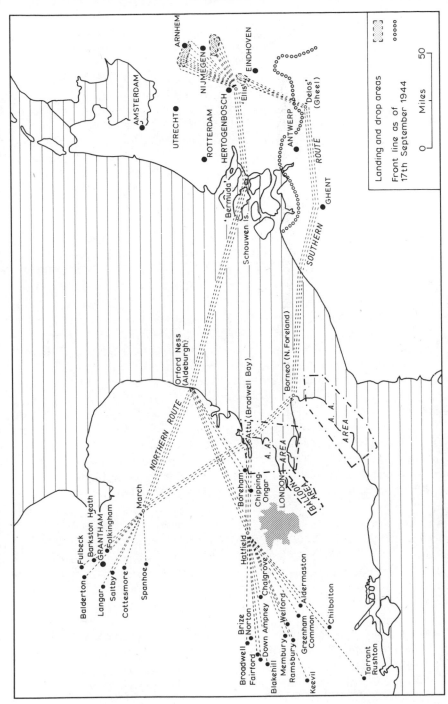

Airborne Assault on Holland, Operation Market Garden: (i) Approach drops, and landing zones (LZs) for the gliders. After careful examination of terrain studies, and enemy defence overprints, the troop carrier commander and the airborne commanders made the initial selections at a conference the next morning. They had to consider accessibility to assigned objectives, ground formations, avoidance of flak and enemy defences, and concentration of the airborne forces. Again compromise was necessary. It was generally desirable for paratroops to drop directly on an objective, or as close to it as possible. In this case, however, DZs could not be close to the main objective bridges because flak concentrations protected those bridges. For the same reason cities had to be generally avoided. Rivers and canals might be hazardous for parachute troops, but streams and ditches in the target area were also a great advantage: they were effective anti-tank obstacles.

The 1st Airborne Division had the honour of taking the bridge at Arnhem. Its commander, Major-General R. E. Urquhart, C.B., D.S.O., in conjunction with Lieutenant-General Browning in charge of the whole operation, drew up the simplest plan which would meet the requirements. Even this however involved at least two, and as it turned out, three, lifts. All the Division was to be used, together with the Polish Parachute Brigade. One factor governed the journey to the objective and the arrival there. The German airfield at Deelen and the town of Arnhem itself were very well protected by anti-aircraft guns. Situated as the bridge was, just to the south of Arnhem, comparatively slow-flying aircraft stood no chance if they approached too near to it in daytime. It was necessary, therefore, for the dropping and landing zones to be well beyond the range of the guns at Deelen.

Since the country around Arnhem is for the most part well wooded, the number of suitable open fields was not very great. Four were eventually chosen. The first three lay immediately north of the railway running through Arnhem to Utrecht, the farthest of them being about eight miles from the bridge. The fourth zone was south of the railway and somewhat larger than the others. A fifth, close to the city itself and near the small village of Warnsborn, was chosen as the place on which supplies were to be dropped after the landing.

Major General Maxwell D. Taylor, Commander of the 101st Airborne Division, was dissatisfied with General Browning's original plan for the disposition of his division. That plan would have spread the division in seven separate areas along an axis some thirty miles long. General Taylor was anxious to concentrate his forces. Sharing his views, General Brereton stated: 'Such dispersion destroys its tactical integrity, renders it incapable of fighting as a division, and presents insurmountable problems of resupply. Each small group is susceptible of being destroyed in detail.' The Airborne Army Commander raised further objections from the air point of view; the difficulty of making accurate drops on the numerous small drop zones, the problem of finding suitable drop zones in each of the areas, and exposure of the air lifts to hostile fire over a large area.

Finally General Taylor received permission to discuss the problem with Lieutenant-General Sir M. C. Dempsey, commanding the British Second Army, under whose command (through 39 Corps) the 101st Airborne Division would operate on the ground. As a result, the proposed seven areas for the 101st drop were cut to two general areas.

Another factor influencing the selection of drop zones appeared when General Williams determined that it would take two hours for a regiment to assemble after landing, and another three hours—a total of five—for it to reach the city. The principal concentration of 101st Airborne Division troops would be in the area designated Landing Zone 'W', between Zon and St Oedenrode west of the main highway. One regimental drop zone, DZ 'B', would be in the south part of this area about a mile and a half northwest of Zon. Another regimental drop zone, DZ 'C', was chosen in the north part of the area, a mile south of St Oedenrode. All gliders for the division were to land on LZ 'W'. The third regimental drop zone, DZ 'A', was about five miles north of DZ 'B', south-west of the Willems Vaart Canal near Veghel.

Actually General Taylor agreed to divide this regiment's drop zones so that one battalion could come down about three miles to the north-west in DA 'A-1' on the opposite side of the canal and astride the small Aa River. This disposition was to facilitate quick seizure of the bridges in that area from both sides.

All drop and landing zones for the 82nd Airborne Division, with the exception of one rifle company's DZ just west of Grave, were north of the Maas River. Drop Zone 'O' (for two battalions less one rifle company), was immediately north and west of Ober Asselt and about a mile and a half east of Grave; the DZ for the other battalion of that regiment was about a mile and a half east of the main DZ 'O'. The whole area LZ 'O' was for gliders. Drop Zone and Landing Zone 'N' were south, and DZ and LZ 'T' were north, of Groesbeek.

Since dispositions had already been made for the 'Linnet' and 'Comet' operations, only minor changes in troop locations now were necessary. The 101st Airborne Division was in the South of England, the Newbury area in Berkshire, close to IX Troop Carrier Command fields; the 82nd was in the Midlands near Nottingham, also close to troop carrier fields; the British 1st Airborne Division was still at fields in the Swindon, Wiltshire, area, and the 1st Polish Parachute Brigade was in Lincolnshire, near Grantham. Troops began moving to the take-off fields on 15th September, and were sealed in at daylight the next day. The magnitude of the operations is probably better grasped in terms of the number of airfields used. Market Garden used twenty-four; seventeen for American units, seven for British.

Troop-carrier arrangements included rather elaborate plans for navigational aids. Even though the operation was to be conducted in daylight, navigational aids would be used to ensure identification of routes and drop zones. Eureka (radar) and compass beacon equipment was set up at wing assembly points; departure points on the English coast were marked by Eureka, compass beacons, and occult (light flashing a code letter); midway across the North Sea were placed marker boats with Eureka and green holophane lights sending code letters. Aircraft on the southern route would pass over a white panel T and yellow smoke, 5,000 yards before reaching enemy lines, after turning not far from Gheel. Pathfinders would precede the columns to each division area; a pathfinder team from the 82nd Airborne Division would mark DZ 'O', and two teams from the 101st Division would mark DZ 'A' and DZ 'B'. Pathfinder aircraft would carry special radar equipment by which the crews would find their way to the target areas from the boat markers. The division pathfinder teams would mark the DZs and LZs with Eureka, compass beacons, coloured panels, and coloured smoke.

Troop carrier officers gave a great deal of consideration to keeping column time-length short, in order to have the greatest protection from escorting fighters and in order to have carriers over enemy-held territory in the shortest time possible. Formation intervals could be tighter than those used in night operations, and troop-carrier plans provided that the aircraft might fly in three streams—the right and left each separated from the centre by one and a half miles.

Air formations had to allow a certain amount of manoeuvrability and, at the same time, give good concentration for paratroops and gliders on the ground. The C-47s were to fly in nine-ship elements in a V of Vs comprising serials of up to forty-five aircraft, in trail, with four-minute intervals between the leading aircraft of each serial. Glider columns would form into pairs of pairs echeloned to the right, in serials of up to forty-eight aeroplanes towing gliders, in trail, with seven-minute intervals between heads of serials. Altitudes had to be decided with a view to avoiding small arms as well as heavy anti-aircraft fire, to dropping troops and releasing gliders at minimum safe altitudes, and to assuring clearance of incoming aircraft with those returning from the target area.

Initial plans called for the 38th and 46th R.A.F. Groups to tow 335 Horsas and thirteen Hamilcars on D-day; 293 Horsas, fifteen Hamilcars and ten Wacos on D + 1, and sixteen Horsas and ten Hamilcars on D + 3. The actual take-off figures differed only slightly from these.

By 0900 on D-day, 17th September 1944, the weather was fit for take-offs from all bases. Gliders towed by Dakotas, Halifaxes, Stirlings and Albemarles started taking off from Brize Norton, Fairford, Harwell, Keevil, Tarrant Rushton, Broadwell, Blakehill and Down Ampney at

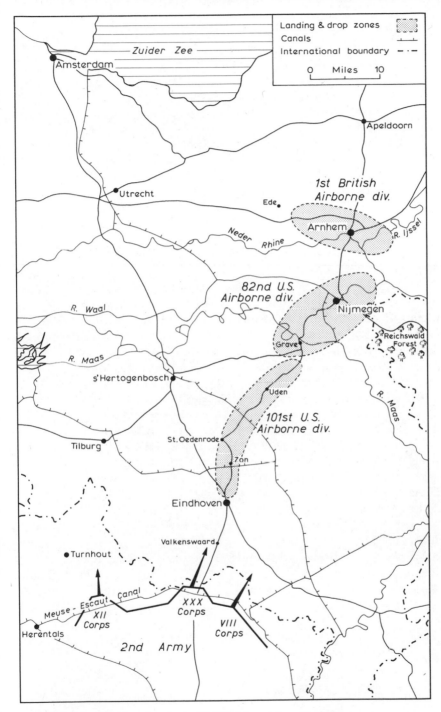

Operation Market Garden: (ii) Divisional Landing Zones

0945. All 359 gliders scheduled for D-day take-offs got off successfully. One combination had to turn back because of engine trouble, took off again, but had to return to be re-scheduled for the D + 1 lift.

While these flights were taking off, others carrying the 82nd and 101st Airborne Divisions were taking off from other fields in England bound for landing and drop zones in the Netherlands.

The fleet of gliders—that was part of an even larger armada including hundreds of planes carrying paratroopers—began going through patches of cirrus cloud, and before it had crossed the English coast heavy turbulence caused twenty-four gliders to release. One crashed on landing. Twenty-two landed satisfactorily at various fields and were recovered and scheduled into the D + 1 lift.

Just beyond the coast, flight serials broke out into a bright clear sky. Before long other mishaps occurred. Two tow-ropes parted, the gliders landing in the water. Three tow-planes developed engine trouble and cut their gliders loose. One of these landed in the water, and one on Schonwen Island.

Men in one of the gliders sloshing about in the waves began to see water-spouts nearby. A German coastal battery was ranging in on their glider. The firing continued for two hours, but the Germans still had not hit the glider when a British Sea Rescue service craft managed to get to the glider and remove the men, saving all hands. Similar rescues saved the men in the other three gliders.

Eight hundred and twenty-one B-17 bombers ahead of the air-lift attacked known German anti-aircraft positions and any gun that dared to fire on the transports; 371 R.A.F. fighter-bombers cannonaded barges, trucks, and anti-aircraft guns; 322 bombers hit other targets. Three thousand tons of bombs beat down the German anti-aircraft guns that morning. Allied fighters, 550 U.S. alone, raced through the skies, eyes peeled for German fighters. Two enemy flights near the Rhine were sighted, but they dared not challenge the Allied armada. Transport pilots, less concerned with flak than in any previous airborne mission, flew unswervingly towards glider release and parachute drop zones.

There was very little flak until Groesbeek. Thereafter the gliders began to take some hits. Flak severed one tow-rope, but the remaining gliders all made it to within gliding range of the landing zone, cut off, and started manoeuvring for landing. A light wind caused a small percentage to overshoot the landing zone.

In *Defeat in the West* by Milton Shulman, the German war-reporter Erwin Kirchoff, describes the landings:

> It was early on the Sunday afternoon of 17th September. The cinemas in the small Dutch towns were slowly filling up, and the streets and highways, along the canals and small streams, were crowded with young people on bicycles. And then out of the blue sky roared several hundred enemy

fighter-bombers. Their aim was to attack the German defensive positions and locate the flak positions. Barely had they disappeared beyond the horizon when, coming from the west across the flooded coastal areas, appeared the planes and gliders carrying regiments and brigades of the enemy's airborne army .... The troops bailed out from a very low altitude, sometimes as low as 60 metres. Immediately after that the several hundred gliders started to land. In those first few minutes, it looked as if the down-coming masses would suffocate every single life on the ground.

Two Hamilcars touched down on ground too soft to bear them, their wheels ploughed into the ground, and the gliders nosed over. The accident made unserviceable the 17-pound artillery pieces each carried.

An enterprising young musician jumped from one of the first gliders and started playing the regimental march, of the King's Own Scottish Borderers, 'Blue Bonnets Over The Border'. The rest of the glider formation skidded to a stop to the tune. He continued to march and blow, oblivious of German fire and whizzing gliders, until all his regiment landed.

Thirty minutes after the last of the over 325 gliders had landed, personnel had cleared the craft of all material they had transported.

A Dulwich schoolmaster, turned glider-pilot, landed General Richard Gale in a ploughed field. Dust and earth forced its way up into the big black Horsa. A landing wheel was whipped off in a ditch; the glider hit a post and swivelled round on its nose. 'Fine work, my boy,' said the general, and stepped out. All tried to free the general's jeep from the twisted wreckage but could not do so. They got out of the field and crossed waist-high through a crop of corn to the village road. Through the village was the country house that the general had picked from a map as his temporary headquarters. When they got there, Griffith kicked open the door and lurched in with his tommy-gun, his eyes peeled for Germans. Inside were two pairs of short-sighted eyes, peering out from the faces of two spinster ladies in their night-dresses, who held candles up at him and said, 'Bon jour'.

Soon they were fussing over the *Général Anglais*. The general began fixing his communications. Then the two old ladies insisted on serving him a breakfast of bacon and eggs.

All the primary paratroop objectives had been taken. The general ordered his Red Devils to dig in and 'infest the area'. Gale's batman, concerned that 'his general' should have suitable transportation, spotted a chestnut mare not far from the Horsa. Off he went and soon had his general mounted in true cavalry style. The general badly needed some means of transport over the tricky farmland with its hedges and woods. The horse was 'just the job'.

At the dawn muster the troops found the general walking the horse round the garden of his headquarters. He tied her up among the jeeps

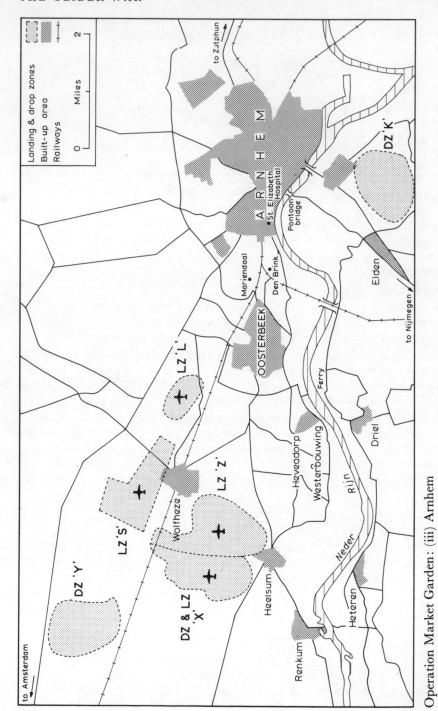

Operation Market Garden: (iii) Arnhem

that had collected in the courtyard. But on her next journey out, she got hit by shrapnel.

One glider, piloted by Lieutenant A. T. Turrell and his men, was shot down between Nijmegen and Arnhem but succeeded in making a good landing. Thirty Dutchmen helped to unload the glider, among them a girl who to do so abandoned her search for a green parachute among those lying about. She wanted it, she said, to make a dress of that colour. Under the guidance of a Dutch priest and a local official the party set off for the division, on the other side of the Rhine. On the way they met six Germans whom they disarmed and locked in the local gaol, after first making them take off their uniforms and put on civilian clothes. All eventually reached the neighbourhood of Arnhem by crossing the Lower Rhine in a ferry.

'We had left in very filthy weather indeed, low cloud and rain, but after a while it improved', says Major R. Cain of the South Staffords, who was soon to win a Victoria Cross, '. . . a little while after mid-Channel he saw the coastline of Holland in front. It was a buff-fawny colour, with white and grey streaks . . . The next thing he recognized was the Rhine. Then they got flak puffs all round them and bits of tracer. Cain ordered all strapped in. Geary, the glider pilot . . . put her into a dive approach. It seemed to be about treetop level when he pulled her out straight . . . and shouted "Hold tight" and they landed in a ploughed field. . . . They got out and took up all-round protective positions. . . . All the area was divided up into square fields with little tree-lined earth roads dividing them. It was very neat and very square. The trees were elms. He could hear very little firing and what there was was a long way off. There was no other activity.'

It was under heavy fire that Lance-Sergeant Maddocks of the Staffords, for example, had to saw off the tail of his glider in order to unload a Vickers gun.

The glider-pilots, having safely brought the troops to the battle, were now as heavily engaged as their passengers. Those who had flown in the first lift helped to hold the landing zones and then, when the second lift came in, fought side by side with the King's Own Scottish Borderers and eventually formed part of the defence of Divisional Headquarters, established at Hartestein. With them were two troops of the 4th Parachute Squadron R.E., one of whose officers, Captain H. F. Brown, earned a Military Cross for the manner in which he led the sappers, fighting as infantry.

When General Browning, piloted by Brigadier Chatterton, took off from Harwell airfield his glider looked like the inside of a gypsy caravan. Bicycles, bazookas, bedding rolls, radios and an assortment of items for his command-post cluttered it. The glider surged as the Stirling bomber powered down the airstrip. Browning had arrived for the 'show' immaculately dressed in a barathea battledress, his

Gliders lying at the end of the tracks they made in Dutch fields when landing

Alan Wood, war correspondent with the airborne troops, typing his despatch in a wood near Arnhem

Sam Browne belt and holster glistening, trouser creases knife-edged, with a swagger stick in his gloved hand. All were in high spirits.

Aloft, the fantastic sight awed him. Thousands of gliders and planes stretched in every direction. Spitfire and Tempest fighters whizzed by, gaining altitude to hover over and protect the plodding glider formations.

Some of the combinations had to fly through clouds; there turbulence caused seven gliders to cut off and land before reaching the coast. Two gliders ditched later over the sea, one managed to make a good water landing, the other broke up on impact with the water. The glider convoy stretched some fifty miles among the many other aircraft carrying parachutists.

On release short of Nijmegen General Browning's pilot, Brigadier Chatterton, started circling down, creating a great imaginary funnel, ending his downward flight in a skid that brought him abruptly into a small cabbage garden behind several farm cottages. A few Dutch peasants wandered up and watched almost disinterestedly as General Browning and others in the glider got out and started towards a forest some distance away, where the headquarters was established for the XVIII Airborne Corps.

Chatterton's glider had flown in an American serial carrying the staffs of operation 'Market'. Twenty-eight other gliders had landed in the same zone. Now Messerschmitts attacked the area, killing an R.A.F. photographer. Up to then the immense armada had mesmerized the German ground troops into inaction, but they awakened and reacted, lobbing artillery rounds on to the area. Shortly, German forces assembling nearby began to fire at Chatterton. Then in the distance Chatterton and his passengers heard a great roaring like a waterfall, and they ran out into the open, disregarding the German fire. Coming towards them overhead they saw a vast armada of aeroplanes, each towing two gliders. It was the American transport column looking like a swarm of angry bees. The sight staggered the British, as well as the Germans. They stopped firing and watched with awe.

At 0950 on D-day the first of 482 C-47s started taking off from Grantham airfield. Those not towing the fifty gliders carried parachutists. Gliders carried elements of the headquarters of the 82nd Airborne Division and the XVIII Corps. It took fifty minutes for them all to get into the air. By the time the last of the planes had lifted its wheels, the lead-plane was almost a third of the way to the landing and drop zones near Groesbeek in Holland. By 1350, thirty-three of the fifty gliders had landed, with 209 officers and men, eight anti-tank guns, and twenty-four jeeps, with trailers and radios. Within a half hour the headquarters' radios were functioning in a wood 1,000 yards west of Groesbeek.

At 1400 that same day fifty-three gliders carrying headquarters elements of the 101st Division, and its artillery, signals, engineer, reconnaissance and advance parties, began to land two miles north-west of Zon. Seventy gliders started on the mission. Two had separated from their tow-planes while over England and had landed there. Fifteen others had cut off between England and the objective, some shot down by German gunners. Three crashed on landing. Nonetheless, 252 men made it to the landing zone, and thirty-two of the forty-three jeeps sent on the mission arrived undamaged on the LZ.

Because of fog earlier in the morning, the gliders did not start taking off until after 1000 on D-day + 1.

The flak over Holland was thicker than the day before. Nineteen gliders were lost before the serials reached the landing zones. Flak cut two tow-ropes and knocked one Horsa from the sky. It killed the pilot in one tow plane of the 545th Squadron of the 46th Group, but the second navigator, although slightly wounded, took over the controls and in a quick conversation over the radio with the glider-pilot, decided to try to complete the mission. Flak now tore away the Horsa's ailerons, but both managed to make it to the LZ where the Horsa released.

Now, with the first navigator assisting, the second navigator flew the aeroplane to Martlesham Heath, where he successfully landed.

Meanwhile shells hit the landing zones. Two truck loads of panzer grenadiers arrived only a field away from one of the zones. Then in the distance there was the drone of aeroplanes that grew louder by the second to grow into a tremendous roar as serial after serial of tow-planes passed near and over the landing zones, releasing their gliders.

Fifty Germans in nearby positions, overawed at the sight, gave themselves up. The gliders descended through heavy fire, but few gliders had any difficulty in landing. The fire was so intense, however, that in the case of two gliders it was decided to abandon them without unloading. Before they were abandoned they were set afire so that no equipment would fall into German hands. Before the day was over forty-nine gliders had been set afire, although it was only in the case of these two that the equipment was lost.

Hamilcars discharged their tanks, and soon the two lorry-loads of grenadiers turned tail. One tank headed for a nearby village to deal with snipers in a church tower. With eight rounds the snipers disappeared.

On D-plus-1 by far the largest glider lifts of the operation, 450 each in the 82nd and 101st Divisions, took off. The 82nd took off between 1000 and 1100 carrying two glider field artillery battalions, one parachute field artillery battalion, part of the anti-tank battalion and the medical company.

The Germans had attacked from the Reichswald and seized a part of the landing zone early in the day. The parachutists had made a mid-morning attack and had driven the enemy off the landing zone,

A landing glider crashes on its nose and turns over

U.S. troops examine a crashed glider, behind the German lines in Holland

but the Germans still had much of it under fire. General Gavin sent a message to England in an effort to have glider pilots notified to land on the west side of the landing zone. Heroic paratroopers, realizing that the German presence was imminently dangerous to gliders soon to be landing, fought off the encircling enemy forces. Sensing the danger, 1st Sergeant Leonard A. Funk rallied the Americans in the vicinity. He marched at the head of the force, shooting his way across 800 yards of open ground. Spotting four 20-mm guns, Funk, with two others, then attacked and destroyed each gun and crew. Then he turned on three anti-aircraft guns close at hand and, leading a small group, he put them out of action, killing fifteen of the enemy.

Flak hit glider pilot Flight Officer Lawrence W. Kubale in the right side of his head. He blacked out momentarily. Coming to, he found the sergeant, a gliderman who was by no means a pilot, at the other controls doing his best to fly the glider—and so far succeeding. Blood streaming from his right temple into his eyes, shrapnel in each of his arms, in severe pain, Kubale nevertheless took over again. He skilfully managed to land right on target when released.

Other gliders that landed near the Reichswald came under intense and damaging fire. While several hundred gliders were landing on the correct landing zone, twenty-five gliders of the 319th Field Artillery Battalion continued over the zone, beyond the Reichswald, and landed about five miles inside Germany. About half the men got back to the division within a few days. The glider pilots explained that they had failed to get a green light signal from the tugs, and thought they should not release.

Four hundred and twenty-eight gliders of the 101st made it to the landing zone. They brought in 2,579 of the 2,656 men of the 327th Glider Infantry Regiment, and parts of division support units that had taken off. Twenty-six men had been injured or wounded and fifty-one remained unaccounted for. This massive lift brought in 146 jeeps and 109 trailers, in addition to the sorely needed infantry.

While it was never commented on in after-action reports, a psychological phenomenon, a sort of mass compulsion, apparently took hold among glider and C-47 pilots. Pilot after pilot witnessed cut-offs going on in the flights ahead and alongside, and this caused an 'if they can, why can't I' compulsion to develop, thus leading to the aborting of forty-five per cent of the glider mission. To an extent, this phenomenon reflected directly the standard of discipline of participating air units. It was not a high standard by anyone's measure.

On D-plus-2 the 82nd had no glider support mission. The 101st had ill luck with theirs. Three hundred and eighty-five took off. Over the fields of England flew the armada. As far as the eye could see stretched the chain of aircraft. Below they could see the coastline and the Channel with its treacherous currents and then Belgium. Flying in close formation the air fleet then encountered heavy fog banks. Visibility was so reduced that at times only the first few feet of the tow-line could be seen. Tug-ships changed their course abruptly without the glider pilot expecting it, jerking so that the gliders flopped over and had to cut loose. Then came flak and heavy machine-gun fire. Soon they could see black smoke and dirt and knew that they were nearing the landing zone. They felt naked up there, knowing that thousands of faces, both friendly and enemy, were upturned to see them pass. With the spit of a thousand devils, the fire surrounded the gliders. It penetrated through the tail assembly, the floor, the very men themselves. Ships and gliders went down but the huge formation never faltered. Eighty-two broke their tow combinations over England, seventeen landed in the Channel and sixteen in Germany, thirty-one in friendly territory, and twenty-six remained unaccounted for. Between 209 and 213, or only half the force, made it to the landing zone. The lift cost the division twenty-nine killed and forty-one injured in crashes, and a total of 225 men remained unaccounted for.

However, the division was finding better reorganization and unit effectiveness than hoped for in its glider operations. Previously the division had left newly landed glider troops to try to find their assembly areas by themselves. In an experiment, it sent five officers and twenty enlisted men as a glider reception task force, in the first glider to land on D-day. From then on these men hovered near the glider landing areas, some in jeeps, some afoot. As gliders came in, they sped to the gliders, met their passengers, quickly orientated them, and pointed out directions to their assembly areas or units. Regardless of the amount of training in orientation before missions it had been found there was loss of time on landing, and some units became lost after leaving their gliders, especially when pilots did not bring gliders down in the expected fields. The new system proved highly effective in getting the glider units organized and ready to fight.

On D + 2 day most of the British missions were parachute re-supply drops, with the exception of a forty-four-glider operation. Many of these gliders had taken off on previous days, but because of rope breaks or other mishaps had not completed the journey. Some were not to fare better on D + 2. Seven ropes broke, two of them in a cloud while over water. Each ditched successfully.

Take-offs had been delayed until late in the morning because of bad weather. Flak was unusually heavy. It severed one tow-rope. The two pilots in another glider were shot in the legs but managed to land on target. One glider was shot down, out of control. Five others were forced down in Belgium and Holland short of the landing zones. Then another tow-rope broke, or was cut by flak.

No Allied fighters gave cover to the flight, at that time a puzzle to the transport pilots who all were finding the flak much heavier than the preceding two days. The fighters had gone up according to schedule, it was later found, and had got to the rendezvous point on time. There were no transports in the sky. The fighters are reported to have assumed that the transport operation had been cancelled because the weather was so bad. They returned to their bases. Enemy flak positions were therefore not attacked as in previous days. This may account for the heavy losses to air transport. Thirteen re-supply aeroplanes did not get back to their bases, and 106 of the 105 that did return had flak damage.

D + 2 brought British glider operations to a close in a battle that was to prove so disastrous to British troops at Arnhem. Six hundred and ninety-six gliders had taken off in the mighty effort. Six hundred and twenty-one made it to landing zones or very close thereto. Of 203 gliders that released successfully for one of the landing zones on D + 1, 189 landed where planned, a remarkable achievement, while twelve landed very near in the adjacent landing zone.

The weather sharply curtailed air operations for four successive days, with none at all possible on D-plus-5. But on D-plus-6 the largest lift took off, carrying American troops. The 82nd Division lost twenty-one gliders before the column left English shores, forty-three were lost from there to the landing zone at Groesbeek, and ten were unaccounted for. The 101st fared better. Of its eighty-four gliders that took off in England, seventy-seven got to their landing zone near Zon.

In the entire 'Market' operation, 902 gliders of the 82nd started off from England. Seven hundred and sixty-three landed within 1,000 yards of their landing zone, 102 outside this radius. Some thirty-seven were unaccounted for. Of the 988 gliders that carried elements of the 101st Division, in the seven days of air transport operations 767 landed 5,000 men on their landing zones or close thereto. Twenty-nine had been destroyed getting to the LZs, forty-one were injured, and 225 remained unaccounted for.

Operation 'Market' was an airborne operation of unprecedented magnitude. A total of 34,876 troops had gone into the battle by air— 13,781 by gliders, 20,190 by parachute, and 905 by aeroplane on a prepared landing strip. Gliders brought in 1,689 vehicles, 290 howitzers and 1,259 tons of ammunition and other supplies.

The contribution of American glider pilots, once they had landed, became a contentious problem of major proportions. More than 1,700 glider pilots made the one-way trip—and once on the ground represented about five per cent of Allied strength in the drop area. This was the equivalent of a glider regiment in numbers; but actually they were a real detriment to the operation as a whole.

If the glider pilots available to the 82nd Airborne Division on D-plus-1 had been organized and trained to participate effectively in ground combat, those pilots might have been assigned a defensive sector for the time being on D-plus-1 along the Reichswald front. This might have released parachute troops there for an attack on the Nijmegen bridge. Such an attack conceivably could have resulted in the earlier capture of the bridge and the relief of the British 1st Airborne Division at Arnhem. British Airborne Corps considered that the British system under which glider pilots were assigned to the Army rather than the Air Force, and were organized into the equivalent of battalions, companies, and platoons, and trained to fight as infantry, was far superior to the American. It reported that the stand made by the 1st Airborne Division, and its subsequent withdrawal across the Lower Rhine, would have been impossible without the assistance given by the organization and training of the 1,200 glider pilots. Commanders of both the 82nd and the 101st Airborne Divisions expressed a need for better organization and control of glider pilots after landing. It was a problem which had been anticipated in manoeuvres, it had appeared in operations in Sicily, Italy, and Normandy, and after repeated recommendations for improving the situation, the problem was as evident as ever in Holland. General Gavin described it in this way:

> . . . One thing in most urgent need of correction, is the method of handling our glider pilots. I do not believe there is anyone in the combat area more eager and anxious to do the correct thing and yet so completely, individually and collectively, incapable of doing it than our glider pilots.
>
> Despite their individual willingness to help, I feel that they were definitely a liability to me. Many of them arrived without blankets, some without rations and water, and a few improperly armed and equipped. They lacked organization of their own because of, they stated, frequent transfer from one Troop Carrier Command unit to another. Despite the instructions that were issued to them to move via command channels to Division Headquarters, they frequently became involved in small unit actions to the extent that satisfied their passing curiosity, or simply left to visit nearby towns. In an airborne operation where, if properly planned, the first few hours are the quietest, this can be very harmful, since all units tend to lose control because of the many people wandering about aimlessly, improperly equipped, out of uniform, and without individual or unit responsibilities. When then enemy reaction builds up and his attack increases in violence and intensity, the necessity for every man to be on the job at the right place, doing his assigned task, is imperative. At this time glider pilots without unit assignment and improperly trained, aimlessly wandering about cause confusion and generally get in the way and have to be taken care of.
>
> In this division, glider pilots were used to control traffic, to recover supplies from the LZs, guard prisoners, and finally were assigned a defensive role with one of the regiments at a time when they were badly needed.
>
> I feel very keenly that the glider pilot problem at the moment is one of our greatest unsolved problems. I believe now that they should be assigned to airborne units, take training with the units and have a certain number of hours allocated periodically for flight training.

General Ridgeway, commander of XVIII Corps (Airborne) did not go along with the proposal to place glider pilots under the command of division commanders for full-time ground training. 'British practice to the contrary notwithstanding,' glider pilots, General Ridgeway thought, were where they belonged: in the troop-carrier squadrons. They could receive whatever ground training they needed with their associated airborne division. This apparently was no change from the policy which had created the problems of so much concern to the airborne division commanders.

The problem of re-supplying the troops by air had not yet been solved satisfactorily in Operation Market. Airborne commanders were agreed that re-supply by parachute should be regarded only as an emergency expedient. The scattered drops meant that the fighting strength of the division had to be weakened to provide recovery details, and many bundles were lost. Gliders, when they could get in, were, of course, much more reliable, but the use of one-way gliders, each requiring a pilot, was an expensive means.

The most striking feature of the plan was that the whole operation was to be carried out by the light of day. The Allied air forces were supreme in the air, and attacks by fighters of the Luftwaffe were neither expected nor feared. The profusion of Spitfires, Thunderbolts, Mustangs, Typhoons and other fighters was so great that the protection they could give was rightly regarded as overwhelming.

There remained only the anti-aircraft defences of the enemy. As has been said, these were formidable and daily increasing. The dropping and landing zones were at extreme range, and this meant that the transport and tug aircraft would have to follow the shortest possible route. The long, roaring columns would have to fly over the Dutch islands on which for the past four years the Germans had concentrated anti-aircraft batteries to prevent, if they could, the passage of day and night bombers on their way to the Ruhr.

Round the objectives themselves light flak was being concentrated in ever larger and larger quantities. Nevertheless the planners felt confident that the losses which might be incurred from anti-aircraft fire would not be so great as to imperil the operation. As it turned out, they were right, for it was only during the latter stages, when it became necessary to drop supplies to the men on the ground, that casualties became severe.

In retrospect, the final analysis of this grand battle, particularly at Arnhem, shows it to have been a credit to the Allied ground forces, although in its immediate perspective it seemed a dismal failure. The German High Command (striving for time by efforts on other fronts), hoped to establish, upon the Maas, the Waal and the Lower Rhine, three successive lines on which to stand and fight. They were in the full throes of preparing to do so when out of the skies, which Goering

These gliders, used in the invasion of Holland, were collected to be repaired for use in the airborne assault on Berlin

had once boasted would ever belong to the Luftwaffe, a blow fell with devastating suddenness. In the space not of days but of hours their scheme of defence collapsed. At one bound the British 2nd Army leapt nearly sixty miles towards the German frontier, and became deeply ensconced in what the enemy had fondly hoped would be his front throughout the winter.

Before a week had passed, the Allies had secured all the bridges over two of the three rivers, and possessed that most valuable of all assets in war, a firm base for future operations.

The enemy's reaction to the airborne attack, though immediate and violent, achieved no more than a limited success. As has been told, he could claim the recapture of the most northerly of the bridges and the thrusting back of the 1st Airborne Division with heavy casualties over the Lower Rhine. This is a fact which must be neither minimized nor exaggerated. The loss of many gallant and highly trained men in an operation of great daring and much hazard, must be set against the gain to the general conduct of the campaign as a whole. That this gain was very considerable, no one, not even the enemy who was constrained to praise the conduct of the Division, will deny.

The resolute seizure of the bridge at Arnhem, which was under British control for three days, combined with the maintenance of a defensive position north of the river for nine days, forced the enemy to devote large resources, among them the remains of two S.S. Panzer Divisions, to the task of ejecting the audacious Urquhart and his men. Had the Germans not been under this necessity, their counter-attacks farther south against the American 82nd and 101st Divisions could have been pressed with much greater vigour and might possibly have succeeded, at least for a time. That they failed must be written largely on the credit side of the ledger when calculating the profit and loss incurred by the operation; or, to vary the metaphor, because a duellist pierces the chest but not the heart of his adversary, he has not failed in his attack, for he has, nonetheless, inflicted a grievous, perhaps mortal wound. To the British 6th, and the 17th American, Airborne Divisions was reserved the honour of inflicting that wound on the Germans less than six months later, north of Wesel on the other side of the Rhine. Their swift and overwhelming success would scarcely have been possible if the battle of Arnhem had not been fought.

OPERATION MARKET

U.S. IX Troop Carrier Command—17–30 September, 1944

Aeroplanes		Gliders
3,989	dispatched	1,899
3,743	effective	1,618
87	destroyed or missing	
845	damaged	

TROOPS*

20,011		10,374
	total carried 32,519	

GLIDER CARGO

	Trailers	Jeeps
carried	526	830
effective	465	710
	2,856 tons	

R.A.F. 38 and 46 Groups—17–25 September, 1944

Aeroplanes		Gliders
1,341	dispatched	697
1,191	effective	621
55	destroyed/missing	
350	damaged	

TROOPS

186		4,215
	total carried 4,401	

GLIDER CARGO

	1,431 tons	1,026 vehicles

Casualties—17–30 September, 1944

AIR UNITS

	Killed	Missing	Wounded or Injured	Total
IX TCC Crews	31	155	66	252
IX TCC Glider Pilots	12	65	37	114
RAF TC Crews	31	217	17	265
British Glider Pilots	59	636	35	730
2d Air Div	1	63	34	98
Total	134	1136	189	1459

GROUND TROOPS, 17–25 SEPTEMBER, 1944

	Killed	Missing	Wounded or Injured	Total
82nd Airborne Div	215	427	790	1432
101st Airborne Div	315	547	1248	2110
1st Airborne Div	286	6041	135	6462
1st Polish Parachute Brig	47	173	158	378
Hq Brit Abn Corps & Signal Pers	4	8	—	12
Total	867	7196	2331	10394
TOTAL	1001	8332	2520	11853

* Includes British troops, exclusive of those carried in British planes and gliders.

CHAPTER XIV

Bastogne—Gliders Leap the Ring

When the German counter-offensive broke through the Ardennes in mid-December 1944, in the drive that was to end in the Battle of the Bulge, Eisenhower had just two divisions in his strategic reserve, the 82nd and the 101st U.S. Airborne Divisions. They were recuperating in the Rheims area after the 'Market' operation. Pressed for troops to stem the Germans, Eisenhower reluctantly threw the 82nd into the lines near Stavelot-Saint-Vith, while the 101st moved to Bastogne.

By the night of 20th–21st December, German panzer units had closed the ring on Bastogne and had overrun the 101st's field hospital. General Anthony McAuliffe, commanding the division, began sending his wounded to the civilian hospital in the city as a temporary measure, for all his medical personnel had been captured. He requisitioned supplies from civilian food stocks, but could do nothing about rapidly diminishing ammunition. A check-up on the afternoon of the 22nd found that except for one battalion with several hundreds rounds of ammunition, his artillery was down to less than ten rounds per gun. Re-supply by air drop was the only way to get the ammunition. He got a message through requesting 104 plane-loads of ammunition and rations.

The Air Force organized supply operation 'Repulse', to fly supplies to the division and other isolated units fighting to turn von Runstedt's offensive. In the next two days some planes managed to get through the heavy weather and drop parachute supplies to the 101st. On Christmas Day the weather was so foul that a 116-aeroplane mission had to be cancelled. Meanwhile German tanks hit the 101st in a desperate effort to penetrate its defences. The division fought back, but now artillery and anti-tank ammunition was perilously low, and there was practically no gasoline. Worst of all, the hospital could not handle the growing number of wounded, now counted at 400, many urgently in need of surgery. Eisenhower radioed his Air Forces in England to make every effort to get supplies to the 101st. However, reports predicted bad flying weather over England the next day, although it might have been possible for planes to take off from fields in France. But there were not enough parachute containers in France, and a para-packing unit, which had been alerted to move to the Continent, itself was held up in England by the weather.

Anxious for his wounded, McAuliffe radioed a request that surgeons and medical supplies be flown in by glider, the only possible way any surgeons could get to the 101st. Apparently about this time, perhaps on the suggestion of the division commander, McAuliffe's G-4 radioed the Air Force to try to get ammunition in by glider, as supplies going by glider needed no such special packaging as was necessary for a parachute drop. The Air Force had retrieved gliders from the Holland operations and had hundreds sitting on French airfields, and it remained now to load them and take off.

It was the 26th December, and still dark outside. At one base in France Lieutenant O. B. Blessing was sleeping off the Christmas holiday. A crew chief yelled, 'Hey, Lieutenant, they want to brief you!' He did not hear the first call, he was sleeping so soundly. The Sergeant came over and shook him, and repeated the message. Blessing got to the briefing shack as fast as he could throw on his clothes, with no inkling of what was 'cooking'. At 1452 he was in the air with a load of 'ammo', the most surprised pilot alive. Everything had happened so fast he was not yet fully about his wits.

Blessing's glider was one of eleven winging to Bastogne. In the mist ahead, several gliders flew with surgeons and aid men, jeeps fitted with litters, surgical kits, ether and other medical supplies. These gliders landed before the Germans encircling the division caught on that gliders were coming in.

Blessing had a smooth flight and almost regained some composure; then he stiffened with fright, as suddenly 'all hell broke loose below!' He gave a split second's glance at Flight Officer Charles F. Sutton, his co-pilot, who looked no less frightened. Sutton, he realized, was 'praying enough for both'. So, a bit more confident, Blessing once more glued his eyes ahead.

He eyed the tracers. Still in tow, he manoeuvred as best he could between the obviously heavy concentrations, but just before releasing, he heard clattering among the steel tubing, and the tail shuddered. He turned and saw light coming through many holes, but miraculously the tail held on and he landed successfully.

Lieutenant Wallace F. Hammargren was coming close to releasing. As he raised his hands towards the black, pool-ball sized release-lever knob, the tow-rope parted a foot away from the nose of the glider, probably hit by flak. A second or so later the pilot flashed the white light from the tow-plane's astrodome, giving Hammargren the release signal.

225

Another pilot, Lieutenant William Burnett, and his co-pilot James C. Crowder, came in low over some tree tops. Enemy 20-mm explosive-tipped shells started fragmenting as they hit the fabric, ripping it to shreds on one side. North-west of the landing zone a piece of flak broke the flying wires in the tail, and the glider became sluggish. Burnett barely managed to make the turn towards the field. He landed successfully.

Most of the other gliders also became targets for the last few minutes, but all came in with their loads intact, landing more than 32,900 pounds of cargo.

But this glider effort did not begin to meet the needs of a situation rapidly growing more serious. Aeroplanes at bases in England, loaded with para-packed supplies, soon stood ready, but the weather gave no indication of improvement. The need was so great, however, that although the mist swept across the runways and cold fog blanketed vision, 301 aeroplanes took off on instruments, and luckily dropped 320 tons of supplies within the ring around the 101st. The weather was so thick on the return flight that it forced a number of planes to land at fields in France to wait for better weather before returning to English bases.

The next day, 27th December, fifty glider-plane combinations from the 439th T.C. Group started for Bastogne from fields in France. Again, for most of them the flight proved uneventful until they were near the release point.

Lieutenant Charles Brema ran into intense, accurate automatic weapons' fire, coming from Germans near a railroad junction at Bras, and from woods half a mile east of Remagne. He released at 1230, made a 270° left turn, and by this time was out of range of fire. He touched ground racing towards trees ahead, but could not brake the glider. The trees did; after a telephone pole had first clipped off part of one wing, the trees took the whole wing and then the other, perceptibly slowing him with each impact. Sweat oozed from under his hands, tightly holding the wheel.

Nearby men from the 101st rushed towards the glider and pulled open the door. Brema thought they wanted to see if he was still alive, or perhaps congratulate him for making it in without getting killed. Instead, they started pulling and hacking at the lashings binding the ammunition to the glider floor, and ran off with it, leaving him unceremoniously to his own devices. He took a little time to check the glider. Not a bullet-hole could he find, nor had the glider suffered any damage in landing. He felt let down.

Other gliders were on their way down, and realizing that the pilots would get little more help than he had, he ran from one glider to another, as each landed, to give what help he could to each pilot.

Another pilot, Lieutenant David H. Sill, with the 92nd Squadron,

Wounded soldiers being placed aboard a cargo glider attached to a field hospital

caught flak for seven minutes; it increased to a high intensity, and lasted until about four minutes before he released. Then the flak seemed miraculously to stop looking for him. When Sill cut away at 3,200 feet, he could see the smudge-pot markers below. He made a 360° right turn, then a 180° left. Gliders were all around making various patterns coming in. While still well above the ground his glider got a jarring bang in the rear and, glancing out, he saw another glider passing a few feet above him on the left, its right wheel dangling. He landed successfully about a mile from General 'Nuts' McAuliffe's command post.

Lieutenant Gans had an uneventful flight until he saw the red light on the top of the tow-ship start flashing—the signal they were ten minutes away from the landing zone. Then black puffs began to pop all about their line of flight. Soon he saw 'white trails' from tracers off in the distance and planes overhead—whose he was uncertain. The tow-plane pilot flashed the white light from the astrodome, the signal to release. Machine guns began chattering. Gans cut off. He saw where to land, but let two other gliders go in ahead, followed, hit a fence, pulled a wheel off, and stopped.

As Lieutenant Mack Striplin's glider got close to the landing zone he could see German 88s below starting to shoot at his combination. He could hear machine guns chattering. When he had cut off, he saw a strange sight during the run-in—'silvery star-shaped balls' or tinfoil-like objects, floating in the air (probably a 'window' dropped by high-altitude aircraft to deceive German radar). One was below, not more than twelve feet from the glider. Striplin flew through the bizarre phenomena. The balls did not dissipate, but soon passed from sight.

Of fifty that started, thirty-five gliders landed close enough to the defenders at Bastogne to get their supplies through. Reports are singularly silent about the remaining gliders, although one mentions that four were shot down. The gliders had brought in 106,291 pounds of cargo. Some 45,000 pounds in fifteen gliders did not make it. That all of the fifteen were shot down is entirely possible, particularly if these were near the end of the air serial, for by that time the Germans were fully alerted. When the planes turned back, they suffered serious casualties; and before they had reached home seventeen of the fifty that started that morning had crashed.

Heavy fog continued over the United Kingdom. Of 238 aeroplanes that were ready, only 188 managed to get off. They dropped 162 tons by parachute without losing a plane, but they too had to land at Continental bases for the night. By now supplies had been loaded in British containers so that the 38th and 46th R.A.F. Groups could be used in getting supplies to Bastogne.

But that evening all further air supply missions were called off, for a corridor connection had been opened and trucks were getting through to the 101st. Over ninety-four per cent of the supplies sent by air—1,046 tons—landed successfully in the divisional area.

General McAuliffe paid several visits to the hospital. He found the surgeons who had come in by glider 'dead on their feet', working around the clock to serve the wounded.

CHAPTER XV

Russia—Glider Pioneer?

While this glider transport experiment (Russian transport of infantry in gliders attached to bombers) first attracted attention and caused much comment among aviation writers and experts, the military leaders among other great powers took little heed of the glider potential, except for the war-minded Germans.

Keith Ayling in *To Fly to Fight*

Just after dark one day in the spring of 1943 gliders took off, their destination secret, from an airfield whose name, if it had one, is now lost. Russia was fighting for her life. No one was yet convinced that her armies had conclusively stemmed the Nazi onslaught. The gliders carried Matjus Sumauskas, President of the Supreme Soviet of the Lithuanian Soviet Socialist Republic, Henrikas Zimanas, editor in chief of *Komunistas*, and seventy others. They were all Lithuanians, members of Operative Group 11 organized to launch partisan movements in Nazi-held Lithuania.

Some 600 miles behind German lines, the gliders cut away from their tow-planes. It was black below. Some came in to fairly good landings. One crashed, killing all. Zimanas' glider hit an obstacle and was virtually demolished, the pilot killed, and passengers badly bruised or severely injured. The accident hurt Zimanas' spine and leg. Despite his injuries, and the arrival of an evacuation plane, he remained with the mission, assisting as best he could as a radio operator while the other partisans made their way to the Kazyan forest. Regaining strength, although limping and in severe pain, Zimanas caught up with the main force in the Kazyan forest. He then went with it to Lithuania.

Nothing was ever known in the West, during the war, of these isolated but daring partisan operations behind German lines that were launched frequently with gliders. Through these operations the transport glider was finally coming into its own in Russian military operations, the culmination of years of preparation.

Like the Germans, the Russians had long been avid gliding and soaring enthusiasts. Russia was one of the few countries to compete with the Germans with any degree of success in the development of gliding. The meagre amount of information allowed to seep out of Russia gave no idea of the great activity centred around glider development there. Russian progress appears to have anticipated that of Germany by perhaps as much as five years, a fact of immense historical significance.

In Russia the state took a direct interest in soaring, and under its support Russian glider pilots began to gain international recognition shortly before World War II. In 1925 the Soviets held their first national glider competition in the Crimea.

While Germany originally used the glider as a subterfuge to improve its aeronautical technology and skill resources, the Russians embarked upon quite a substantial glider development programme for entirely different reasons. Germany's interest in the glider was rooted in those of its qualities that could serve military ends, and took absolutely no notice of its commercial value. In Russia, it was the other way around. Military use became a coincidental offshoot. Russia's commercial aeroplanes could fly passengers and cargo into areas that had no trains and where roads were impassable in bad weather. The aeroplane was solving historical communication problems that had reined-in domestic development over the centuries. The aeroplane was meeting a vital economic and political need at a critical point in Russia's history. Russian expansion of commercial air transportation strove to keep up with the increasing demand to fly more and more passengers and cargo.

Short in technological skills, lacking the industrial capacity and production know-how to turn out the increasing number of aeroplanes demanded of a strained economy, the Russians turned to the transport glider as offering a way to double air cargo capacity, using substantially less resources in air frame materials, aircraft, engines and fuel than would be necessary to achieve the same cargo lift with powered transport aeroplanes.

Already Soviet-built gliders had been towed long distances in single tow. Now experiments began in double and triple tows, with the thought that ultimately a single aircraft could tow many transport gliders carrying passengers in 'glider-train' formation. So rapidly did they progress, that by 1939 they had managed the art of towing as many as five single-place gliders with a single aircraft, a feat never matched elsewhere and an accomplishment not surpassed outside of Russia since.

Although in the 1920s Soviet interest focused chiefly on sport gliding, from the 1930s the government decided to expand Soviet gliding activities. In 1931 a dramatic upsurge occurred when at the Ninth Party Congress, held in January, the Konsommol passed a resolution calling for an unheralded expansion of the gliding movement. The

Konsommol announced a threefold purpose in its resolution. First, through training programmes it sought to build an enormous pool of glider pilots. Second, through research and development and testing of new glider models it hoped to gain useful information for its aeronautical research programme. Third, it was setting out to capture as many world records as it could.

To back up the programme, in 1932 the government built a glider factory in Moscow. It set production goals at 900 primary trainers and 300 training gliders per year. It named Oleg K. Antonov, an aircraft engineer and designer, who was to become famous for his glider designs, to head design and engineering at the plant.

Shortly after the Konsommol resolution was passed, eighty leading glider and light plane designers assembled at Koktabel. They studied twenty-two glider designs, and selected seven for construction and tests to be made in 1932. In retrospect, the pace at which the whole movement progressed gives some indication of the importance the government placed on the programme.

In thirty-six days of tests, Soviet glider pilots flew 662 flights, averaging more than an hour each in the seven gliders to be tested, and in other gliders from distant parts of the Soviet Union, and establishing six new Russian records. During that year, in a single flight V. A. Stepanchenok in a G-9 glider looped 115 times and flew upside down for more than one minute. Soviet glider pilots went on to perform new and unexpected aerobatics and carried out long distance tows and a multitude of other feats. By 1939 Olga Klepikova flew a glider 465 miles to capture the world distance record, a feat that was unbeaten for twenty-two years. On the same occasion B. Borodin flew two passengers for more than four hours in a single flight, and with this feat the transport glider was born. It was then up to some perceptive person to recognize the significance of the flight; and it appears that this was not long in happening.

Although Soviet authorities saw the transport glider as a solution to commercial needs for more air lift, they apparently concurrently saw that the transport glider had some military potential. Military and commercial development began simultaneously in the very early 1930s, perhaps in 1931 or 1932, and ran on closely parallel paths; the Moscow glider factory was their design and production focal point.

The idea for a multi-passenger towed glider, as opposed to the two-passenger soaring glider already flown, must have blossomed in 1932 or 1933, inasmuch as Groshev (designer of the transport glider GN-4), undoubtedly had a large glider, an innovation, on the drawing board in late 1932 or 1933. In 1934 the Moscow glider factory produced this aircraft, the GN-4; a five-place glider that could transport four passengers and was designed for towed flight. Historical exploit though it was, the GN-4 appears to have been a modest development compared with others then on the drawing board, for General I. I. Lisov, in his *Parachutists—Airborne Landing*, published in Moscow in 1968, reveals that as far back as 1932 the work plan for the *Voenno Vozdushniy Sily* (VVS) design bureau included the G-63 glider, a craft that could carry seventeen troops or a like amount of cargo. What is even more remarkable is that the bureau was daring enough to include a requirement for a 50-man glider, the G-64, which was to be towed by a TB-1 bomber. While there are those who would criticize such bold statements as an attempt to bolster Russian ego with another first, or discount them as pure propaganda, there is evidence based on what was to come that the statements did not come from unrealistic fantasy. In 1935 Russia's magazine *Samolet* (Flight) discussed the use of gliders for carrying passengers, citing an 18-passenger glider, with a photograph in support. The article goes so far as to give an illustration of a transport glider train drawn by a four-engined aeroplane. This would mean that the 1932 VVS design requirement was in part realized by 1935 or earlier, for gliders cannot be designed, built and tested overnight. On 9th October 1935 *The New York Times* reported that a G-31 18-passenger glider with a 92-foot wingspan, built by the experimental institute in Leningrad, had been test-flown several times. It was to have been flown from Leningrad to Moscow the same month. This was undoubtedly the glider reported in *Samolet*.

In his book *Without Visible Means of Support*, Richard Miller mentions that the Russians experimented in 1934 with a 13-passenger troop glider, grossing 8,000 pounds.

In that same year the Soviets could boast ten gliding schools, 230 gliding stations and 57,000 trained glider pilots.

Around 1934 a new concept took hold, fostered by Lev Pavlovich Malinovskii, head of the Scientific Technical administration of the *Grazhdanskiy Vazdushniy Flot* (Civilian Air Fleet). Malinovskii conceived the idea of using a low-powered freight glider plane, easy to produce and cheap to operate, that could solve some of Russia's long distance fast freight needs. The fully laden glider would carry around a ton of goods, and be powered by a single 100 h.p. engine. The engine would assist the tow-plane during take-off. Once safely airborne, the glider would cast off and under its own power deliver its cargo to a distant terminal.

Because most of the models were underpowered, only one or two went beyond the experimental stage. Several apparently grew into sizeable 10-passenger models, and there is a strong likelihood that these models, with engines removed, became the first of the larger 20-passenger transport gliders developed in Russia, and observed during the mid-1930s.

While Russian designers and engineers were busy at the task of creating and producing the new weapon, military leaders went about the task of building airlanding and parachute forces to use them. By 1933 the first of these units appeared. Russia startled the world when 1,200 troops landed by parachute with all weapons and equipment during the manoeuvres around Kiev. Later in the year, aircraft transported a complete division, together with tanks, from Moscow to Vladivostok, a distance of 4,200 miles. Minister of War Kliment Voroshilov was therefore fully justified in stating at a congress in 1935: 'Parachuting is the field of aviation in which the Soviet Union has a monopoly. No nation on earth can even approximately compare with the Soviet Union in this field, far less could any nation dream of closing the existing gap by which we are leading. There can be no question at all of our being surpassed.'

That gliders were used in these manoeuvres is not confirmed, although they may have been, and because of the secrecy surrounding them, and because they were so similar to aeroplanes in appearance, their presence among the powered aircraft could have passed unnoticed. Terence Otway states, however, that 'by 1935 [Russia] had gone a long way towards creating an effective airborne force including parachute troops carried in gliders.'

In the Caucasus manoeuvres of 1936, the paratroopers participated publicly, but from then on all exercises and manoeuvres of the arm were carried out in strict secrecy. Keith Ayling reports in *They Fly to Fight*, a large number of troops carried in gliders, in one instance, in 1936; undoubtedly the same Caucasus manoeuvre.

After dropping the veil of secrecy over airborne developments, contrary to foreign observer indications, the Russians did not entirely neglect the fledgeling airborne arm, for by 1940 they approved an airborne brigade of 3,000 men of which more than a third were glider troops. By mid 1941, in a doctrinal turnabout, glider troop units as such disappeared from Soviet troop lists, although glider manufacture continued. Only recently has information filtered from behind the Iron Curtain that in 1941, just before the war started, Russia had already built a glider tank transport, the world's first. The tank flown was a light tank; and the glider carrying the tank was successfully flown. Shortly after this flight Germany invaded Russia, and Russia made no further experiments with that glider. However, the daring experiment, far ahead of those of any other nation manufacturing gliders, gives some indication of the extent of Russia's interest in, and progress with, the glider as a military weapon.

To what extent German military leaders proselyted from Russian transport glider developments is not certain, but certainly these developments could not have gone unnoticed, in view of a curious succession of events involving both Russia and Germany. The Treaty of Rapallo of 1922, through a much overlooked clause, enabled the German military arm to produce and perfect in Russia weapons forbidden by the Treaty of Versailles. For this purpose in 1924 the Soviets turned over to the Germans the remote, disused Lipetsk aerodrome, about 310 miles south-east of Moscow, where they established a flying school and also tested aircraft. Through these activities the Red Air Force gained information about German technical developments.

Also, in 1923 the Germans opened a 'Moscow Centre' liaison office in Moscow, manned by German officers who reported to the Defence Ministry in Berlin. Junkers and other German aircraft manufacturers built factories in the Soviet Union, staffed by German officers and aircraft engine experts. Many officers, such as August Plock, Herman Plocker and Kurt Student, who were later to become generals and who occupied important posts in Hitler's Luftwaffe, served in Russia in the 1920s. General Student, who masterminded Hitler's glider attack on Eben Emael while an infantry officer, visited the Lipetsk airfield every year from 1924 to 1928.

Three factors strongly suggest that early German development and use of the transport glider followed Russian developments by three to five years. The Russians must have had their transport glider on the drawing board perhaps as early as 1932, to enable them to produce their 5-passenger GN-4 in 1934 or earlier. The Germans produced their 'Obs' (flying observatory) in 1933 or 1934, a glider that was not as yet a true transport vehicle, but closer to a scientific laboratory. Secondly, foreign observers saw Russian transport gliders in flight in 1935 or 1936, carrying perhaps as many as 15 to 18 passengers. The 9-passenger German DFS 230 glider did not appear before 1938, and it proved to be a substantially smaller model than those seen in Russia up to that time. Thirdly, the Russians had large airborne organizations in planning in the early 1930s, and actually flew them in the large airborne drop at Kiev in 1935, while it was not until 1938 that the Germans finally organized their 7th *Flieger* Division.

Although Russian military leaders conducted few, and only marginally useful, air assaults during the war, and the glider saw only limited use as a military transport to support these operations, it did play some role.

For the Dneiper River crossing operations of 24th September 1943 alone, the Russians planned to use thirty-five gliders to transport heavy guns and equipment. The glider landings had been sandwiched in between the first mass parachute leap and the second. Apparently the glider phase was not implemented. Apart from this, it was used extensively in partisan support operations and in many raids.

German forces found guerrillas annoying and persistent. Although guerrillas lived off the land to a great extent, the regular military force kept them supplied with weapons and ammunition by glider, and where possible by powered aircraft. The magnitude of these operations, and especially the importance played by the glider, can be judged by the fact that in the counter-guerrilla operations in and around Lipel alone the German troops overran one field that held more than 100 gliders.

Gliders transported rations, weapons, medical supplies, and at the same time provided partisans with key personnel and important orders and information. Gliders landed by night on emergency air-fields and during the winter on the ice of frozen lakes. This support enabled the partisans to carry out successful attacks on railroads, roads, airfields, bridges, convoys, columns of troops, rear area com-mand agencies, and even troop units. The Germans suffered heavy losses of personnel and materiel. The Germans flew reconnaissance missions to discover air-drop and landing fields in partisan-held areas, attacked airlift operations wherever they were identified, used de-ception by setting up dummy airfields and giving fake signals, and finally activated a special anti-partisan wing of 100 Arado-66s. The results achieved against the guerrillas—especially in the central theatre of operations—remained unsatisfactory. In the final analysis, this use of airlift by the Russian Air Force must be considered a success, for the relentless night airlift operations enabled the partisans to carry out their tasks.

After the war Russian interest in gliders did not immediately wane, and new models were reported, though sources of these reports are few and hard to find. Until as late as 1965 the Soviets had three glider regiments, which they have since deactivated. They have also put in mothballs the best equipment in their glider fleet for possible future use.

CHAPTER XVI

Some Gliders that Never Fought

While glider development went on in Great Britain, Germany, the United States, and Russia, there was little notice or knowledge by these great powers of glider development elsewhere. Yet some surprising developments took place in countries far distant from the locations of major glider production and their theatres of operational use.

These nations undertook the development and production of gliders without the benefit of experience gained by the major producers. Each did a surprisingly creditable job.

Japan is perhaps the first of these other countries that should be mentioned. Unknown to even her friendliest Axis partner, Germany, Japan embarked on a glider development programme in 1941. She had precious little antecedent upon which to base her efforts.

The Japanese, until 1935, had never taken sports gliding seriously. In that year Hirth, the famous German soaring pilot, arrived in Japan with his Goppingers I and III soaring gliders, to show the Japanese something of the art of soaring. He performed with both of these gliders at Tokorozawa and so impressed the Japanese Air Force generals that they sought his advice about introducing glider flying into the training of pilots, as a step prior to the pilots learning to fly powered aircraft.

Apparently the Japanese Air Force thought enough of the possibilities of using the glider, to order the production of several soaring models patterned on the German Goppingers. When the Japanese invaded China, Japanese military authorities turned their attention to the pressing matters of the enterprise, and glider development stopped.

In 1940, the word of the German accomplishment at Eben Emael filtered into Japan. Several months later, German generals vaunted the achievements of the daring glider operation at Eben Emael to Japanese and other Axis partner attachés, when they took them on a tour of the shattered Allied defences in Belgium and France. The Japanese attachés' reports on the German achievements with gliders further impressed Japanese generals as to what the glider could accomplish. From this time on, the Japanese Army and Navy initiated steps that, though never vigorous, nonetheless assured a continuous attention to the subject.

In 1941 the Army constructed its first troop-carrying glider of consequence, the Ku 1. The Navy followed shortly thereafter with a contract to the Japanese Aircraft Corporation to produce the MXY 5, a 13-passenger glider.

Soon the Army launched into the development of the Ku 8, a glider that carried twenty-two men, and one which, after several modifications, became their mass production model. Four hundred were built. The Japanese Army also decided to produce a tank-carrying glider, the Ku 6. Not much is known of this glider except that at least one model was built and it flew with a tank on several occasions. The Army planned to use it to counter the American invasion of Japan. They had in mind flying the glider and light-tank combination into areas where the Allies threatened to make landings, or where landings had already been made, to turn them back by quickly rushing the tanks to the scene.

By 1940 the Japanese had organized both glider and parachute airborne units, starting with small experimental units of squad size. Soon they organized larger, battalion-size 'raiding' units. These were ultimately consolidated into two 6,000-men divisions, that each had two glider regiments plus other units. Each regiment had 900 men; rather small, by Allied standards, for glider requirements.

Japanese prisoners of war interrogated by the A.A.F. reported observing Japanese gliders, and glider training going on, in Manchuria, but no Japanese combat glider operations ever took place there.

When MacArthur launched his long-vaunted campaign to carry out his promise to return to the Philippines, the Japanese moved some of their glider forces to the south. They planned to place them in a wide-ranging strategic reserve, to take off in a matter of hours, to repel one or more of MacArthur's possible thrusts while forces were still struggling over the beaches.

Japanese gliders, tow-aeroplanes and airborne units, began the long, frequently interrupted trek, starting from Nishitsukuba. The various units converged first on the island of Cheju do in Korea. Originally the next stepping-stone was to be Okinawa, but Allied air activity there made this move undesirable and they landed at Cheju do instead. They next flew to Shanghai and then to Taiwan.

By November 1944, however, MacArthur had already set foot on Leyte. The Jap ground forces there were in serious trouble, and the Japanese now decided the forces *en route* would be launched against U.S. forces in Leyte; in exactly what mission was not yet determined.

Meanwhile the first echelon of the ground support units of their glider assault force had also arrived at Taiwan by ship. The Japs

The Australian DHA-G2 suction-wing test-glider

Kokusai Ku-8 used by the Japanese Army Air Force

began a glider infiltration to Clarke field sixty miles north of Manila. Towing with Type 97 bombers, the Japs managed to get twelve gliders to the Philippines; and about the time the last had arrived, the Jap Command at Clarke got wind that the Allies had sunk a ship carrying the second echelon of 300 men, a much-needed ground support unit with supplies, before it had reached Taiwan. Only three survived.

The loss of this force, combined with the fact that the Jap situation on Leyte had deteriorated, made a glider foray with what could now be only a token force, foolhardy. Thus the plan was cancelled.

By January MacArthur was in Luzon, Manila captured, and the last of the Japs about to be driven into the sea. A desperate, hopeless venture, they now planned to try to hold onto the north end of Luzon, hopefully to retain a beachhead for re-invasion. They planned to land glider forces at Clarke field to bolster Jap strength there. However, they called off the landings when U.S. forces landed at Lingayen Bay, 100 miles to the north of Clarke, on 9th January 1945, eliminating the last of Jap ports in the Philippines.

In last-minute desperation, all hope of winning the war lost, but anxious not to lose Okinawa for the negotiations ahead, the Japs looked desperately about for some means to bolster the Okinawa garrison, heavily pounded by the U.S. Navy and under ground attack by the Marines and the Army. They prepared an assault force of eight gliders to take off from airfields around Yokota, Japan. They scheduled the landings for 20th August 1945. Meanwhile atom bombs incinerated Nagasaki and Hiroshima, and by 15th August the war had ended.

A more aggressive use of gliders by the Japanese forces did not take place for many reasons. Most important was the lack of aircraft to tow the gliders. Another, and almost equally important reason, lay in the lack of fighter cover for any planned glider operations. By the time the Japanese had produced a substantial glider-airborne arm, the tide of war was flowing swiftly against Japan. Militarily Japan was exhausted, her resources were severely drained and she was unable to afford any frills. Probably underlying was the same factor that coloured Allied thinking, a lack of belief in or enthusiasm for the new weapon held by the Japanese top command.

AUSTRALIA

Australia—geographically isolated, gravely endangered by Japanese advances in the Philippines, Malaysia, Indonesia and Burma—was interested in the possibilities that the glider held for army forces that would fend off Japanese landings on any of her isolated shores. The Australian Army planned the use of glider-borne units that could be flown quickly from key airfields across wide expanses of desert to threatened areas.

In 1942 the Air Force contracted with de Havilland Aircraft (DHA) to produce a 6-place glider, the DHA-G1. Several were built. A later modification, the DHA-D2 was also built. When the Japanese advance in the Far East slowed down, the Australians gradually stopped the development of transport gliders, but not before they had built an unusually versatile glider, considering their lack of technical experience in the field when they first entered it.

ITALY

It is uncertain when the Italians took an interest in the transport glider. However, by 1943 they had produced the AL-12, an especially trim and flyable glider. It carried ten men, but apparently only one glider was built.

FRANCE

The French Army, impressed with what the Germans and the Allies had done with gliders, planned the building of transport gliders immediately after France's liberation. A contract was made with the Fango works. They constructed the Castel-Mauboissin 10 or CM-10, an all-wood glider that carried a jeep, a trailer, and three to six men. It was an advanced development considering that France entered the field a decidedly late comer.

However, budgeting restrictions, combined with a change of heart on the part of the military, began to have its effect, and soon a programme that projected the building of some 100 Mauboissins was cut back and only six were ultimately built. Most were finished after the war ended.

When the army discontinued production of gliders, some funds were allocated to turning the existing gliders into powered aeroplanes. The ultimate was a glider-turned-jet, the CM 101R.

CHAPTER XVII

Varsity—Assault Across the Rhine

Early in 1945 the Allies agreed on a three-phase campaign to end the war against Germany. It included several airborne assaults on enemy positions across the Rhine, north of the Ruhr River between Emmerich and Wesel. 'Varsity', one of these operations, would send British and American airborne divisions to assist the British Second Army, making an amphibious crossing of the Rhine near Wesel. The plan for this operation was ambitious. It called for landing 17,000 glidermen and parachutists and thousands of tons of supplies, armour and other heavy equipment in just four hours. As such, it was the most enterprising airborne operation ever planned. In a doctrinal turnabout, airborne drops were to follow, not precede, the beginning of the ground assault by the British Second Army.

Dynamic General Sir Miles Dempsey, the Army's commander, established the objective for the airborne troops, and set the tone for the operation. Rather than let the airborne divisions take the safer, but less daring, alternative of dropping close to the Rhine, where they would soon have the assistance of his ground troops (a plan suggested by some of his more conservative staff officers), he chose otherwise.

He ordered his airborne forces, the British 6th and the American 17th airborne divisions, to land near, and secure, the Diersfordter Wald, a wooded area four miles east of the Rhine. This meant that the airborne forces were making a relatively deep penetration, which raised the possibility that the Germans might cut the divisions off from the main ground assault. However, the risk was well worth the gamble, he felt.

Although scarcely 100 feet higher than the river surface, the woods covered the highest point near the Rhine. This meant that this excellent observation spot had to be denied to German artillery observers, and made available for Allied use. The woods, moreover, camouflaged and protected German artillery batteries that could rake Dempsey's men as they crossed the river. Until airborne troops cleared the woods of the enemy, the Second Army would find it next to impossible to bridge the Rhine, because of the fire the enemy could place on bridge sites.

It would take several hours, after the amphibious crossings had begun, for General Dempsey's troops to capture bridge sites on the eastern shore and move bridging equipment up. Airborne landings to capture the woods could take place some time in the morning; the time was later set at 1000.

The staff selected six glider landing zones and four paratroop drop zones. Nine zones were on, or near, the east side of the woods, and one paratroop zone was on its west side. All ten zones were in an area less than six miles long and five miles wide—an unprecedented degree of concentration.

Firm, level fields and meadows, averaging 200 to 300 yards in length, formed a checker board throughout the zone. Small hedges, light fences, and ditches skirted many of them. No Rommel's asparagus showed up on aerial photographs, nor other man-made military obstacles; nor were any found in the landing zones after the landing. A double-track railroad cut diagonally across the area from north-west to south-east. A few hundred yards to the east of the railroad, a high-tension power line on 100-foot pylons presented a major hazard to gliders and billowing parachutes. The River Issel bordered the eastern edge of the area, and running south-south-east, was a water-barrier sixty feet wide. Although many other minor hazards existed, it was most important to avoid depositing the airborne troops in the wood, in or beyond the Issel, or against the high-tension line.

Being aware that Wesel was a logical place to cross the Rhine, the Nazis had massed an estimated ten of their best remaining divisions within twenty miles of the assault area. These divisions had been so reduced by attrition, however, that their combat effectives were fewer than 50,000 men; their full strength being 150,000. Among them were two or three panzer divisions with perhaps 100 tanks, and self-propelled guns; these were reported to be more than ten miles from the assault area. A maximum of 12,000 troops, which included two divisions and a brigade group, were thought to be within a ten-mile radius of the airborne assault. If they concentrated in the Diersfordter Wald to oppose the amphibious landings, the airborne attack at their rear and on their flanks would cut them off. Because it was believed that the Germans were expecting an airborne assault, it was more likely that they would keep their main strength behind the River Issel, with only a holding force in the wood. In that case the airborne troops might be encircled.

'Varsity' involved both British and American air units. The United States IXth Troop Carrier Command had orders to transport the Airborne Divisions. It assigned 226 C-47s and seventy-two C-46s for

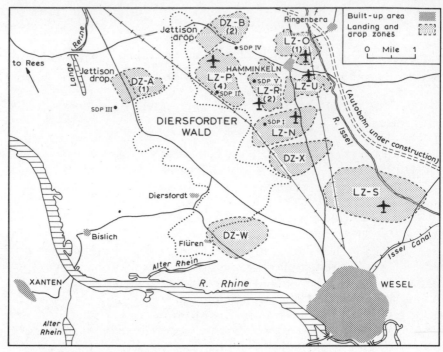

Operation Varsity (Wesel, Germany)

lifting the 17th Division paratroops; 243 C-47s for the British division; and 610 C-47s, many of them to use the double-tow technique, to tow 906 gliders carrying the 17th Airborne Division glider elements. The 38th and 46th Groups of the Royal Air Force supplied 440 aircraft to tow an equal number of gliders carrying the glider troops of the 6th Airborne Division. The flight path was not excessively long, and only the last six miles of it were over enemy territory. But to deliver simultaneously two divisions of troops within two hours and thirty-seven minutes required precise timing, since the British troops would fly from England and the Americans from bases around Paris.

Brigadier Chatterton's Glider Pilot Regiment had been reinforced after its losses at Arnhem by a high proportion of pilots of the Royal Air Force, who contrived, in a short space of time, to learn both to fly a glider and to fight as soldiers. Thus it was that, when that bright spring morning dawned, every pair of pilots in the 440 British gliders that took off knew not only how to fight, but exactly where to fight.

The troop carriers based in England had orders to enter the Continent at Cape Gris Nez and fly a dogleg course to Wavre—thus avoiding the radar range of German-held Dunkirk. The flights from England and France were to merge over Wavre in Belgium. This

Transports and gliders fill the air as the 17th Airborne Division sets off for the Rhine

Gliders facing in all directions, as they landed, in a patchwork of German fields

location caused the least possible detour for the transport wings stationed in France, and could be reached by all wings without their interfering with each other's courses or assembly areas. From Wavre three traffic lanes, one and a half miles apart, led north-east for ninety-two miles to Weeze—the principal assembly point, located fourteen miles west of the Rhine.

At 2000 hours on 23rd March the British began a heavy artillery barrage against the bank of the Rhine and the drop zones and landing zones that had been selected for the airborne operation. An hour later this artillery barrage was lifted, and the first wave of the British Second Army assault boats pushed out into the Rhine. To the south, the United States Ninth Army assault began at 0200. All the crossings were completely successful: there was little German resistance from the opposite bank of the river. By dawn, nine small bridgeheads had been secured in the Wesel-Emmerich area, some twenty miles across, although there was fierce fighting at some points. German paratroops held Rees, ten miles north-west of Wesel, throughout D-day and kept the British 51st Division pinned close to the river. Enemy troops also held Wesel.

At 0710, aircraft of the R.A.F.'s 38th and 46th Groups, flying Stirlings, Halifaxes and C-47s, started off from the runways of airfields in East Anglia. They towed 381 Horsas and 48 Hamilcars up into a bright clear sky, carrying the Airlanding Brigade of the 6th Division. U.S. Air Force aircraft flew the parachutists of the divisions. Aircraft were taking off from eleven fields in all, the many columns marshalling in the sky over Hawkinge in Kent to form one gigantic fleet. It crossed France near Calais, then headed towards Brussels. Simultaneously American planes began lifting the 17th Airborne Division from twelve aerodromes around Paris. They marshalled, and headed towards Brussels to converge with those coming into view from Calais. Everything was going smoothly. A thousand fighters swept the sky above the plodding columns.

Brigadier G. K. Bourne could see the Rhine, a silver streak, and beyond it a thick, black haze, for all the world like Manchester or Birmingham as seen from the air. For the moment, he wondered whether the bombing of Wesel, which had preceded the attack upon that town by commando troops, had been mis-timed. If this were so, then all the landing zones would be obscured by clouds of dust blowing from the rubble created by the attack.

The landing zones were indeed dusty, but the dust did not prevent glider pilots from making successful landings. By 0945 the formation was approaching its objectives, flying over the Rhine at an altitude of 2,500 feet. Three hours and ten minutes after take-off, the leading British gliders neared the landing zone. A *Times* aeronautical correspondent, riding in a Halifax reported:

Away at the right a farm building was burning itself out. Near by, a field was strewn with white, blue, and red parachutes, but of their former wearers there was no trace; they had already advanced into the pall of smoke which hung like a gigantic curtain over the battlefield, hiding all that was going on underneath, blotting out the horizon and smudging the blue sky with dirty grey-brown fingers. In the middle of the field sprawled an up-ended glider.

As we approached the dropping zone the danger of collision became very real. The Halifax rocked dangerously in the slipstream of machines in front, and perspiration trickled down the pilot's face as he tried to keep the tug in level flight while the glider was preparing to cast off . . . . 'Two miles to go,' the pilot shouted. 'O.K., tug,' came the reply. 'Can you take us a little lower?'

The nose of the Halifax dipped down slightly. Then we heard the voice of the glider pilot again. 'Hello, tug, I am casting off now.' 'Cheerio, old man. Good luck. See you again soon.' The Halifax gave a bound forward as it was relieved of the load of the glider. The Horsa started to dive steeply away to the right, and we turned upwards and to port, climbing swiftly to get out of the tangled stream of gliders and tugs . . . . We were over the battle area now, and in a few seconds gliders and the ground were lost in a sea of smoke. All that remained were the tugs, with their tow-ropes dangling behind them.

Occasionally one could see the flash of a gun . . . . The contending ground forces now had the stage to themselves, for in the smoke and dust of battle the air forces could not intervene further. As we turned for home a few puffs of flak appeared . . . A Halifax in front had one wheel of its undercarriage hanging down; . . . obscured by smoke a Hamilcar glider had force-landed in the corner of a field. Ant-like figures were busily engaged in unloading a gun and light tank.

For half an hour after we had started back the unbroken stream of tugs, gliders, and parachute-troop-transports still flowed eastwards.

It was now nearly time for Brigadier Bourne's glider to cut off. In accordance with orders, but against his will, for he wanted to see what was happening, he had strapped himself in. They began to go down in a steep glide, and he listened with strained interest to the excited converse of the two pilots, neither of whom had been on operations before. Presently, he heard the first pilot say to the second, 'I can see the railway.' Then he felt much relieved; and soon he saw the landscape flying past the windows. They landed very fast, went through a couple of fences and stopped with a jerk. All—consisting of the Defence Platoon of Divisional Headquarters—nipped out and took cover under a low bank, on top of which was a post and rail fence. There was a lot of shooting about a mile away. They had arrived only about 600 yards from the preordained spot. After landing, the airborne troops moved off, reached two farms, outside of which they observed docile German prisoners standing in lines, and went to their headquarters at the Kipenliof farm. Throughout the action there was a lot of sniping from the eastern edge of the forest.

Sergeant J. H. Jenkins found the 24th, D-day morning for 'Varsity', fine and clear. He had an uneventful take-off and soon linked up with the main stream. What a stirring sight! Glider combinations as far as the eye could see, with an umbrella of fighter escorts that put heart into all of them.

They eventually crossed the Rhine at Rees, as planned, and then their troubles started. Monty, in giving effective cover for his ground assault, had laid smoke screens, which with some thin low cloud, completely obscured the ground below. They were therefore in the hands of the tug crew, and prayed that the navigator's dead-reckoning would give the correct release point. Suddenly they saw the green aldis lamp flashing from the rear gunner's turret and, with a 'This is it, Skipper', the co-pilot pulled the release knob. The airspeed dropped and, selecting a quick trim, Jenkins took a hurried look at the starboard wing tip, noticed it was pointing at a slightly darker patch in the cloud, and turned sharply until they were heading for it.

They glided down, completely isolated, and only their compass-reading told them they were heading in the right direction. Then the fireworks started—a series of ominous thumps from all around, and a swishing sound nearby as another glider plunged earthward, with pieces falling from its burning fuselage. The altimeter was reading a fraction under 2,000 feet and still they could not see the ground. The co-pilot stuck his head through to the rear and called for safety belts to be fastened. It was then Jenkins decided to take a chance. He would do a blind box-turn on wing tip and compass and lose 200 feet on each of the east, north and west legs. He would then turn south again, on the original heading and pray that they had not drifted too far off track. He followed this plan, and at 1,300 feet they were on their 180° 'reading' once more.

The co-pilot, by this time, had discarded his safety belt and was coolly standing up in the cockpit, peering down into the murk. Suddenly he let forth a great shout—'Church spire ahead, ten degrees starboard Skipper!' Thank God for the R.A.F., and the co-pilot in particular. Jenkins looked across and for the first time saw a miracle—the smoke and cloud was still a blanket, but just about half a mile ahead, or so it seemed, there was a small circular opening, about the size of a dinner plate, and up through this hole that beautiful church spire was pointing triumphantly to the heavens. They altered course slightly, turned over the spire at 600 feet, put on full flap and went in.

The ground suddenly appeared a few hundred feet below, the stones in the cemetery standing out stark and white! Down and down they went, air speed now down to seventy-five and, leaving a chunk of their starboard wingtip up a tree, rumbled into a soft ploughed field. They finally came to rest about 100 yards from their planned touchdown. In seconds the passengers were scrambling out, two being sniped as they did so. The co-pilot and Jenkins followed suit—after automatically

A glider snagged in a tree after the Rhine crossing

Troops of the 1st Allied Airborne Army leaving the glider in which they landed

setting the flaps to neutral—and hastily set up the Bren in one of the deep furrows alongside. As they lay there with tracers shooting overhead, the co-pilot casually remarked: 'Comforting thought that most of the "muck" is a foot above the tracer, don't you think!'

After things had quietened down sufficiently to unload they remembered the Thermos of tea. Jenkins made a dash for this and on returning to the lea of the farmhouse wall unscrewed the cap, to find to their great mortification that a bullet had gone clean through the bottom and the contents had saturated the outer covering. 'Oh well, it was probably cold anyway!' said 'Andy' Anderson, his co-pilot.

Some gliders landed within 200 yards and others within fifty yards of their objective. This nearness was despite an artificial haze that was caused by the bombardment and bombing of Wesel which, in places, reduced the visibility to less than 220 yards. Some landings were more, and others less, eventful. The gliders carrying the coup-de-main parties of the Royal Ulster Rifles and those carrying the Oxfordshire and Buckinghamshire Light Infantry were particularly successful. The former delivered a party in six gliders which landed with pinpoint accuracy at their objective, on both sides of a bridge over the Issel. The latter landed on the west side only of a second bridge. This bridge was speedily captured, but subsequently it had to be blown up, at night, to stop a German counter-attack headed by a Tiger tank.

Despite the careful planning and execution of the operation, unforeseen circumstances were inevitable and important; they were mostly in favour of the Allies. It happened that many men of the 513th Parachute Regiment were dropped by mistake on the divisional landing zone before the gliders arrived. They did not waste a moment in checking their whereabouts but went immediately, and with utmost resolution, into action against a bewildered and fiercely resisting enemy. The paratroopers took a lot of casualties, but by the time the British gliders started swooping in the field was safe.

The haze, smoke, and dust over the combat area had not only reduced visibility but also partly shielded incoming gliders. Although many gliders were released as much as 1,000 feet higher than was planned, ninety per cent of them landed on or near their zones— many within 100 yards of their objective. Six missed the landing area by more than a mile, but came down in territory held by American airborne troops. About ten of the 416 gliders carrying British units were shot down, and 284 were damaged by flak, partly because they were released too high. Ground resistance was vigorous and effective, and only eighty-eight gliders came through completely unscathed. Fires completely destroyed thirty-seven that had landed.

The glider contingent would have had an even harder time had it not been for the presence of British paratroops on DZs A and B, and of American paratroops dropped by mistake on the landing zones near Hamminkeln. Thus, the operations were not a good precedent for glider landings on zones not previously occupied by paratroops. Nevertheless, the gliders did bring in 3,383 troops, 271 jeeps, 275 trailers, 66 guns, and a wealth of other equipment, including trucks and bulldozers.

By nightfall of D-day all organized German resistance in the British sector, from the western edge of the wood to the Issel, had been broken. The airborne invaders had become united with the forces moving up from the Rhine, six bridges across the River Issel had been seized intact, and more than 600 prisoners taken.

The 17th Airborne Division, which had been thrown into the lines in the Battle of the Bulge, had only recently been withdrawn from the lines and was in a rear area training and re-equipping. As soon as it was assigned to the 'Varsity' assault, the training, which had heretofore been exclusively of a ground nature, was altered to include airborne training. The 194th Glider Loading and Infantry Regiment of the division initiated lashing instruction. It received enough gliders to lift one rifle company at a time. Companies conducted exercises involving tactical glider landings with emphasis on rapid orientation, assembly, and combat firing on ground similar to the Wesel area.

Other pre-operational activities came into being. The Regimental S-2 set up a war tent and fitted it with necessary sand tables, map boards, and lighting equipment. Stringent security measures governed the operation of this installation.

The regimental commander instituted pertinent administrative measures with emphasis on a series of show-down inspections, ordnance repairs and vehicle maintenance.

Shortly the regiment got its allocation of 345 gliders for the air movement, forty-one less than it needed. The regimental G-3 subdivided the allotted CG-4As among the units of the regiment and prepared loading plans. In view of the fact that a total of 386 CG-4A gliders was required to fly a glider regiment, only fifty per cent of the 1/4 ton trucks and trailers of the regiment were included in the air echelon.

The land tail and base echelon of the regiment were prescribed and organized in accordance with instructions from Division.

The wing glider officer, 53rd Troop Carrier Wing, to which the 435th, 436th, 437th and 439th Groups were assigned and the senior glider officer of each of these groups, visited the regimental war tent, where they met the leaders of the glider units they were to fly into Wesel, and then the S-3 briefed them on their respective ground missions. It later transpired that these officers had not been previously briefed on the impending operation by their own air force commands. This occasioned some misunderstandings between the regiment and 53rd Troop Carrier Wing. Liaison was also established with the three assigned regimental departure fields near Paris.

Liaison likewise was made with the 1st Airborne Brigade of the British 6th Airborne Division, and most pleasantly so. The Commando Brigadier visited the 194th Regiment at Chalons. The time and place and way the two units were to conduct their efforts at Wesel became a matter of discussion. Because it was considered likely that the initial contact would be made at night, a ready means of mutual identification was deemed essential. It was felt that the traditional beret of the Commandos would afford a most suitable silhouette; and in order that the Commandos should have some similar means of identifying the airborne troops during hours of darkness, it was decided that the latter should attach their parachute first aid kits to the front of their helmet nettings, thus providing a distinctive outline.

The marshalling areas, occupied by the three battalions of the regiment controlling the fields, were located one on each airfield. In general, the marshalling areas were most satisfactory; each consisted of a pyramidal tent camp enclosed by wire. Strict security measures prevailed relative to the regiment's camps, despite the fact that the more relaxed air units themselves had not, as yet, adopted their additional operational security measures. Briefing of the platoon leaders and enlisted personnel commenced immediately upon arrival. So complete and intense was the preparation that each gliderman was given thorough instruction on every phase of the operation, from the overall theatre picture down, including his own individual assignments.

The loading of gliders commenced at 0600 on D-1 but as had been so frequently the case before, problems developed with the glider pilots. Glidermen were responsible for the proper loading and lashing of equipment in the gliders. At the same time the glider pilot was responsible for seeing that the load in his glider was a flyable load. Thus, in order to avoid any discrepancies, arrangements had been made with the Air Force units for their glider pilots to be present at their respective gliders during the loading phase. As it developed, however, very few pilots were present. This was occasioned by the fact that it was not until 1300 on D-plus-1 that the pilots were briefed that an actual operation was on. Until then the pilots had believed that the presence of the airborne on the field was in the nature of a 'dry run'.

By 1300 on D-plus-1, the airfields' military police cordoned off the fields and the pilots were briefed. Glider infantry battalion commanders attended the briefing. Immediately following this, the glider pilots marched to the airborne marshalling area where they received a five-hour briefing on their ground missions. Upon completion of this instruction, and realizing that the operation was not a 'dry run', the glider pilots immediately proceeded to the runways, located their gliders and now seriously checked their loads. This resulted in a considerable amount of confusion and readjustment of loads, which adherence to the original plan would have averted.

The loading was finally co-ordinated properly by mid-afternoon, and commencing at 1800 on D-plus-1 crews 'stacked' gliders and tug aircraft on the runways in parade-like take-off formation.

At 0730 the next morning after a hearty breakfast, and the usual policing of the tent area to leave it neat and clean—for whom, none knew—the 194th climbed into gliders and the leading gliders took off in double tow.

Only a few minutes after the lift of the American airborne units had begun, a pathfinder plane took off from Chartres. Within ten minutes the first planes swept over Chartres in serial formation and headed for the assembly point at Wavre. Having taken off from the other fields around Paris, six additional serials took up their positions behind the leader. Not one of the C-47s in the formations failed to take off or had to turn back.

The first four paratroop flights, made up of 181 C-47s, carried to DZW 2,479 troops of the 507th Parachute Infantry Regiment and the 464th Parachute Field Artillery Battalion. This drop zone was located on the south side of Diersfordter Wald and two and a half miles north-west of Wesel. When the aircraft arrived, DZW lay under a pall of smoke. The fliers caught glimpses of the Rhine, but the ground beyond the river was invisible except through an occasional rift in the smoke. Ground fire was slight; and although twenty-nine planes were hit, not one was shot down. Most of the planes of the first serial, however, lost their way. They dropped 693 men at about 0950. Although these troops landed about two miles north-west of the drop zone, they rejoined the rest of their battalion within an hour. The second and third serials placed their paratroops squarely in the drop zone. The fourth serial reached the zone about 1005 and dropped the 464th Parachute Field Artillery Battalion accurately, but in a somewhat dispersed pattern. By 1300, however, the artillerymen had nine of their twelve howitzers in position and firing.

Within three and a half hours the 507th Parachute Infantry had taken all its assigned objectives; at 1300 it made contact with advanced elements of the 15th Division. By 1803 the United States paratroops joined forces with the British airborne troops on the northern border of their sector, and at 0200 on the 25th a patrol to the southeast reached the British troops in the Wesel area.

The last three of the seven serials carrying American paratroops lifted the 513th Parachute Infantry and the 466th Parachute Field Artillery Battalion to drop them on DZW. This drop zone was on the east side of the Diersfordter Wald, about one and a quarter miles east-north-east of DZW. The whole air echelon, which comprised 2,071 men and sixty-four tons of supplies, was flown from Achiet in seventy-two C-46s. The pilots completely missed their assigned crossing point over the Rhine, partly because of poor visibility and partly because of their lack of experience in flying their new planes in large formations. As a result, they deposited their paratroops between one and a half and two miles north of DZW, in the British sector, south-west of Hamminkeln.

At 1008 as the first aircraft began to drop its troops, the serial was raked by intense and accurate flak and small-arms fire. This fire continued from positions along the Issel while the C-46s were making their right turn after the drop, and some shooting followed them until they got back to the Rhine. The C-46s caught fire easily, so that the German guns destroyed nineteen planes and damaged another thirty-eight of them.

Upon landing, the 513th Parachute Infantry attacked the enemy in the vicinity of DZW. By 1230 a nucleus of the regiment had formed, and had begun to move toward its pre-planned position in the drop zone. By 1530 most of the regiment had reached the proper area.

Among more than 1,000 planes in the armada, 610 C-47s were towing 906 Wacos. Gliders of the 680th and 681st Glider Artillery Battalions and the 155th Anti-aircraft Battalion followed close on the tails of the last of the gliders transporting the 194th Infantry. All headed towards LZS, about two miles north-west of Wesel. In all but the last fifteen minutes in the air all was uneventful. Much of the flight was over France, and ground held by the Allies. Intelligence had done its work well, and wherever Germans dared challenge the armada, fighters and bombers took them over. U.S. and R.A.F. endeavours became increasingly evident as the gliders approached Wesel. Plumes of dust rose high as bombs hit enemy guns.

Howard Cowan of the Associated Press recounted, in his article 'The Approach to Wesel':

> The wings of the glider vibrated violently—almost shook you out of your seat, and you knew something was wrong when the pilot began manoeuvring desperately to break up a 'tail flutter', a malady that shakes these things to pieces in a matter of seconds. And you closed your eyes and clenched your teeth and prayed.
>
> Then, without an instant's warning, your seat dropped from under you. Your helmet flew off and you were on your knees on the floor. That's just the way a glider rides. The man next to you wasn't wearing a helmet and blood is streaming down his ashen face. He's a casualty even before we've been landed—his head bashed against the metal framework.
>
> For three agonizing hours it went on this way. You'd watched the Seine and Maas Rivers slide past and knew the next big stream would be the Rhine. Before you were ready, it was below snaking across the shell-pocked plain.
>
> Things began happening fast—too fast. Above the sustained roar of wind ripping past cloth-covered ribs of the glider, you began to hear crack! pop! snap!...
>
> You shook hands, wished each other luck, and glued your eyes on the pilot, waiting for him to push the lever which would cut the glider loose from the tow-plane.

The haze thickened, from shells fired into the landing area by Dempsey's artillery trying to silence enemy ground fire; added to this, smoke from smoke-generators protecting the Army's river crossing operation crept over the landing zone. The crescendo of anti-aircraft fire seeking the glider increased mile by mile from the Rhine on. Glidermen now saw black mushroom clouds rising above the man-made haze as planes, mortally wounded, hit the earth and burned angrily in their death throes. Flying in at 600 feet altitude, planes and gliders were too low to get essential landing visibility. The O.K. for planes to climb came in time to get gliders to 1,000 feet, and then at 1,036, the lead glider cut away from his tow-plane.

As Cowan's glider was about to release:

Bursts of rifle fire were accompanied now by the popping of machine guns and a guttural whoomph of 88-mm shells. You unconsciously lift off your seat and brace as if to meet hot metal singing through the smoke. You find yourself dodging and weaving from something you can't even see.

Then the pilot's hand goes up and forward.

'Going down!' he shouts, and the nose pitches forward steeply. The speed slackens and the roar of the wind dies down and the battle noises suddenly are magnified into a terrifying din.

'Now,' says the Sergeant, 'is when you pray.'

The right wing tilts sharply as the shadow of another glider flits past. It almost hits us.

Smoke is thick and acrid—almost like being inside a burning house. You can see half a dozen buildings aflame on the ground. Dozens of gliders are parked at crazy angles on every field. Everyone with a weapon has it cocked and across his lap.

Then, before you know it, the ground is racing underneath. You are in a pasture, crashing through a fence, bounding across a gully, clipping a tree with a wingtip. You've made it—landed and nobody hurt.

You relax for a moment, but realize a split second later that that was a mistake. Bullets are ripping through the glider.

'Get outta here! Get outta here!' someone shouts, and prayers give way to curses as first one and then another kicks savagely at the door.

Men spill onto the grass haphazardly and begin crawling toward a ditch just beyond a barbed-wire fence. You're getting shot at from a house at the other end of the meadow.

Hot lead whines overhead. Bullets uproot little cupfuls of moist green turf around you until you are digging your toes in and clawing the earth with your fingers to move forward. Your pack snags on the bottom strand of the barbed-wire fence and it seems hours before you're free.

You roll into the shallow ditch. A foot of red, slimy water makes no difference. It actually feels good trickling down the open throat of your woollen shirt and filtering into the toes of your boots, and you're tempted to drink it, for your mouth is parched.

Everyone is out of the glider. You check up and find that two men are hit—both medics. One has a bullet through the top of the head—it went in and out through the top of his helmet—but he's still conscious. The other was shot through the calf of the leg.

You're fairly safe for the time being unless another glider swooping in

A Hamilcar glider, emptied of its cargo

Hamminkeln railway station on D-Day plus one. A glider has landed across the track

lands on you. It shears off the top of a nearby tree and makes a neat landing 100 yards down the field.

The firing slackens as minutes tick by and more gliders come in. Soon you muster enough courage to crawl out of the water—it's getting cold and uncomfortable by now—and take a cautious look around.

You find the area cleared and shooting over, at least in this pasture.

Someone gets a jeep to take the wounded to an aid station, and the rest of the party strikes out for the regimental command post.

Now that the enemy fire was becoming so intense, glider after glider began releasing a mile short of the set release point. The air above became dense and eerie with their shrieking dives. Pilots desperately searched for their correct fields, and went in fast. Where a pilot could not find his landing area, he frantically sought for an open space somewhere. Landing areas were now crowding up with gliders piling in, with those that had landed, and with those that had been torn to shreds. Pilots unable to find their right fields, or even their proper zone, had now dexterously to come in without slicing an incoming glider or a parked one. Gliders began colliding in the air. Despite the circumstances, pilots bravely did what they could to bring their cargo to the battle intact.

The flight up to the last few minutes for Flight Officer Olin P. Vossler of the 98th Squadron of the 440th Group was like a training flight. Just before he released he could hear the crack of what he later thought must be an 88, then a lot of machine-gun fire. Seconds after release he heard bullets ripping the floor, and hitting the frame. Suddenly his glider shuddered and 'stopped' in mid air from a direct hit. It raced madly towards the field where, to his dismay, he saw five Horsas and some CG 4s on the ground ahead and telephone poles and lines crossing his path. He hit two different poles, knocked them over, and became tangled in telephone lines that must have helped to stop him.

He yelled to the 'doughs' inside to 'run like hell!' and get down flat as far from the glider as possible; 'it's liable to explode!'. He and his co-pilot ran to a foxhole nearby. When the firing let up he sneaked close to the glider, to find a one-and-a-half-foot hole through the right wing, and holes in the nose and tyres. He found his squadron glider captain and they crawled into a foxhole for the night. 88s began pounding the gliders in the various landing fields. Glider pilots saw many paratroopers hanging from the trees, lifeless in their harnesses.

Lieutenant Clarence J. Benkoski, pilot, and Jacob Zichterman, co-pilot, got the green light and cut off. A glider two positions ahead had a wing shot off and went straight down into the trees, ablaze.

The gliders and tow-ships were catching intense flak and small arms fire, so Benkoski steepened the bank to get away. Then their tow-ship received a burst in the left wing-tip, and immediately thereafter their glider drew a 20-mm burst directly behind Zichterman's seat, that tore through the jeep's front right fender and on through the top of the glider. At the same time they were hit by small-arms fire. Zichterman saw a triangular field and suggested that they land there.

They were hit about two-thirds of the way down, hit anti-glider posts in landing, and approached an irrigation ditch. Benkoski pulled back on the stick and got enough lift to receive only a slight bump; he continued through another fence to stop ten feet beyond. They got out of the glider and lay low for about two minutes. The jeep driver got into the vehicle, and they all lifted the nose while he drove it out; the mechanism attached to the jeep, for lifting it, was fouled.

They made their way to the assembly-point, where prisoners were being marched in by droves and guarded in the woods. They then proceeded to their assigned road blocks. Zichterman picked a spot about seventy-five feet from the crossroads in the north-east quadrant, and dug in between the 57-mm anti-tank gun and a machine gun.

All hell broke loose after dark. At 2355 they were attacked by a tank firing a machine gun and an 88 gun, two 20-mm 'flak wagons' and an estimated seventy-five men with automatic weapons and two mortars. Bazookas drove the tank back, causing it to back over one 20-mm wagon. A 57-mm close by fired one shot but couldn't get the tank in its sights.

The tracers set fire to a glider behind them and to a house to the left. This lighted up the area and Zichterman could distinguish German forms on the corner, and dodging around the house on the south-west corner of the crossroads. He fired his carbine at them at minute intervals, a few rounds each time, but didn't see any direct effect.

Two Germans voluntarily came through a defensive road-block to one of the glider pilots. He started to take them prisoner. The glider infantry sergeant who was in charge of the defensive positions told the pilot they were not taking prisoners. The pilot sent them down the road and shot them with his 45.

Later at about 0300 two more Germans came up to surrender. He tried to get them to halt. They didn't. He killed them with a machine gun.

When morning came and they came out of their holes, there were thirteen dead Germans and about sixteen injured were routed out of a house. Zichterman helped round up prisoners and searched a few houses.

They were told they were going back to the Rhine. They crossed the Rhine on a 'Limey' truck ferried on a barge, and slept on the western bank. The next morning they rode to the British reception post aboard a duck, took a truck to Helmond and from there a plane to England.

Benkoski felt that the glider pilots had been left in 'a hell of a situation', to have to go on a mission that promised tough fighting without adequate weapons—merely the light arms issued to a glider pilot. He considered that he should have had a light machine gun, a bazooka, a Browning automatic rifle, grenades and some sub-machine guns. His after-action report closed with, 'Let's get some of these weapons in the squadron, plus two 57-mms that fire from the shoulder.'

Despite all, and because of better discipline and greater experience, plus their fortitude, glider pilots did a magnificent job. A high per-centage came in right on target. By 1140 the last of the 572 gliders in the first glider serials was on its way towards the ground. They had delivered 3,492 men, 202 jeeps, 94 trailers, and munitions and artillery. The Germans hit 140 of some 295 planes towing gliders, and twelve C-47s crashed in and around the glider landing zone. Eighty-three gliders had landed outside the designated landing area.

CHAPTER XVIII

The German Effort Continues

By 1941 German ground commanders at the extremities of the many extended, far-away lines of communication were critically in need of supplies and equipment. The Wermacht was advancing deep into Russia. Field Marshal Erwin Rommel had landed his Afrika Korps in Africa, and German forces there, with their mounting successes, were being given the strongest logistical support Germany could furnish. One way of surmounting the problem of long, guerilla-interdicted supply lines (consuming days of shipment time in Russia) was to use air supply. Again, with the British Navy in control of the Mediterranean, the most practical way to supply Rommel and sustain his drive towards Alexandria was by air. Aeroplanes played a major role in delivering supplies, but gliders began to assume more and more importance as time went on.

They also played an important role in Russia, where many of the German forces were surrounded. The only practical means to get adequate supplies to these pockets that had no airfield, and no make-shift landing strips that would support power aircraft, was by glider. In North Africa a similar condition developed, especially after German fortunes began to turn sour and Montgomery stitched Rommel's lines to the coast, capturing most of the usable airfields inland. It was at this juncture of the campaign that gliders, especially the Go 242, came into their own.

To make the glider operations and training more effective, the Germans discarded their policy of creating a special task force for each operation, and began to organize glider transport units. This was done for the Go 242 probably early in 1941, and undoubtedly was accomplished about the same time with ME 321.

After the creation of these glider organizations, the gliders began to be used in diversified ways. For example, a limited number of Go 242s were fitted out as maintenance and repair shops. Thus equipped, they were towed to the front where and when needed. Landed, there, they were used for the maintenance and repair of fighter aircraft. In certain instances they supported the panzer unit maintenance facilities.

The overall command of the glider activities resided in the 11th Flying Corps. Here research and development were co-ordinated. The 11th Flying Corps controlled the organizations structuring the glider fleets, and the headquarters of the Flying Corps provided the gliders and pilots, among them those who went to the aid of encircled German forces and area targets such as Kholm, Welikije Luki, and Tarnopol.

From 21st January 1942 Kholm was completely encircled by Soviet forces. The stronghold was defended by a force of about 3,500 men from various units and several arms and services, under the command of General-major Theodor Scherer. This force had tenaciously and successfully defended its position against all Soviet attacks.

The battle area of Kholm was so limited that transport aircraft could not land. Unfortunately, the only airfield in the pocket was situated in the immediate vicinity of the main line of resistance. There, it was constantly exposed to direct fire by all enemy weapons. At the end of February 1942 an attempt was made to land on this field. This operation, ordered by the First Air Fleet Commander against the advice of the Chief of Air Transportation, resulted in the loss of five out of seven Ju 52 transports, and of a part of the aircrews participating in the effort; therefore the Luftwaffe mounted no further ventures of this sort. All German commanders agreed that supplies could only be brought into, and landed on, the Kholm area by glider and parachute.

At the rate of one ton of payload each, the DFS 230s initiated the support operation. Later, the larger Go 242, towed by He 111s of the Fifth Special Purpose Bomber Group, was used for carrying very heavy items of equipment. The load of each Go 242 was about two and a half tons. During the first stages of the operation, nine landed on the airfield. Very often both gliders and cargo were lost through enemy anti-aircraft fire. Even when they landed without mishap, there was no way of taking off again, and the crews remained in the pocket to participate in the defence. As the German-held pocket was reduced, only dauntless DFS 230s were able to make landings, finally landing on one street of the village. Eventually, even this grew to be impossible, when Soviet forces further reduced the perimeter.

Early in 1942, Kesselring met Hitler and Mussolini at Berchtesgaden to map out Axis operations for the Mediterranean area for 1942. At this meeting Kesselring suggested a combined airborne and seaborne invasion of Malta, which Hitler accepted. The next day General Student was called in and directed to plan and carry out the airborne phase of this operation. During April and May 1942, Student drew up his plan and conducted manoeuvres with both German and Italian airborne units in preparation for the operation. Student was to have under his command five German Parachute Regiments, approximating twenty to twenty-two thousand men, and the Italian Parachute Folgore, approximating 3,000 troops. (Student rated the Italian parachute units as usually mediocre; but the Division Folgore as elite troops.) In addition to these parachute units, eight Italian divisions were to participate, including armoured units comprising about 150 tanks and 800 specially trained engineer troops for duty at the beachhead. Included in the parachute units were two German and one Italian engineer battalion, and it was Student's plan to utilize these troops to prepare landing areas for air-landing forces after the initial assault. Five hundred gliders were marshalled for the operation.

After about two months of planning, training, and making necessary preparations (the actual invasion was set for late in August) Student was called to report at the end of June 1942; but to his great surprise Hitler, at this meeting, cancelled the entire operation. Student stated that he believed that the assault on Crete, and the German losses there, played a small part in changing the Fuehrer's mind, but he primarily attributed the cancellation to Hitler's lack of faith in the Italian forces participating. Student believed this lack of faith came as a result of continuing reports by Rommel of Italian deficiencies, and more directly to a personal report made to Hitler the previous day by the panzer commander of the German forces in Africa. While the taking of Malta was vital to the success of overall German operations in the Mediterranean, sufficient troops were not available to undertake the operation, and Hitler preferred to cancel it rather than to risk heavy losses should the Italians crack. This was a great disappointment to Student, who firmly believed that the attack would have succeeded. He was banking on this to demonstrate the effectiveness of the airborne idea and to vindicate the questionable results of the airborne operation against Crete.

In October 1942 Hitler suddenly reversed his policy of rejecting airborne operations, and ordered Student to employ his forces to rupture the coastal road at Alder, halfway between Taupse and Sukhuni, thus interrupted the flow of Russian reinforcements and supplies coming from Georgia. The German forces, having accomplished this, were to move south-east down the coastal road and capture Batum, an oil pipeline terminal port on the Black Sea. This plan entailed the employment of some 16,000 parachute troops of *Fliegerdivision* 7, about 400 transport aircraft and 250 gliders. Take-off bases were selected in the Crimea. At this time *Fliegerdivision* 7 was in Normandy, and was sped to the Crimea by rail. The troops were fully prepared, and the necessary aircraft and gliders were being assembled, when the Russian Caucasian Army started moving so rapidly that the operation had to be cancelled. The parachute troops already assembled were withdrawn to the vicinity of Vitebsk and put into the German line as ground forces. It was Student's opinion that if he had had a few more days the operation could have been undertaken with some chance of success.

In September 1942 Student prepared a plan to use parachute forces in an attempt to effect the capture of Stalingrad. His plan entailed dropping strong forces just to the east of the River Volga to block Russian reserves moving into the city, and also to attack the defenders from the rear. This plan never was any more than an idea; it was immediately rejected by Hitler as being hopeless.

Earlier, at the beginning of 1941, Student was ordered to study the possibilities of taking Gibraltar by means of an airborne assault. After some review a negative report was submitted, declaring that the capture of Gibraltar from the air was not possible. Due to the characteristics of the fortress there were only two possible places where a landing could be made; one an aerodrome just north of the Rock, and the other a small parade ground; however, both of these areas were overlooked by the fortifications, and any forces attempting such a landing would have been decimated before they could attack. The only other possibility would be to bring ground forces through Spain but 'in respect to the neutrality of Spain' nothing further was done to launch an assault on Gibraltar.

For the administration and inspection of all heavy air transport units on the Russian front, a special staff called the *Grossraumtransportfleigerfuhrer* was created at Warsaw during November. Glider units were then shifted to Warsaw, where they were administered operationally by this staff until February the next year. In the central sector, the Russian attack rolled forward from its former base at Dniepropetrovsk, and moved north-west to Zhitomir. The GO 242 gliders of the unit were employed in carrying supplies to the forward areas and evacuating wounded on return flights; meanwhile at Brobriusk, the glider units were doing similar sorties in the Gomel salient. More than half of the eastern front's strength had been concentrated in the Dneiper bend in December. Aircraft serviceability was declining as winter set in, and the unit found itself pinned down by air superiority along the entire length of the eastern front. Transport units had been flying transport and evacuation sorties steadily for six months, but with the launching of the Russian winter offensive in mid December, all possibility of withdrawing any *transportfliegergruppen* for rest or re-equipping vanished.

The Germans employed gliders on the largest scale in the air supply mission and air movement of troops. Gliders were also part of the tactical air arm. Three gliders, for carrying technical supplies, maintenance personnel or ammunition, were assigned to each *Stuka Gruppe*. The gliders were towed with the wing on each change of base. Workshop installations in some gliders were successfully employed. Other gliders delivered saboteurs and SS men behind enemy lines. But the supply of air units and ground units, and the air movement of personnel were their principal missions.

Gliders were allocated as workshop aircraft and used in conjunction with flying workshop platoons. The GO 242 and ME 321 was most adaptable for this purpose. Units were assigned from one to three gliders for the transport of equipment of the technical or headquarters staffs, or as mobile workshops. 'Every *Stuka Gruppe* had three DFS 230 gliders as organic equipment to increase mobility and to assist in transporting equipment during frequent moves.'

The first large scale employment of military air transport for tactical evacuation was during the German retreat from Kuban in Russia, in 1943. Every aircraft and glider which could be made serviceable was used to rescue some 82,000 isolated troops, and much of their equipment, over a five-week period. At the peak, 6,000 to 7,000 soldiers a day were flown to safety. In the Crimea, initially, gliders flew in reinforcements but at the end, in 1944, the operation changed to evacuation. Ju 52s with floats were used in the Crimea, where flights were over much greater distances than in Kuban. Evacuation of key personnel from other pockets became a frequent mission as the eastern front contracted. The total number of troops evacuated was over half a million in the last two years of the war. Additionally, 50,000 tons of weapons and materials were salvaged by air. Only in Africa was tactical evacuation insignificant. From Libya and Tunisia wounded were evacuated by air whenever possible. Large forces, in total, were evacuated from Sardinia, Corsica, Rhodes and Crete, and from Greece and the Balkans in late 1943 and through 1944. DFS and Go 42 gliders were extensively used in these evacuations.

CHAPTER XIX

Mussolini's Rescue—and Other Episodes

Tales of escape and rescue—dramatic, romantic, sometimes fantastic—are to be found in the history of every epoch of every people; but my escape from the Gran Sasso appears even today as the boldest, most romantic, of all, and the same time the most modern in method and style.

Benito Mussolini, *Storia di un Anno*

On 12th September 1943, Hitler called Major Otto Skorzeny, a brawny paratrooper, to Berlin. He had decided that the future welfare of Germany to an extent involved the rescue of Mussolini, now hidden away by his captors for some months. He felt that Mussolini had been betrayed by the King of Italy with the assistance of the King's friend Marshal Badoglio. As related in *Commando Extraordinary*, by Charles Foley, Hitler said to Skorzeny, 'I cannot and will not leave Mussolini to his fate, . . . He has got to be rescued before these traitors can surrender him to the enemy.'

He then turned to Skorzeny and in quietly spoken words told him, 'You, Skorzeny, are going to save my friend. . . . You will avoid no risk. . . . You will succeed and your success will have a tremendous effect on the course of the war. This is a mission to which you will be answerable to me personally!'

With a double handclasp, Hitler sent him off. For the next seven weeks German Intelligence gave Skorzeny every assistance it could to find Mussolini's whereabouts.

For Hitler, the rescue of Mussolini promised a revival of Fascist military energy, a second wind for his deflated prestige, and reassurance to all the other little Mussolinis of the satellite countries, whose loyalty to Nazi Germany might be flagging.

For the King and Badoglio the removal of Mussolini meant the final collapse of the Fascist power, and possession of his person was a trump card in their deal with the Allies. Mussolini's guards had strict orders not to let him get away alive.

Ultimately the Germans located Mussolini and his jailers in a newly built hotel on the Gran Sasso, near Aquila, in the Abruzzi mountains. The area was bristling with anti-aircraft guns, and defence cordons manned by *carabinieri*. The word was that 250 were billeted in the hotel. Their defences were impossible to take. The Italians had overlooked nothing; nothing, that is, except an individual's determination to get through.

There was only one possibility; if an orthodox German land assault was ruled out, only the sky was left. A parachute operation was not possible. The altitude ruled it out. The air was thin and paratroopers would be dashed to pieces. Moreover they had nowhere to land. But gliders!

Air photos showed a triangular patch by the hotel. Skorzeny thought that if it were really flat and smooth, gliders might land. Aggressive glidermen might reach Mussolini before his guards could bayonet him. Skorzeny figured he had three minutes in which to reach Mussolini after landing. The landing triangle was incredibly small, and never before had gliders come down in such a rarefied atmosphere. He estimated that of a hundred men in the attack force twenty might survive; a pitifully small number to attack a position defended by 250.

Skorzeny fought for a glider attack. He was given the green light.

The gliders took off, after an aeroplane pilot had made a reconnaissance over the area several days earlier with Skorzeny. Skorzeny's plan was that the first two gliders and their ten men would land and cover the landing of the third glider. A fourth glider was to follow into the landing area.

The first three glider combinations took off. The fourth and fifth ran into bomb holes and never took off but Skorzeny was unaware of the mishap. The combinations climbed to 12,000 feet, where they entered clouds. Emerging, Skorzeny found that the two leading gliders had vanished. One was being towed by the plane pilot who was to lead the gliders to the objective, so Skorzeny now had to lead the way.

Wedged in his seat, Skorzeny could not see where he was going. He drew his knife and hacked vents in the canvas sides. Through these he peered at the granite mountains below. The Gran Sasso gradually loomed ahead. Yes! there was the hotel on its dizzy perch on the triangular ledge. He signalled to release. His glider swooped gracefully down to the hotel, and to the pilot's disbelief Skorzeny pointed to the ledge. The sloping shelf seemed built more for a ski jump than for a glider landing field. It was studded with big boulders. The pilot gazed ahead in mesmerized disbelief that he had to land *there*! Skorzeny shouted 'Dive; crash, but land! As near to the hotel as you can.'

They got closer, the drag brake sucked out and billowed from the tail, and suddenly the glider, jolting and pitching over the boulders, stopped in a shuddering crash.

Skorzeny forced his way out. He and several others dashed up the escarpment into the hotel, and in an energetic search through the surprised garrison located Mussolini. Skorzeny entrusted the Fascist leader to his brawniest subaltern.

Soon several other gliders landed and glidermen rushed to Skorzeny's assistance. One glider crashed in smithereens. Within a short while a single engined Storch made it into the landing area. Skorzeny squeezed Mussolini behind the pilot and climbed in. Now twelve men clung to the tail of the Storch. It revved its engine. They dug in their heels until the engine was racing madly, and then released the Storch. The little plane manfully rammed the rocks in its way, slithering upward gradually, leaped a deep crevasse, and Mussolini was free.

THE CROSS-ATLANTIC TOW

The feasibility of towing gliders across the Atlantic was demonstrated in April 1943. Carrying vaccines destined for Russia, and aircraft, radio and engine parts, a CG-4A in tow behind a Dakota aeroplane made history in a twenty-eight-hour leap-frogging trip along a secret route across the blustery Atlantic. Actually the trip was conducted in easy stages, the twenty-eight hours being flying time only. Nevertheless, the flight was risky. Snow falls almost constantly along the Atlantic coast of Canada at that time of year. It was either the leap into the snowstorms or, as the co-pilot of the glider, Royal Canadian Air Force Squadron-Leader F. M. Gobiel said, 'otherwise we would have been sitting in Canada fishing until the end of the war. It was then!' Gobiel thought they were adequately prepared, however, since they had tried out some experimental day and night bad-weather flying with the glider before the Atlantic flight.

The worst part was the first leg from Canada. The pilot found he had to climb into a strong wind. This made for a plodding flight speed. After three hours they got to 9,000 feet, and ice began to form on the glider. The first leg took twice as long to fly as scheduled. The glider played 'funny tricks'. Contrary to Gobiel's hopes, the tow-rope never seemed to be 'in a gentle curve in front of your nose' as he had found in the experimental flying. 'One time you may be going to one side, then the other. Then you are going away up and you sit waiting for the jerk when the rope tightens up, and the next second, if the weather is very bad, you are dropping in a beastly swing from maybe 50 to 100 feet above the tug to 25 feet below it.'

Both pilots took turns at the controls, but for power pilots such as they were, it was a sobering experience to find that neither could really loosen up at the controls. There was no auto-pilot to take some of the strain. They had to be on the alert every minute, anticipating the tow-line, the turbulence, the up and down draughts. They had to scramble through the two-foot space left between the cargo and the roof of the glider to get food in the rear of the fuselage. Neither liked the experience. But what they found most frightening was the turbulence. Frequently it was so great they thought the glider was about to be torn to pieces. In one storm, some of the ballast tumbled violently in the glider, hitting the roof and then going 'down through the floor.' At other times the snow was so thick that the sergeant had to fly on instruments only, and as much of the tow-rope as he could see.

This route was the worst that could have been taken, although the shortest. Many gliders might well have been ferried, by the thousands of different aeroplanes crossing the Atlantic during the war over normal routes or via Africa, when the weather was more temperate. But this single flight was the only one ever made by glider across the Atlantic.

OPERATION VASSIEUX

One little-known German glider operation, erroneously recorded by most sources as exclusively a parachute operation, took place in the foothills of the Alps. The French *maquis* forces in the vicinity of Vercors sat astride the routes of withdrawal of the German 157th Division. This division was in Southern France anticipating the Allied airborne operation 'Dragoon' that was to come in August 1944.

On 21 July 1944 the Germans landed ten gliders at Vassieux, some more at Weilern, and others on other *maquis* communication centres, effectively removing the *maquis* threat.

THE ATTEMPT TO CAPTURE TITO

In February 1944 Winston Churchill stated in the House of Commons that the Yugoslav guerillas were containing a substantial amount of German military power. It has since been estimated that the Germans had to keep fourteen divisions in Yugoslavia, to control the country and maintain their lines of communication. This German commitment meant fewer divisions for the Allies to fight on other fronts.

The Yugoslav resistance was led by Tito and centred at his headquarters in Drvar. In an attempt to break the back of the resistance, the Germans decided to capture Tito.

Early in the spring they assembled ten gliders on an unprepared field in the Banta region north of Belgrade. From there they were towed to Kraljevo where with 100 selected men of the 500th S.S. Battalion they prepared for the operation. It was a bold undertaking and the glider pilots, not being the fanatics the S.S. men were, had no taste for the operation. Once landed, they were assured, a 100-

man S.S. unit, and another, the same size of mountain troops, were to march to their help. On the other hand, three partisan divisions were reported in the vicinity of Drvar. The odds were not good.

The night before the operation a severe thunderstorm hit the German assembly area, and while it did little damage, it was the start of a week of foggy unflyable weather that led to one postponement after another. After seven days the Germans called it off.

Several weeks later the Germans scheduled another operation to start from Agram. This time the force was larger; it was to use fifteen gliders, and to be a combined glider-parachute operation.

The fifteen gliders carried a reinforced company of the battalion and several mountain artillery guns. They became the leading serial in the stream of aeroplanes carrying parachutists. From the time the last gliders took off until the first landed was an hour, even though the overland distance between the take-off field and Drvar was not great. Assembling the formation in the air and climbing to altitude to get over the mountains lying between the two points took much of the hour.

The force landed at Drvar on 25 May 1944. They did not get Tito; the Russians had flown him out in a Dakota several weeks earlier.

TAKING THE RUSSIANS TO YUGOSLAVIA

Yugoslavia was the location of a very unorthodox special glider mission described by Ronald Seth in *Lion With The Blue Wings*[1]. Three Horsa gliders were said to be lying on one of the airstrips near Kairouan in Tunisia, and the squadron was instructed to bring them to Comiso, Italy.

In early spring 1944 an American troop-carrier squadron flew the glider pilots to Tunisia. Landing at dusk on the desolate, abandoned airstrip, the pilots found the Horsas lonely and dejected; the last remnants, except for the wrecks and the litter of rusty tin cans, of the masses of men and machines that had packed these North African airstrips, roads and olive-groves, when the 1st Airborne Division had set up here their Headquarters and base for the assault on Sicily.

The Horsas had been at the mercy of wind, rain and Arabs for six months, but there was no question of carrying out a proper inspection. Indeed, there was no one in the party qualified to do so. So the next morning the pilots climbed into the cockpits, tentatively tested the creaking controls, patted the woodwork for luck, and flew off on a 250-mile journey across the Mediterranean for Comiso.

There they loaded each glider with a jeep, and anything else that would make up 7,000 pounds weight. They tested the loading, since they had not been supplied with charts, by arranging the jeep and

[1] This entire section on the Yugoslav operation was taken from this source.

boxes in such a way that a man swinging on the tail could just lift the front wheels clear of the ground. If rough and ready, this simple method always proved satisfactory.

They flew on to Bari in Italy; a hazardous flight, with the tugs barely clearing the high hills, through heavy snow and a north-east gale, providing an experience that was extremely unpleasant. At Bari the reason for this activity became apparent. A strange (in the sense of curious) organization in Cairo had asked that a Soviet military mission, headed by Generals Korneyev and Gorskov, should be flown by glider to Marshal Tito's headquarters in Yugoslavia. The mission had already made one attempt by Dakota, but had been prevented from landing by a heavy fall of snow, which made gliders the only alternative method of infiltration. Code-named Operation 'Bunghole', the tugs were to be C-47s of the 64th Troop Carrier Group, U.S.A.A.F., the glider pilots British, and the gliders British Horsas, thus making it a really Allied effort.

On arrival at Bari, the American tug-pilots insisted that the Horsas could not be lifted over the Dinaric Alps. The flight to Italy had made this self-evident. So, after that, the Horsas were discarded—though they were to die honourably in a vineyard twenty miles north-west of Cannes, later—and were replaced by American Wacos. The squadron's training had been carried out on Wacos, so three were flown to Bari the next day, and loading up to 4,500 pounds test-flights were carried out. General Korneyev insisted that his officers should take part in these flights, in the positions they would occupy during the journey. Except for Staff Sergeant McCulloch's decision to execute a 360° turn over the town from about 300 feet on his landing-approach, the tests passed without incident.

The Russians wanted to be landed in German-occupied Yugoslavia, in a valley called Mendenapolu, the honey field, about two miles north of the little town of Bosan Petrovac midway between Zagreb and Sarajevo, in the eastern foothills of the Dinaric Alps, which hereabouts reach up to 8,000 feet. The landing-zone was 100 miles inland from the Dalmatian coast and 250 miles from Bari.

A diversion raid was to be made on Zagreb by the 15th U.S. Air Force, with fifty Fortresses which were to have a fighter-umbrella of a mixed force of Mustangs, Thunderbolts and Spitfires. The take-off was timed for 1100 hours, thus making 'Bunghole' the first daylight operation.

After two days of non-flying, wintry weather, the skies cleared, and the take-off went forward as planned. The C-47 tugs were under the command of Lieutenant Colonel Duden, U.S.A.A.F., with American pilots, and navigated by an Australian, a South African and a New Zealander, from their respective Air Forces.

The glider combinations rendezvoused with the escort fifty miles to the northward, off the coast, opposite the Eighth Army forward positions in Italy, and together they headed north-east across the Adriatic at 8,000 feet in a cloudless sky giving unlimited visibility. It was extremely cold, and though the far-flung escort of fighters were occasionally glimpsed wheeling and banking high overhead and far below, most of the time the gliders had the sensation of being alone and defenceless in the midday sun.

The forces made landfall dead on track over the island of Zirje. Snow blanketed the Yugoslav coast. The sharp outline of the towering range of the Dinaric Alps came into view while still fifty miles away. There was no sign of civilization in the tortuous foothills, ribbed and ridged with ravines, and patched with forest under the deep white carpet below.

The air became turbulent. The turbulence steadily increased during the next half-hour, until the flight rocked and swayed over the last saddle with 500 feet to spare, with peaks towering on either side. As the hinterland opened up, they knew that they were coming up to the target area. In a few minutes, after obtaining a 'fix' on a large river, the tugs turned about and the gliders cast off about four or five miles away from their objective. As they circled to land, thin wisps of smoke came up from straw fires below them, the first welcome indication that a correct pin-point had been made—welcome, because the tow-rope telephone-type inter-com on all the gliders had been unserviceable from take-off.

Within seconds, and a few yards from each other, the gliders touched down—perhaps flopped in the snow with a sickening jolt would be a better description—reared vertically on to their noses and settled slowly back. The 'landing run' was about twenty feet, and since they were about 4,000 feet above sea level, the ground was covered with soft snow about three feet deep. Thus the first three Allied aircraft landed in Yugoslavia since the German occupation.

After being forcibly embraced by almost unbelievably dirty and bearded Yugoslav partisans, they were hurried to a hut in the forest which lined the valley. The Russians were full of *bonhomie*, laughing and shaking hands with all within reach. The Generals had adopted avuncular poses, and even a Colonel, who had sat throughout the flight nursing a tommy-gun, grinned broadly for the first time.

After a quick meal, accompanied by suitable speeches in various languages that were all unintelligible to the Englishmen, who replied with equal unintelligibility, they set out for Petrovac in sleighs.

BUDAPEST

By the latter part of 1944 the Russians had surrounded Budapest. A German offensive from outside launched on 3rd January 1945, failed to break through to the German garrison in the city. The Germans began a massive air supply operation, primarily by parachute drop, since no landing fields in the area held by the Germans were safe from Russian mortar fire or anti-aircraft guns.

By the end of January, Budapest was a city in seige. Ring upon ring of Russian anti-aircraft guns and searchlights girded the city. Experienced German pilots claimed that of all the belligerents, the Russians had the deadliest anti-aircraft guns and those most feared by German pilots.

The parachute drops were not successful to the extent hoped. A continual pall of smoke and haze hung over the athletic field in the city, and other suitable drop areas close by. Parachute drift after release from the aircraft led to the loss of many containers to the enemy. Aircraft losses were severe.

In mid-January it became evident that parachute dropping of supplies was not the solution to the urgent supply problem facing the beleagured German garrison. A hurried call went out for glider pilots from the many disbanded air transport units. Some had to be plucked from front line combat to join the units into which they had been drafted. Within one week pilots were reporting to Weiner Neustadt and other air fields just south of Vienna. Gliders had to be retrieved from stores accumulated in distant depots when the air transport units disbanded. In a matter of days gliders had been loaded and secured to flat cars, and trains were on their way.

Glider sorties were sporadic, because of many problems. After the gliders began arriving, there were not enough pilots, nor enough technicians to assemble them and get them flight-ready. Frequently there were not enough flyable tow-planes available for glider tows; or fighter cover was not available. By 5th February the Germans managed an eleven-glider operation. Six made it to the release point over Budapest, four of them were shot down in the approach to land at the athletic field.

One of the more spectacular, and at the same time tragic, missions took place on 9th February. Ju 52s, DO 17s and He 111s towed forty-eight gliders towards Budapest. Before they could get to the release point twelve gliders had been shot down or had aborted because their tow-planes had crashed. Thirty-six gliders managed to reach the field and land successfully. However, by this time, the Russian guns had the range of the tow-craft and downed all but two of the remaining thirty-six. Thirteen men were killed, twenty-nine wounded, and ninety-six were missing from the mission.

Again on the 13th, twenty gliders took off to Budapest. None of the tow-planes returned, and the fate of the gliders was never determined by the command at Weiner Neustadt. The irony of these operations is that the glider pilots had little information about the severity of the enemy anti-aircraft fire they would encounter; information was purposely withheld so as not to lessen their determination to complete their mission.

MORESBY—MISSION ABORTED

At 0825 on 5th September 1943 the 503rd Parachute Infantry took off from Port Moresby, in eighty-four C-47 transport planes. An Australian parachute artillery regiment (25-pounders) reinforced the regiment. To assist a three-pronged Australian drive for the important Japanese-held port of Lae, the paratroopers were to seize an airstrip at Nadzab, some twenty miles inland. The air formations included 302 planes; A-20s laid smoke screens to hide the drop zones from enemy observers; B-25s bombed and strafed the landing area; B-17s, especially prepared for the purpose, carried in each bomb bay a 'basket' of twelve bundles of equipment, a parachute on each bundle; containing ammunition, heavy machine guns, and supplies, which would be dropped according to signals from the ground wherever needed. Squadrons of P-38 fighters flew cover above, and P-39s guarded the flanks; heavy bombers carried bomb loads to drop on enemy positions at the nearby Heath Plantation.

Three deaths and a number of fractures occurred in the jump, but the paratroopers found little resistance on the ground and they quickly organized a perimeter defence. An Australian pioneer battalion which had set out on foot six days earlier joined them, and work proceeded on the airstrip. The shuttling by air of the 7th Australian Division from Marilinen to Nadzab (an operation which required several weeks) began thirty-six hours later.

No gliders were used in the Nadzab operation. Eleven, loaded with Australian men and equipment, were waiting to take off at Port Moresby on 5th September when their mission was cancelled. Ostensibly the use of the gliders was cancelled because the outstanding success of the parachute drop made them unnecessary, but a contributing factor was the concern for the safety of the men they would carry. All the gliders were showing signs of deterioration. On the flight from Brisbane, where they were being assembled for the operation, one glider had lost its tail-assembly in mid air, and the crew had been killed in the resulting crash. Thirty-five pilots and thirty-five mechanics, the first glider contingent for the Southwest Pacific, had arrived in Australia in February 1943, and in April another twenty-six pilots and twenty-six mechanics had joined them. Their crated gliders—twenty-seven of them—arrived shortly afterwards. Actually none of these gliders was ever used in tactical operations. Some of the pilots and mechanics were later assigned to various other duties, among widely separated troop carrier units, and others were returned to the United States.

GLIDER RESCUE MISSION

On 13th May 1945, a C-47 flying on instruments struck a ridge in the Orange Mountains in Dutch New Guinea. Of the passengers, the three survivors included a Wave corporal, Margaret Hastings. Search planes located the wreck, but the area in the interior, called Hidden Valley, was inaccessible by trail. Men, followed by supplies, parachuted into the valley to prepare a strip suitable for glider landings, and recovery by snatch technique. Two medical corps men also parachuted in, and rendered aid to the survivors.

Glider crews on Wakde Island prepared for the rescue operation. On 28th June, the first glider landed successfully. They loaded the five passengers, including the survivors, and thirty minutes later were snatched. Then, in two subsequent sorties, the parachuted men were flown out by glider. Sentani airstrip, on Hollandia, served as the base of operations.

LUZON—THE ONE AND ONLY PACIFIC OPERATION

Promptly at 0600, on 23rd June 1945, a C-46 carrying paratroopers of the 11th Airborne Division took off from the Lipa airstrip on Luzon. Six CG-4As and one CG-13 glider brought up the rear of scores of aircraft that followed in a V of Vs on their way to Aparri in northern Luzon. Fighters hummed overhead. This was a first for gliders in the Pacific. Although hundreds were at airfields scattered through the Pacific islands, none had yet been tested in combat. The tactical objective of this mission was to hasten the collapse of organized enemy resistance in northern Luzon. The troops to be dropped were to expedite a junction with American and Philippine guerrillas to the south, to free the Cagayan Valley.

The parachute and glider landing zones were the same, an abandoned enemy airstrip five miles south of Aparri. They flew to the rendezvous point at Camalaniugan, 250 miles by direct route from Lipa, the staging base for the airborne troops. To avoid alerting the enemy, they approached the rendezvous point over the China Sea, adding 100 miles to the course. Glider tow-planes carried neither paratroopers nor cargo. The gliders carried a total of nineteen troops, six jeeps, one trailer, machine-guns, ammunition, radio and medical supplies.

At precisely 0900 the planes reached the drop zone, which pathfinders had marked with coloured smoke, contacted the guerrillas on the west bank of the Cagayan, and then slipped across the river at night. Fighter bombers laid down a smoke screen, blinding the hills to the south-east where the Japs supposedly had artillery which could reach the drop zone. Paratroopers and gliders 'unloaded' from the aeroplanes in a single pass over the field. Glider landings were equally

Men of the U.S. 11th Airborne Division landing near Appari, Cagayan Valley in Luzon

Appari, Cagayan Valley. A jeep and equipment is unloaded from a CG-13A glider

accurate, although the grass on the strip was denser than appeared from photo interpretation. A wing-tip collision between two CG-4As was the only imperfection in the glider phase.

Three days after the drop, the 511th made contact with the 37th Division, sealing off the Cagayan Valley. The captured strip was later used for supply landings, and to evacuate casualties.

FINAL ALLIED OPERATIONS IN BURMA

In April 1945, C.C.F.T. transports and gliders played an important part in the final stages of the campaign in Burma, getting airfields at Pyinmana, Toungoo, and Pegu into operation in time for quick support of the IV Corps advance. At Pegu the transports carried out a familiar role, delivering reinforcements that would enable the ground forces to hold and consolidate their gains. In preparation for these activities, a reserve of 86,000 gallons of gasoline was built up at Meiktila to permit the temporary operation of C-47s from that advanced base. Gliders loaded with bulldozers, runway lighting equipment, jeeps, tractors, scrapers, gasoline, radio equipment, food, and water were ferried into Meiktila, until fifty-five were on hand.

IV Corps by-passed Pyinmana and secured Lewe Airfield south of the city on 20th April. At 0850 the next morning eight C-47s of the 4th Combat Cargo Squadron, after delivering supplies to Meiktila, towed one glider each to Lewe. Each glider contained a tractor, a scraper, two bulldozers, a jeep and trailer, a power saw, gasoline, rations, water, and nineteen men. The first was released over Lewe at 0955, the last at 1015. Some of the gliders were damaged in landing—one beyond repair—but none of the equipment was lost. The machinery was put to work immediately, but the gasoline was left aboard the gliders until it should be needed. This was a mistake because Japanese fighters, making one of their last sweeps over Burma, came over Lewe on the morning of 22nd April and set the gasoline in five of the gliders on fire. This incident delayed work on the airfield for only a few minutes, however, and by noon the strip was 4,500 feet long. The first transports landed at 1600 that afternoon, only sixty-four hours after the ground forces had driven the Japanese away.

While Lewe Airfield was being repaired, a division overran Tennant and Kalaywa Airfields at Toungoo. A bulldozer that had accompanied the advancing column filled enough craters at Tennant to permit glider landings, but most of the equipment with the ground forces was put to work on Kalaywa. On 23rd April six C-47s of the 4th Combat Cargo Squadron, after delivering supplies, lifted six gliders loaded with construction equipment from Meiktila and released them over Tennant between 1015 and 1045. The Tennant Strip was in much better condition than the one at Lewe; a C-47 carrying much personnel and

A DFS 230 German glider with Vassieux in the background. In July 1944
Nazis burned every building in the town, wiping out men, women and
children

equipment landed at 1415, and a 6,000-foot runway was ready by 1600. Improvement of the field continued throughout the 23rd, and on 24th April 56 transports landed with supplies.

C.C.T.F. had one more task in the railroad corridor, though the Japanese evacuation of Rangoon, and its subsequent occupation by air and sea, had marked the success of the 14th Army's offensive. Ground forces reached the well-sited strip at Zayatkwin, thirty-two miles from Rangoon, on 4th May. Although Tennant Airfield was barely serviceable, C-47s of the 1st Combat Cargo Group and 117 Transport Squadron towed gliders from there to Zayatkwin on the morning of 5th May. Handicapped by weather as well as by craters in the runway, the engineers made slow progress. When Lewe Airfield became temporarily serviceable on 8th May, eight more equipment-loaded gliders were towed to Zayatkwin. Momentarily improved weather, and the added equipment, enabled engineers to open the strip to C-47s before nightfall on 8th May, and to C-46s on the 9th. Zayatkwin was the southernmost airfield opened in the IV Corps area during the drive on Rangoon.

CHAPTER XX

What Might Have Been

Whether airborne troops could maintain themselves in prolonged action from an airhead independent of connections with ground troops was a question never answered in the war. After the operation in Holland General Brereton felt that airborne troops should not operate without relief by ground troops for longer than three days. Early in 1945, however, he became anxious to prove the feasibility of an independent airhead, and pushed forward planning for such an operation.

He planned to land his forces by glider, parachute, and aeroplane onto a strategic airhead near Kassel, in Germany. The assault would be conducted in four phases. First, the 13th, 17th, 82nd, and 101st U.S. Airborne Divisions, and the 1st and the 6th British Airborne Divisions would go in by glider and parachute to seize airfields and airstrip sites, and to set up defences. He estimated that this would take three to six days. Next he would land the 2nd, 84th, 103rd Infantry Divisions, and one other, on the airfields and strips. Then he would launch an offensive to the north-west to seize the high ground east of Paderborn, and to cut lines of communication east and south-east of the Ruhr, towards which the Allied armies to the south could advance.

Two airborne divisions, with aviation engineers, would go in on D-day and on D-plus-1. Thereafter, one infantry division would go in each day until all had been delivered. Then all aircraft would be devoted to re-supply and evacuation. Bombers would have to fly an important share of the re-supply missions.

General Eisenhower said that he 'would dearly love to have one big airborne operation before the war ended' and 'it would really be fun to do.' Whether or not the operation would be ordered hinged on finding the divisions. On 15th March the target date was announced as 1st May.

By this time German resistance had disintegrated to such a point, and Allied ground armies were advancing so rapidly, that this vast operation was made unnecessary, and planning now went forward on operation 'Eclipse', the political coup of all time that never came off—the capture of Berlin by an Allied airborne assault. It called for Allied airborne forces to seize Templehof Aerodrome, Berlin's major air terminal, and also to take Gatow, Orenienburg and Staakin airfields, and prepare to take Berlin. Thousands of CG-4As, CG-15s, CG-13s, Horsas, and Hamilcars stood ready to take part in the biggest airborne offensive ever known. It would have scooped the Russian capture of Berlin by ground forces by several months.

The operation was never given the green light. On 23rd April 1945, the Russian armies began to enter Berlin. A momentous opportunity had slipped from the Allied grasp.

One German officer claims that the Russians started marshalling an enormous number of gliders at airfields close behind Russian lines during the months before they launched their ground offensive against Berlin. If this is correct, is it possible that the Russians planned to scoop the Allies' 'Eclipse' once General Eisenhower ordered the operation, especially if it looked as though the Russian ground armies would not beat 'Eclipse' to Berlin?

If it were possible to answer this question in the affirmative, it would mean that Russia intended to have Berlin first, and at all costs, regardless of Allied military or political efforts.

World War II is the only glider war the world will ever see. By the time Allied commanders learned how to use their glider forces, and gained courage to do so, conventional forces had won the war in Europe and in the Pacific, but at terrible cost in time, blood and materials.

It is impossible to measure how the effective use of glider and other airborne forces might have shortened the war, and caused less bloodshed, by capturing objectives in hours (as in the case of Eben Emael) which armoured thrusts took days to reach.

Unfortunately, senior ground generals in Germany, Japan, Great Britain and the U.S. had been schooled in the use of organizations and tactics that were founded in the experience of World War I. There was not a single senior ground commander in the field anywhere in the world, with the exception of General Wingate and possibly Viscount Montgomery, who is known to have given creative forethought to how to employ airborne forces. They were simply ignorant of the potential of the glider as a military weapon. Most never came close to a glider.

General Elwood Quesada, who fought as an American fighter pilot, feels that Air Corps and Army senior generals considered the glider an untested weapon. Generals are known to prefer to fight with weapons tested in at least one previous war. This is a fact of history that has many precedents.

General Patton took delight in beating enemy generals to objectives. He took equal delight in 'getting there' ahead of his fellow Allied generals. He felt airborne operations to be of questionable value, since several times he arrived at proposed airborne objectives before the airborne operations got under way.

Yet had he had a better knowledge of gliders and their potential to air lift supplies, especially gasoline, he would have been furious to be told there were thousands of gliders parked along air strips from which C-47s were taking off to carry much needed gasoline to his armoured columns. These gliders, and thousands of grousing glider pilots sorely in need of something to do, could have been carrying gasoline in gliders in tow behind the C-47s. It would have more than doubled the amount of gasoline being flown forward. Yet it was not done.

Gliders might well have been flying gasoline to the forward tanks of Patton's columns, landing in fields alongside the road. This was never done. It could have been! Patton should have realized that the opportunity to use airborne troops existed, and asked that they be used. He did not.

About the only example of airborne troops being used to paralyze the enemy's system of command, communication and supply, to create diversions, and to create confusion and disorder deep in enemy rear areas, were the glider landings in support of General Wingate's operations in Burma. In this case the troop carrier aircraft were mostly American, the ideas British, and the troops British and Indian. Similar objectives might have been appropriate to Europe and North Africa, but there was an important difference. Because of the jungle in Burma it was difficult for the enemy to move reinforcements into the area where troops were landed, and the threat of armoured counter-attack was not great. Quite the contrary was true, of course, in Europe, but that disadvantage might have been overcome through the skillful use of tactical aviation to isolate the battlefield and to provide close ground support.

Though the opportunity certainly presented itself several times in Europe, airborne troops were never used to block retreating enemy forces until the main ground forces could destroy them. It is possible that the drop of two or three airborne divisions between Falaise and Argentan, about 12th August 1944, could have closed the escape route of the Germans in the pocket there and so brought about their complete annihilation.

The Burma operations implied something of this concept on a small scale. Leaders thinking in bigger terms, however, always were disappointed. As related earlier, General Arnold and General Marshall were both anxious to try a bold, deep airborne penetration for the invasion of Normandy.

Undoubtedly, the tagging of gliders as 'gliders' did much harm to their cause in the United States. Despite efforts to divorce the glider from the widely held belief that it was just an overgrown sailplane the connotation was there, and it led to serious confusion and doubt relative to the level of performance and merit of this new weapon in the power-orientated air force. 'Better,' as Colonel Dent has stated, 'for the whole programme, had the glider been referred to as a motorless transport, which it actually was.'

Nothing that occurred in airborne operation during the war ever proved that glidermen were anything but as efficient, *or more efficient* than paratroopers. Unlike parachutists they landed with guns that did not have to be laboriously put together, and squads did not have to be untangled from parachutes and gradually assembled. Glider units landed ready to shoot, and—barring accidents—they were not dazed or disoriented as many a paratrooper is liable to be, especially if he has landed on his tail and snapped his neck a bit. Wind conditions never were a serious factor in planning a glider operation as they had to be for a parachute operation.

Britain's General Frederick A. M. Browning felt that the advantage of gliderborne troops over parachute troops, wherever it was possible to use the former, had been demonstrated. His viewpoint was that troops carried by gliders landed in formed, even if small, bodies and carried with them a more liberal supply of ammunition, transport, and comparatively heavy weapons than did paratroopers. Glidermen could land in most country that was suitable for parachute troops, although their range might not be so great. Gliders could be released at a distance from their landing zone, thus the aircraft might not have had to run the same risk of flak that they would experience when carrying parachute troops. Gliders themselves, that had been released in the correct place, were difficult flak targets. There was probably more risk, he considered, in parachute troops being dropped in the wrong place than there was of gliders being released incorrectly.

The German generals, Student particularly, supported the viewpoint voiced by General Browning.

Not so the Americans, for many reasons few of them being based on the logic of Generals Browning and Student.

Even up to the time of 'Eclipse', that lost opportunity, American glider-supported airborne thrusts (less so the British ones) never did reach the zenith they should have simply because U.S. military leaders never had an open mind about their employment. The Air Force, especially in American theatres, was 'gung ho' on bombers and fighters, wedded to conventional piston-propelled aeroplanes performing in mass formation according to tactics developed in World War I. Also, content at having won the struggle for independence as a service and backed by the world's most formidable industrial might geared to turning out ample quantities of aircraft to win the war conventionally, they needed no gliders, no V-bombs, and could do without jet propulsion. It was about as simple as that. Our Air Force left it to the Germans to do most of the basic innovation in aviation during the war.

No up-and-coming Air Force commander could afford association with the transport arm of the Air Force without risking professional suicide. Air commanders became generals by flying bombers and fighters, not by flying the slow C-47, and certainly not by flying a glider. At least this proved to be the case in the U.S. armed forces. Contrarily, the Germans did have General Student, and the British had Brigadier Chatterton, both glider pilots who attained high rank. Not one American glider pilot assigned to air transport units rose above the rank of major, from what can be determined in existing sources. A few in the glider-pilot training programme and in glider production became colonels.

The weight of Air Force resources was thrown into backing the 'air-power through bombing' concept. Air transport received only passing recognition and support; the glider effort, initially none. Much of the Air Force's attention to air transport, as concerned with the transport of airborne troops into battle, came as a result of the intention to drop parachutists, much less because of an interest in towing gliders.

As long as the Army Air Forces were committed to a policy of 'proving' the decisive capabilities of strategic bombing, attention to troop carrier needs could not be more than secondary. General Arnold, truly enough, was an airborne enthusiast. But he was more of a strategic bombardment enthusiast. In his study of recommendations for the postwar establishment, Colonel Julian J. Ewell, who had commanded a regiment in the 101st Airborne Division and now is a Lieutenant General, noted in November 1945, 'Troop carrier and airborne are inseparable. Each has many other commitments but in the actual combat operation they must co-operate perfectly. The relatively slow growth of America's airborne potentialities in this war has been primarily due to Air Force indifference to their own troop carrier needs.'

Although the British did better than the Americans in producing gliders and had a better organized glider element, and when alone may have been more enterprising in their use, their glider effort for many reasons—the availability of tow-planes for one, and the necessity for integrated planning and operation between the U.S. and Britain— was tied to American thinking and action in the use of gliders.

Many British general officers rode gliders into combat. Brigadier Chatterton flew General Hopkinson, who was a qualified paratrooper, to Sicily and General Browning to Nijmegen, in Holland. Lieutenant S. C. (Bill) Griffith, later to become famous in the world of cricket, flew General Gale, commander of the 6th Airborne Division, into Normandy.

Only two American general officers were flown into combat by glider. One was killed in the crash of his glider in Normandy. General Anthony McAuliffe with typical elan, realizing that the glidermen of the 101st needed an example, and perhaps aware of how the airborne general officers had neglected this aspect of leadership, flew into Holland in a glider. The parachute idea had taken hold among the senior American airborne commanders. It became the way to go about things, for there was no present or future glory in riding a glider into combat to compare with the awards forthcoming via the parachute route.

Is there another, and possibly more important lesson to be learnt from experience with the glider in World War II, and with the helicopter in Vietnam?

The U.S. Army has its own helicopter, its own helicopter pilots, and pilot generals. They operate under the same major command as the troops they fly into combat. There is a singleness of command purpose; they go in as a combat team, and there is no question that this will be so, or heads are chopped.

The glider story during World War II would have achieved many more successes, more efficiently, had all glider operations and personnel belonged to the Army. Glider pilots could have been better organized, trained, and disciplined, and happier. Generals like Ridgeway and Gavin would have seen to this, and would have satisfied the glider pilot's yearning to do more than corral and guard prisoners, and unavoidably get underfoot and be bothersome to airborne commanders in the heat of combat. While U.S. glider infantrymen were being killed in Holland, and the British Glider Pilot Regiment suffered 157 killed and 469 wounded as they fought alongside British infantry, some U.S. glider pilots were camera-shopping in Nijmegen, where they had drifted after the landings. They caused a serious morale problem to ground commanders, as it might well be understood. Glider pilots do not deserve criticism for such happenings. They were part of a system that was at fault.

In a manner of speaking, the same kind of basic ailments that plagued the glider programme in the Air Forces, also affected the sound development of the glider ground combat organizations, their infantry and artillery. The glider trooper ended up as a most unwanted stepchild, forced to take a back seat to his more glamorous, parachute-jumping, airborne counterpart. Moreover, the organization and training of the glider troops—plagued by lack of doctrine, vacillation and change in higher echelons, that constantly modified the glider organizations, and hard pressed for high-calibre men—was hampered further by the problems that hobbled the glider promotion programme. A paratrooper could get his jumps, a paratroop unit or part of it could get its airborne training, if there were only a single C-47 aeroplane available. To the gliderman, a plane parked and ready as a glider tug was of no use without a glider to haul, and there were long periods when whole airborne divisions were out of balance in their training cycles because paratroopers could undergo training but not glider troopers. And there were times when there were ample gliders, but the aeroplanes had been spirited off.

A glider infantryman had three strikes against him on his one-way journey into combat; the towing aeroplane could be hit, lose power, or crash, and have to let loose its glider. Or it could for almost any minor reason cut off the glider to leave it to its doom. If the glider pilot found a good reason he could do the same. The sweating glider trooper had no say in the decision, although his interests, and the interests of his command, would be least served by his continuing, even taking into consideration the vagaries that may have caused the glider pilot to abort the mission. Many glider pilots released without reason, some certainly out of cowardice. Finally, the poor glider passengers had no parachutes.

In contrast, paratroopers had more options than their glider companions, and they knew it. If the aeroplane turned back, they went with it to a safe landing. If shot down, there was a good chance most could manage to get out of the plane before it cracked up and parachute to safety. Above all, paratroopers wore parachute boots, a highly prized symbol of which all other G.I.s were envious.

In all fairness, I did witness airborne generals riding in glider training and orientation flights given to airborne divisions stateside. This to their credit. But there was more safety to jumping into combat, and certainly more prestige, and every general looked for this and left the glider colonels to ride gliders into combat, especially after the death of General Pratt in the Normandy glider landings. Events have since proved their apparent wisdom, since most U.S. World War II jumping generals have gone far.

The glider still has a place in war. The question is, will military men accord it that place? The answer in most nations is—probably not. High cost, noisy, powered aeroplanes and helicopters best epitomize, thrive in, and are thriven on by parasitic industries that support a technology from which the richest profits flow. A six-passenger helicopter is manufactured at ten times the cost of a 15-passenger glider. The 'flying crane' helicopter can carry a tank 150 miles. The glider can carry a tank 1,500 miles at one tenth or less of the cost. The helicopter has the advantage that it can move about freely under its own power, also, it is more versatile than the glider in wooded areas where there are few clearings, but its high cost and short range make it a luxury.

No one has tried jet-glider tows for military or commercial long-haul operations. The thought will raise all sorts of objections. None-

(*above*) Hamilcar gliders ready for the take off. (*below*) After the war—
Horsas waiting to be salvaged

theless, technology could produce such a combination, and it would have many applications. Industry and government alike will ridicule a jet-glider tow combination, but they are satisfied that a glider-rocket combination being designed into the orbital space laboratory (through the glider return vehicle programme) provides an economical way to handle manned rocketry. Blessed with the dollar sign, this glider has industry's blessing and it will be built and used.

Gliders still have military uses. They are still the only aircraft that can haul heavy cargo thousands of miles and land this cargo on any kind of open area that is a few hundred feet long, and that can be released at a high enough altitude and far enough away not to be discovered until they are on the ground. Gliders can fly as large a force, and carry as much heavy equipment, as the military want. The failure to see this stems from psychological, philosophical, emotional and mental obstacles—better called the conventional-thinking, establishment-minded, hierarchical-orientated, military mentality found in all armies.

Land warfare still has many places where gliders can be used. Wherever there is an extensive land mass as in Eurasia or the western hemisphere, or large water-areas to bridge, gliders can be useful. The threat to an army of glider armadas descending on its communications is not to be taken lightly. Certainly U.S. doctrine calls for no such imaginative use of a discarded weapon, but who can speak for the military innovators of other nations, to whom the glider could give cheap transportation. Certainly Russia, to whom the glider is a proven guerilla weapon, has not discarded her glider guerilla-support doctrine. With what other weapon would they replace it? There is none.

It is now more than twenty-seven years since the last glider operation. For a time after World War II the Air Force and the Army maintained an active but wary interest in gliders and glider operations. Until the early 1950s, officers and men in some of the courses at Fort Benning, Georgia, were still being given glider orientation rides.

By this time the Air Force had developed transport aeroplanes that could land on rough landing strips and in open fields. Better planes for dropping parachutists were being produced. Artillery and tanks, that gliders might have flown into operation, were being carried in huge cargo planes and dropped by parachute over objectives. The need for the glider as a support aircraft for parachute operations had disappeared, at least as far as the parachutists or airborne-minded generals and staff planners were concerned.

Soon the helicopter had appeared, as a transport for troops (much to the dismay of the paratroopers) and as a weapon-carrier, doing much the same job as gliders had previously done at far less cost, and which the powered troop transports could not do as well as had been hoped.

Canada held on to many of her gliders into the 1950s. Australia continued experimental work with its de Haviland for some years after the war. It is reported that the Indian armed forces were flying transport gliders left there by the U.S. until some time in the 1950s. England disposed of hers in the late 1940s.

Several sources claim that the Soviets have not dispensed with the military glider; that a small, but select, group in their air-force is composed of trained glider pilots—a group that will serve as a cadre if the Soviets decide on a rapid expansion of their glider fleet. To facilitate such expansion, these sources claim, a substantial number of gliders in storage are available.

Few vestiges of these gallant, misunderstood, often maligned aircraft now exist. One forms part of the airborne museum at Saint Mère Église, France, the wing protruding through the wall of the museum to form a cover for the entrance. The Caproni Museum in Milan displays a Caproni transport glider. The U.S. Air Force Museum at Wright-Patterson Air Force Base, Ohio, has a CG-4A that someday may be displayed. The 101st Airborne Division Museum at Fort Campbell, Kentucky, has one exhibited and the 82nd Airborne Museum at Fort Bragg, North Carolina displays the fuselage of a CG-15A. The cockpit of a Horsa is exhibited at the Airborne Museum at Aldershot in England. The Museum of Army Flying at Middle Wallop will display a replica of two-thirds of a Horsa fuselage including the cockpit. These are the final tributes to a once great glider armada, now all but a memory.

APPENDIX

Tables and landing patterns in this appendix are abstracted from the operations report of the U.S. 82nd Airborne Division for 'Market Garden', the airborne invasion of Holland. They show the detail in which the operation was planned and consummated by tracing elements of Company A of the 325th Glider Infantry Regiment from their loading plan to the area in which they landed.

Tables B, C, D, and E are representative tables taken from the glider loadings, flight and landing plan taken from the invasion report of the 82nd Division. Company A is found in Table B. This and the others, as well as landing pattern charts in the Appendix show in minute detail the fortunes of the various gliders that took off on that eventful mission.

Fortunately for Company A, it fared better than some of the others. Twenty-four of its twenty-five gliders landed in LZ 'O' (see Map 16) where they were supposed to land according to Table B. Examination shows that many gliders carrying other units of the 82nd had serious mishaps, and some landed sixty miles away from the zone (see Map 17), a long hike through enemy saturated country from their regiment's landing zone.

Most equipment shown on Table E lifted by the gliders landed in serviceable condition. Casualties, despite the misfortunes to the gliders evident in Table D, were surprisingly few, although the fate of some of the passengers was not reported since they landed so far from the designated zone.

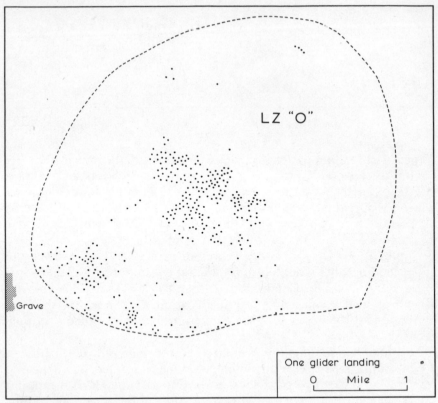

LZ "O"

One glider landing

0   Mile   1

Grave

Glider Landings of U.S. 82nd Airborne Division in Operation Market Garden: (i)

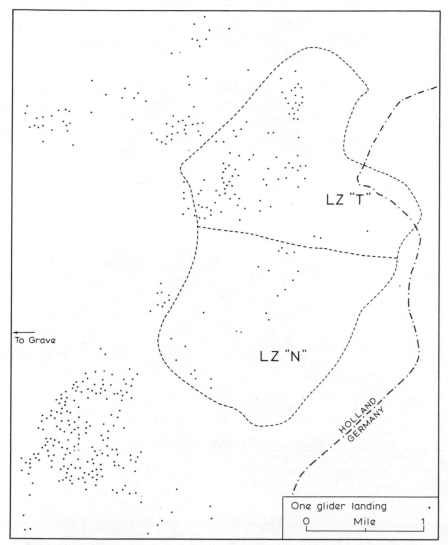

LZ "T"

To Grave

LZ "N"

HOLLAND
GERMANY

One glider landing

0   Mile   1

Glider Landings of U.S. 82nd Airborne Division in Operation Market
Garden: (ii)

Table A

Abstract from the Glider Loading Plan of Company A, 325th Glider Infantry Regiment, 82nd Airborne Division

Glider No. 1

1 Wpns Plat Sgt T/Sgt	240
3 Basics	720
1 Sgt LMG Sq Ldr	240
2 Amm Bearers LMG	480
1 Gunner LMG	240
1 Supply Sgt	240
1 Officer FA Fwd Obs	240
2 EM FA Fwd Obs	480
1 Asst Gunner LMG	240
	— 3120

Equipment:

1 Litter w/2 Blankets	26
1 Can Water	50
1 Box K Rations	46
1 LMG	50
2 Shovels	10
2 Picks	14
22 Chests MG .30 Cal Am	440
	— 636
Total	3756

Glider No. 2

1 Mortar Sqd Ldr Sgt	240
2 Amm Bearers Mortar	480
1 Gunner 60mm Mortar	240
1 Asst Gunner 60mm	240
1 Mortar Sec Ldr S/Sg	240
1 Mortar Sec Msgr	240
1 Wpns Plat Ldr Lt	240
3 Basics	720
2 Msgrs Wpns Pl Hq	480
	— 3120

Equipment:

1 Litter w/2 Blankets	26
1 Can Water	50
1 Chest MG .30 Cal Am	20
4 CLs 60mm Amm	416
2 Shovels	10
1 Box K Rations	40
1 Axe	7
1 Mortar	50
1 Pick	7
	— 626
Total	3746

Glider No. 3

2 Sqd Ldrs 60mm Mor Sgt	480
2 Gunners 60mm Mor	480
2 Asst Gunners 60mm	480
4 Amm Bearers 60mm	960
2 Basics	480
1 Arm Arti	240
	— 3120

Equipment:

1 Litter w/2 Blankets	26
1 Can Water	50
2 Shovels	10
1 Box K Rations	40
3 CLs 60mm Amm	312
2 Mortars	100
3 Chests MG .30 Amm	60
2 Picks	14
1 Axe	7
	— 619
Total	3739

Glider No. 4

1 Capt Co Comdr	240
1 Sgt Comm	240
2 Msgrs (Co)	480
7 Riflemen (Pl)	1680
2 Basics (Rad Op)	480
	— 3120

Equipment:

1 Litter w/2 Blankets	26
1 Can Water	50
2 Boxes K Rations	86
3 CLs 60mm Amm	312
1 Axe	7
83 Sandbags	28
2 Shovels	10
1 Radio SCR 300	40
3 Picks	21
1 Box K Rations	40
	— 620
Total	3740

SERIAL N⁰ A-14   TIME OF DROP · 1617   FIELD · BARKSTON HEATH   LZ · O   ROUTE · S   GP N⁰ 61ˢᵗ

ORGANIZATION	TAIL NUMBER	GLIDER				PERSONNEL				JEEP		TRAILER		GUN		DISTANCE FROM LZ
		INTACT	DAM	DES	MISS	OK	KIA	EVAC	MISS	SER	UNSER	SER	UNSER	SER	UNSER	
Co "B" 325 Gli Inf	43-42638	X				14										
"	43-39947	X				14										LZ
"	43-40510		X			14										"
"	43-41466	X				14										"
"	42-56514	X				13										"
"	43-26947	X				14										"
"	43-41074		X			14										"
"	43-340463	X				13										"
"	341525	X				14										"
"	43-40562	X				12	1									"
"	43-42108	X				13										19 mi SW
"	341536		X			13										LZ
"	43-41539	X				14										"
"	43-37388	X				13										"
"	43-41710	X				13										"
Co "A" 325 Gli Inf	327282	X				14										"
"	43-41217		X			14										"
"	336703	X				14										"
"	319879	X				14										"
"	339657	X				15										"
"	265283		X			13										"
"	43-41484	X				15										"
"	279393	X				13										"
"	341942	X				14										"
"	319832	X				14										"
"	341583		X			15										"
"	319865	X				14										"
"	340390	X				15										"
"	256551	X				14										"
"	256336	X				14										"
"	42-43657		X			13										"
"	43-19103		X			13										"
"	42-73566	X				13										"
"	43-19761	X				13										"
"	43-40389	X				14										"
"	43-77545	X				14										"
"	43-19811	X				14										"
"	43-40446		X			14										"
"	341395	X				14										19 mi SW
"	256344	X				14										LZ
TOTAL		31	9			550	1									
PERCENTAGE		77.5	22.5			99.82	.18									

TABLE C

SERIAL N⁰ A-16   TIME OF DROP · 1631   FIELD · FULBECK   LZ · O   ROUTE · S   GP N⁰ 440ᵀᴴ

ORGANIZATION	TAIL NUMBER	GLIDER				PERSONNEL				JEEP		TRAILER		GUN		DISTANCE FROM LZ
		INTACT	DAM	DES	MISS	OK	KIA	EVAC	MISS	SER	UNSER	SER	UNSER	SER	UNSER	
Ha&Ha Co 325	339987	X				7				X						17 mi SW
"	336728		X			13										19 mi SW
"	42-77594	X				3				X						30 mi SW
"	339675	X				9										28 mi SW
"	274065				X			3				X				LZ
"	341903	X														LZ
"	340094	X				4				X						"
"	339661				X			11								
"	342631			X		4						X				28 mi SW
"	42-77762			X		5		1			X					"
Co "C" 325 Gli Inf	341202	X				16										LZ
"	339729	X				13										"
"	336428	X				14										"
"	342133		X			14										"
"	277511	X				12										"
"	372285	X				12	1									"
"	274083	X				13										"
"	279161	X				13										"
"	256227		X			13										"
"	273070	X				11										"
"	340430	X				12										"
"	277564		X			13										"
"	327454	X				13										ENGLAND
"	277495	X				12	1									LZ
"	336958	X				13										"
Ha&Ha Co 1ˢᵗ Bn 325	42-77730	X				15										12 mi SW
"	341063		X			14										13 mi SW
"	279183	X				11										ENGLAND
"	277589	X				11										LZ
"	274061	X				3	1			X						13 mi SW
"	343095	X				7						X				19 mi SW
"	246492				X			4			X					
"	342147				X			3			X					
"	277959	X				4				X						19 mi SW
"	341159			X		2	1				X					LZ
"	341864				X			5					X			
"	339914				X			6					X			
"	277449	X				5						X				19 mi SW
"	341496	X				7						X				"
"	341059	X				3					X					
TOTAL		26	5	3	6	333	4	33		6	4	5	2			
PERCENTAGE		65	12.5	7.5	15	89.7	1.1	9.2		60	40	71.4	28.6			

TABLE D

ORGANIZATION	TAIL NUMBER	GLIDER				PERSONNEL				JEEP		TRAILER		GUN		DISTANCE FROM LZ
		INTACT	DAM	DES	MISS	OK	EVAC	KIA	MISS	SER	UNSER	SER	UNSER	SER	UNSER	
Btry"B"320 FA Bn	43-41489			X		3					X					3 mi NE
"	43-41683			X		3					X					4 mi NE
"	43-41089			X		7										"
"	43-41421			X		13										"
"	43-41502			X		2			1		X					"
"	43-41940				X				2						X	
"	43-41432			X					2		X					3 mi NE
"	43-41xxx			X		1	1								X	4 mi NE
"	42-77890			X		1			1		X					3 mi NE
"	42-77818				X				2						X	
"	43-20131			X		2					X					3 mi NE
"	43-19801				X				2						X	
"	43-40093	X				2				X						LZ
"	43-40546	X				2								X		"
"	43-41379	X				2				X						"
"	43-36937		X			2								X		"
"	43-41374	X				2				X						"
"	43-41459		X			3				X						"
"	43-40212		X			4						X				"
"	45-42154	X				4						X				"
"	43-41905				X				4				X			
"	43-42127				X				4				X			
"	43-41684				X				4				X			
"	43-42110				X				4				X			
"	43-41677				X				4				X			
"	43-40219				X				2		X					
"	43-42007				X				2		X					
"	43-40162				X				2		X					
"	43-40085				X				2		X					
"	43-41629				X				2		X					
"	43-41146	X				5										LZ
"	43-40447		X			5										"
"	43-40213	X				5										"
"	43-40461	X				5										"
"	43-37390	X				5										"
"	43-41964		X			5										"
"	43-41994	X				5										"
"	43-36791		X			3	1	1								"
"	43-40554		X			4										"
"	43-41607		X			4										"
TOTAL		10	8	9	13	99	2	1	40	4	11	2	5	2	4	
PERCENTAGE		25	20	22.5	32.5	69.7	1.3	.9	28.1	26.6	73.4	28.5	71.5	33	66.6	

TABLE E

ORGANIZATION	TAIL NUMBER	GLIDER				PERSONNEL				JEEP		TRAILER		GUN		DISTANCE FROM LZ
		INTACT	DAM	DES	MISS	OK	KIA	EVAC	MISS	SER	UNSER	SER	UNSER	SER	UNSER	
Hq & Hq Btry Div Arty	43-40150	X				2	1			X						LZ
"	43-40153		X			4	1					X				"
"	43-40376	X				2				X						"
"	43-40138	X				4						X				"
"	43-19831		X			3				X						"
"	43-41705		X			3		2								60 mi SW
"	43-37304	X				3				X						LZ
"	43-40141	X				5						X				"
"	43-40393		X			3				X						"
"	43-40523		X			2				X						"
"	43-40220		X			5						X				"
"	341340			X		2	1			X						"
"	40139		X			5						X				"
Btry"B"456 FA Bn	42-77900	X				2				X						"
"	43-42094	X				5						X				"
"	42-7499	X				4								X		"
Btry"C"456 FA Bn	43-41157	X				2				X						"
"	43-41389	X				8								X		"
"	43-27375	X				9								X		"
"	43-36726	X				2				X						"
"	43-41191	X				5								X		"
"	43-39738	X				9								X		"
"	42-77660	X				2				X						"
"	43-41398	X				5								X		"
"	43-41181	X				10								X		"
"	43-40240	X				3				X						"
"	43-36946	X				9						X				"
"	42-79454	X				2				X						"
"	42-56358	X				2				X						"
"	43-40236	X				5								X		"
"	43-40241	X				10								X		"
"	43-41520	X				2				X						"
"	42-56120	X				6								X		"
"	43-40429	X				7						X				"
"	42-56226	X				2				X						3 mi SW
"	43-43090		X			4		2				X				LZ
"	43-41969	X				5				X						"
"	43-39233	X				2						X				"
"	43-36917	X				4								X		"
"	43-41863	X				3										"
TOTAL		31	8	1		171		5	2	17		10		11		
PERCENTAGE		77.5	20	2.5		96		2.2	1.8	100		100		100		

BIBLIOGRAPHY

Only the major written sources are given here

Warren, John C. *Airborne Operations in World War II, European Theater* (U.S.A.F. Historical Study 97)

Ibid., *Airborne Missions in the Mediterranean, 1942–1945* (U.S.A.F. Historical Study 74)

Morzik, Fritz-Gerhard; Hümmelchen, *Die deutschen Transportflieger im Zweiten Weltkrieg* (Frankfurt am Main, Bernard & Graefe Verlag für Wehrwesen, 1966)

Němeček, Václav, *Sovětskè Letadla* (Prague, *Naše Voysko*)

Taylor, William H. *Glider Operations on Two Fronts.* A.A.F.S.A.T. Special Intelligence Report, No. 54, September 1944

Masters, John. *Road Past Mandalay* (New York, Harper, 1961)

Greene, William. *Warplanes of the Third Reich* (Garden City, Doubleday, 1970)

Otway, T. B. H., D.S.O. *Airborne Forces*, from the series *The Second World War*, 1939–1945, Army (The War Office, 1951)

Ministry of Information, Great Britain. *By Air To Battle.* (London, His Majesty's Stationery Office, 1945)

Air Enthusiast for March, April, May 1972

AAF Historical Office, Headquarters Army Air Forces, Army Air Forces Historical Studies: No. 47 (unpublished); *Development and Procurement of Gliders in the Army Air Forces 1941–1944*

Management Control Central District-ATSC September 1945. *The History of the Glider Program at Northwestern Aeronautical Corporation*

Headquarters U.S. Army Air Forces in Europe, AAF Sta. 197, APO 633, U.S. Army 15 Oct. 1945. *Air Staff Post Hostilities Intelligence Requirements on German Air Force*, 'Tactical Employment Troop Carrier Operations, Section IV, F, 1, 2, 3, 4, 5, 6, 7, and 8'

U.S.A.F. Historical Division Liaison Office, March 1962. *U.S.A.F. Airborne Operations World War II and Korean War*

U.S.A.F. Historical Study No. 1, *The Glider Pilot Training Program, 1941–1947*

Wright, Lawrence, *The Wooden Sword* (London, Elek, 1967)

Chatterton, George, *Wings of Pegasus* (London, MacDonald, 1962)

Seth, Ronald, *Lion With The Blue Wings* (London, Victor Gollancz, Ltd., 1955)

INDEX